THE

LOST BOYS

affirm
press

First published by Affirm Press in 2019
This edition published in 2020, reprinted in 2022
Boon Wurrung Country
28 Thistlethwaite Street
South Melbourne VIC 3205
affirmpress.com.au

10 9 8 7 6 5

NATIONAL
LIBRARY
OF AUSTRALIA

A catalogue record for this
book is available from the
National Library of Australia

ISBN: 9781922400109 (paperback)

Cover design by Karen Wallis, Taloula Press © Affirm Press
Maps by John Firth
Typeset in 10/17 Sabon
Colour separation by Splitting Image Colour Studio, Clayton, Victoria
Printed and bound in China by C&C Offset Printing Co., Ltd.

Aboriginal and Torres Strait Islander readers are advised that this book
contains images and names of deceased persons.

Every effort has been made to ensure that the facts presented in this book are
correct. Any new information supplied will be included in subsequent editions.

THE
LOST BOYS

The untold stories of the under-age
Anzac soldiers who fought in the First World War

PAUL BYRNES

affirm
press

To Mary, always

CONTENTS

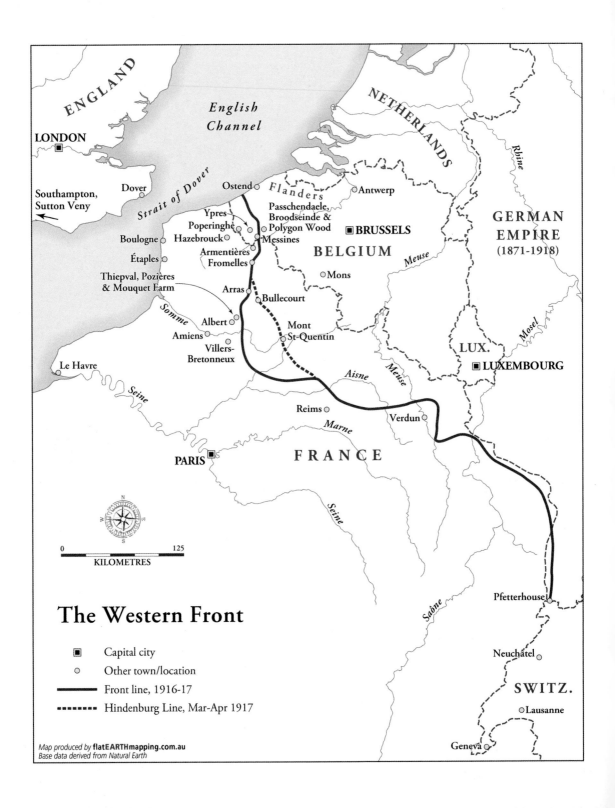

ENGLAND

*English
Channel*

LONDON ■

Southampton,
Sutton Veny ←

Dover

Strait of Dover

Boulogne ○

Étaples ○

Le Havre ○

Seine

Somme

Thiepval, Pozières
& Mouquet Farm

Amiens ○

Villers-
Bretonneux ○

Albert ○

Arras ○

Ostend ○

Flanders

Ypres ○
Poperinghe ○
Hazebrouck ○
Armentières ○
Fromelles ○

Messines ○

Passchendaele,
Broodseinde &
Polygon Wood

NETHERLANDS

Rhine

Antwerp ○

■ BRUSSELS

BELGIUM

Mons ○

Meuse

GERMAN
EMPIRE
(1871-1918)

Bullecourt ○

Mont
St-Quentin ○

Aisne

Meuse

Mosel

LUX.

■ LUXEMBOURG

Reims ○

Marne

Seine

Verdun ○

PARIS ■

FRANCE

Saône

Pfetterhouse ○

Neuchâtel ○

SWITZ.

Lausanne ○

Geneva ○

N
W E
S

0 ———— 125
KILOMETRES

The Western Front

■   Capital city

○   Other town/location

───   Front line, 1916-17

▪▪▪▪   Hindenburg Line, Mar-Apr 1917

Map produced by flatEARTHmapping.com.au
Base data derived from Natural Earth

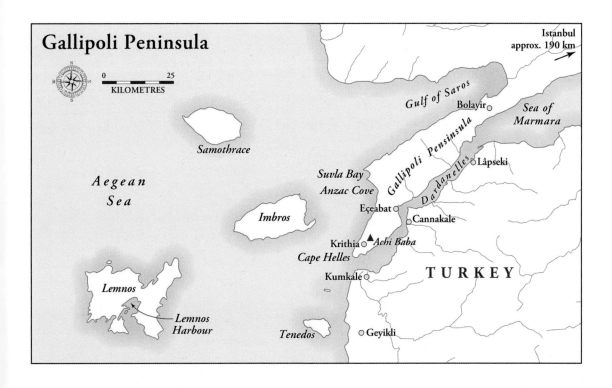

Gallipoli Peninsula

KILOMETRES
0 — 25

Istanbul
approx. 190 km →

Gulf of Saros

Bolayir ○

*Sea of
Marmara*

Samothrace

*Aegean
Sea*

Gallipoli Peninsula

Lâpseki ○

Dardanelles

Suvla Bay
Anzac Cove

Imbros

Eçeabat ○

Cannakale ○

Krithia ○ ▲ *Achi Baba*

Cape Helles

T U R K E Y

Lemnos

Kumkale ○

*Lemnos
Harbour*

Tenedos

○ Geyikli

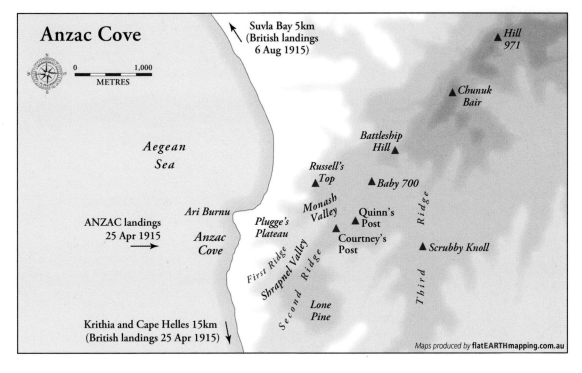

Anzac Cove

METRES
0 — 1,000

Suvla Bay 5km
(British landings
6 Aug 1915) ↖

▲ *Hill
971*

▲ *Chunuk
Bair*

*Aegean
Sea*

*Battleship
Hill* ▲

*Russell's
Top* ▲

▲ *Baby 700*

Ari Burnu

*Monash
Valley*

*Quinn's
Post*

ANZAC landings
25 Apr 1915 →

*Anzac
Cove*

*Plugge's
Plateau*

▲
*Courtney's
Post*

*Third
Ridge*

▲ *Scrubby Knoll*

First Ridge

Shrapnel Valley

Second Ridge

*Lone
Pine*

Krithia and Cape Helles 15km
(British landings 25 Apr 1915) ↓

FOREWORD

They shall grow not old as we that are left grow old:
Age shall not weary them, nor the years condemn.
At the going down of the sun, and in the morning
We will remember them.
'For the Fallen', Laurence Binyon

PRIVATE MILLER MAFFEKING FERGUSSON, from Quorn, South Australia, arrived in France on 9 April 1917 as a reinforcement. Nearly a month later, on 5 May, he received multiple gunshot wounds during the 27th Battalion's attack near Bapaume in the Somme Valley. He was taken back to the 3rd Casualty Clearing Station but died a few hours later. He is buried in the nearby Grevillers British war cemetery. He had claimed to be eighteen years old when he enlisted, but he was really sixteen years and four months old. His two older brothers, Thomas and William, also served; both survived. Miller's distinctive middle name – although misspelled – commemorates a famous siege in the Boer War, which concluded with a British victory six months before he was born. Private Fergusson was one of several thousand under-age boys who served in the Anzac forces in the First World War. Most of their stories have never been told.

In the First World War of 1914–1918, thousands of Australian and New Zealand boys lied about their ages, forged a parent's signature and went off to fight in a war on the other side of the world. They found they could die as well as any man, but they could never grow old. Like Peter Pan's lost boys, they have remained forever young.

One hundred years later, they're all gone, but how well do we remember them? Australian historians have written little about them, perhaps because in a war of such profound horror and loss, this story is just one tragedy among many. Tens of millions died in those four years, many of them civilians. Why should we remember these headstrong lads, many of whom were almost men? No-one forced them to go, after all.

Nor is it surprising that boys as young as twelve wanted to go. Teenage boys have always been in a hurry to prove their manhood, to escape family authority, to take part in adventures. What's surprising to us now is that their parents let them go: did they not care about their children? Did they value patriotism and duty above their own offspring? Has the world changed that much? This book is an attempt to understand, rather than condemn, but there is much to understand. Australia in 1914 was almost a different country.

The idea for this book began in Ypres in Belgium in June 2017, almost a century after the first rumblings of the Battle of Passchendaele. I was there to research another project on the Western Front when I came across a list of 170 under-age soldiers who were on the Australian War Memorial's Roll

---

of Honour. I knew what that meant: none of them came back. The Roll of Honour records the Australian dead from all conflicts – more than 100,000 names, of whom 62,000 died in the First World War. Those 170 boys represent a tiny percentage of the 62,000, but the list is a work in progress. The legal age of enlistment in 1914 in Australia was between nineteen and thirty-eight, so the Australian War Memorial initially only included boys under eighteen. When eighteen-year-olds are included, the list will grow.

Each under-age boy on that list had a short biography, enough to form an idea of each soldier. These fragments were remarkable: heartbreaking, but full of daring, ingenuity and recklessness, random horror and capricious luck. The more I dug, the richer the details became. Jennifer Milward, who put that list together, aided enormously with that task.

> They may have been too young, too wild and too full of romantic ideas for their own good, but these boys had grit.

A few stories on that list stood out. There was William Arthur Leslie Richards, aged sixteen, who joined a Newcastle battalion in which his former teacher was now his officer. There was fifteen-year-old Jack Harris from Sydney, who died at Lone Pine, eighteen hours after arriving on Gallipoli, because his officer had a death wish. And there was Leslie Thomas Prior, from Melbourne, who could not stay out of trouble. He died at Bullecourt, a battle that should never have happened, three months after his fifteenth birthday. He was the second-youngest Australian to die in the First World War, and the youngest to be killed in action.

As appalling as some of their stories are, they are not all tragedies. Some of the boys lived through the war and re-started their lives. The youngest Anzac is a New Zealander, Leslie Shaw, who enlisted at thirteen and eight months. He survived the battlefields to live an adventurous life after the war.

This book offers just a small selection of these boys' stories, arranged as a chronology, taking the reader through the war from Gallipoli to the Armistice. I have tried to address aspects of history through each story, assuming that some readers will have little knowledge of this war. I have done that partly because I hope young people will read it.

Anzac Day remains an important day in our culture, but the ways and means of commemoration in Australia have long been dominated by militarists, rather than pacifists. We remember our soldiers with sorrow, but not why they went or who sent them. We justify their suffering with words like 'hero' and 'sacrifice'. The stories of these boy soldiers are sometimes heroic, but that was not my purpose in writing about them. If we remember them, we should also remember that they should never have been there. It's right to ask why they went and who allowed them to go, lest it should happen again. In that sense, it was *not* a different Australia that sent them.

As they prepared for war, some of these boys had splendid photographs taken by professional photographers who worked around the training camps in Australia and behind the lines in France and Belgium. Many families have kept these as cherished records and reminders of their loved ones. I thank those who shared them. They are all acknowledged at the end of the book.

I have tried to find relatives of most of the people in this book, with limited success. I would be pleased to hear from anyone who can add more to these stories.

They may have been too young, too wild and too full of romantic ideas for their own good, but these boys had grit. Their stories are a microcosm of the Australian experience in the First World War: they ate the same food and fought the same fights as the older men, suffered the same privations, indignities and losses, endured or did not as temperament and fate decided. Some of them became men in the process, old before their time. Others never got the chance. ❧

INTRODUCTION

HALF A SOLDIER

The minstrel boy to the war is gone,
In the ranks of death you'll find him
His father's sword he hath girded on,
And his wild harp slung behind him
'The Minstrel Boy', Thomas Moore

Not all the under-age hopefuls were boys. Sixteen-year-old **MAUD BUTLER** of Kurri Kurri, New South Wales, twice tried to stow away on Egypt-bound troopships.

Australians could not wait to go to war in 1914 – especially those who would not have to fight it. Politicians, preachers and newspaper editors, by and large, saw a clear duty, even an opportunity. If Britain was at war, so were its dominions, including Australia. The fact that Australia was free to decide not to participate, even if 'at war', barely entered the discussion: in the words of a popular song of the time, 'Australia will be there!'

One-third of all Australians had been born in Britain. Their leaders, even more British-born, were keen to show the Mother Country that Australia had overcome her convict origins and produced a vigorous 'race' of southern whites, loyal to the Empire. Australians in general were ready to be taken seriously on the world stage. Many thought that would require a 'blood sacrifice', including William Morris Hughes, the politician who would lead the country for the second half of the war. The letting of youthful blood on foreign soil was supposed to prove to other nations that Australia had come of age.

Britain called and Australia was British. Germany was 'belligerent' and militaristic and cruel and needed to be taught a lesson. If the Royal Navy lost its dominance, who would protect Australia from the Asian hordes to the north? Damn it, man, look what they are doing to poor little Belgium! There had been years of propaganda in this vein leading up to the outbreak of war. God was on our side, said the vicars and priests, and He would protect His own. Sign here, laddie.

An Irish Australian might have observed that it was not that different to what Britain had already done to Ireland, but few dared. Irish Australians joined up nearly as fast as everyone else. Men of adventurous

> Men of adventurous spirit did not want to be left behind, to be handed a white feather – the hated symbol of cowardice – or suffer the ire of loved ones.

spirit did not want to be left behind, to be handed a white feather – the hated symbol of cowardice – or suffer the ire of loved ones.

Australia's leaders had foreseen the need to train an army and from 1909, the government required all men between eighteen and twenty-five to attend a military training camp once a year. Boys between twelve and eighteen were to be trained in a compulsory cadet scheme. There was widespread public opposition to this cadet scheme, which suggests that not everyone believed in the militarisation of children and youth – at least not yet.

Australian and British authorities believed a world war would come in 1915, when Germany completed its preparations for war. When it came six months early in August 1914, Australia was willing, but far from ready.

Prime Minister Joseph Cook promised Britain a contingent of 20,000 men, but the Australian *Defence Act 1903* prohibited overseas service. A new army would have to be formed and equipped from scratch. This had to be done quickly and without conscription. Men would have to volunteer – which they did in vast numbers in those first months.

The news that Australia was going to war generated enormous excitement. The crowds in Melbourne broke into patriotic song as they waited for the latest cables to be posted on the noticeboards outside the *Age* newspaper.

Thousands jostled outside Victoria Barracks in Sydney and Melbourne in the heady weeks of August 1914. The recruiting halls were only in the cities, so country men jumped on trains, buses and bicycles. The poorest walked long distances. Stockmen from vast cattle stations in the north rode hundreds of miles to the nearest railhead. They joined an army that barely existed. Sydney recruits slept in the grandstands at Randwick Racecourse in that first month, waking to the sound of racehorses doing track work.

The government decreed that any white man aged from twenty-one could enlist if he passed the size and fitness tests, and they would even take nineteen-year-olds with a letter signed by a parent. They did not bother to ask for proof of age, not

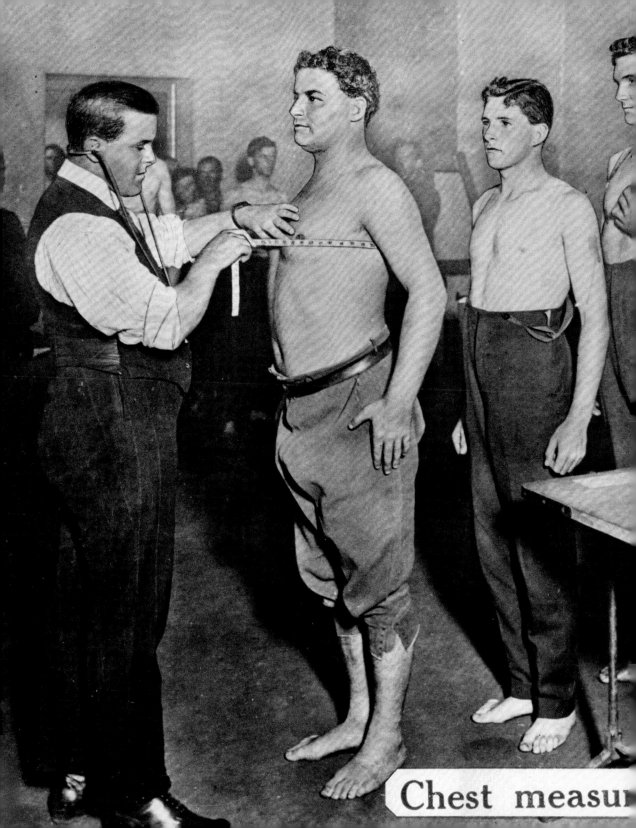

Chest measur

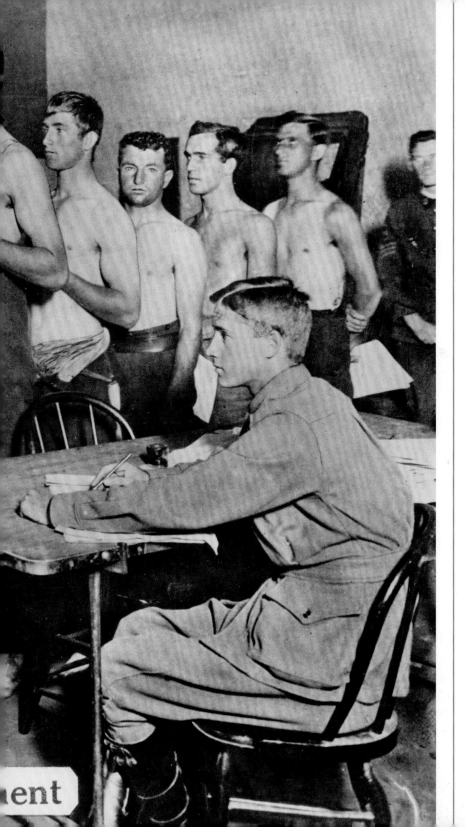

Major Frederick Maguire, medical officer, measures recruits for chest size at Victoria Barracks, Sydney, in February 1915.

ent

that many men could have provided it. This was a gift to under-age boys: they did not even have to work out an appropriate date of birth. A parent's signature was easy to forge, since there was no way a recruiting officer could easily check it. From a modern standpoint, it looks like a system designed for abuse, but it was more likely a set of careless decisions, made in haste. The first contingent was supposed to be ready to sail in a month.

From the start, the Australian soldier was proud that he was a voluteer. It became a badge of courage that distinguished the Australian Imperial Force (AIF) – as the brass decided to call it – from almost all other armies in the conflict. Australians wore the uniform because they wanted to. Initially, that made them almost impossible to discipline, but it also helped to unite them.

The first Australian battalions were based on geography: recruits in New South Wales joined New South Wales units, Victorians joined Victorian units, and so on, but they sometimes met in training camps. At Broadmeadows in Melbourne, Liverpool in Sydney, Enoggera in Brisbane and Blackboy Hill in Perth, New South Welshmen and Victorians met Tasmanians, Queenslanders and South and West Australians, often for the first time. Petty state rivalries gave way to a sense of common cause. They were not yet a band of brothers, but they might soon be – and from a country established as a series of penal colonies, that was something.

In this heated atmosphere, some teenage boys saw a perfect opportunity to escape all bonds of authority and run away to the war. Some dreamed of duty and glory; others wanted to do things they were not supposed to do, like fighting, drinking and fornicating. Governments and generals didn't necessarily see a problem. Teenage boys had a long history in European warfare: they made good recruits. Boys were more easily motivated to fight and they would carry out orders quicker than older men. They lacked inhibition, but not aggression.

And for the recruiters, it was often hard to tell a strapping sixteen-year-old from a strapping nineteen-year-old.

At first, the Anzac recruiters had their pick of the strongest and fittest men. Teenage boys were not required. And yet from the start they were accepted by a system that did not take seriously the idea of protecting them, if only from themselves. It's clear that many people in a position of authority, with what we would now call a duty of care, thought it was reasonable and proper that they be allowed to go. Was this callousness or belligerence, or a profoundly different idea of nobility and duty? Were people so different in 1914 that it is hard now for us to understand?

The *Official History of Australia in the War of 1914–1918* notes that many young boys made it into the ranks: 'It is equally certain,' wrote Ernest Scott in Volume XI, 'that hundreds who were below the military age enlisted and were passed for service, long, lean sinewy fellows whom nothing could prevent from being "in it"...'

In fact, many *were* prevented from being in it, their lives saved by the intervention of mothers and fathers who insisted on the return of their sons. Some boys then ran away and re-enlisted in a different city or a different name. More than one told his mother that he would run away and change his name if she refused permission to go – then she would never know what happened to him.

Some joined up to follow a brother or father already serving. Some appear to have needed the money, which was relatively generous, at six shillings a day when overseas – six times that of a 'Tommy' (British soldier). Military historian Peter Pedersen says Australians were the best-paid soldiers of the war.

Many of the first under-age recruits were boys who had come to Australia with their families from Britain. Their sense of patriotic duty was strong, but boys of Irish and German descent enlisted too. Aboriginal people were not supposed to be admitted, but it depended on where and when they tried to enlist – and perhaps on the lightness of their skin. The Australian War Memorial has identified at least 1000 Aboriginal

'My duty was to send him ashore but the little fellow was brought aboard again the next day rolled up in the blankets. I took him to Egypt and the child cried bitterly because I would not allow him to go to the front.'

soldiers from the First World War, some of whom were under-age, like John Alfred Richards, from Moree, just over sixteen years old when he enlisted in March 1916.

Many parents were proud that their sons were in uniform, whether or not they were under-age. In September 1915, the Sydney *Daily Telegraph* ran a picture of Private Roy Norman Tucker, of Bonnyrigg, wounded at Gallipoli and then in hospital at Heliopolis in Egypt.

His mother wrote that he had been anxious to go when war broke out but his parents refused, promising to reconsider later. They let him go at fifteen and ten months. 'The great determination and pride which he showed swayed us,' Mrs Tucker wrote. 'I am sending along the boy's photo in the hope that its publication might serve as a pattern to others.'

The Australian newspapers carried hundreds of articles in those four years about under-age enlistees, almost none of which condemned the practice. Politicians were largely silent on the matter too. Boy soldiers did not become a political issue until later in the war, when they started dying.

Almost the only voices against war in Australia were a few leftist publications like *The Australian Worker*, which saw a capitalist plot.

It's worth noting though that more than half of all eligible men in Australia never joined up over the course of the war. Some were religious pacifists or politically opposed to a war between capitalists, some were the sole breadwinners for large families, and some were isolationists, believing it was not Australia's war. They were often labelled cowards – although it took courage to resist the tide.

Women were largely in favour of the war, but not all. Feminist groups split into pro- and anti-war camps. Some suffragettes, like Vida Goldstein and Adela Pankhurst, fought against the war, despite harassment and censorship. These women were a minority, albeit an influential one. It's much easier to find women noisily supporting recruitment for the war. Some became brutal accusers, dispensing white feathers to any man not in uniform, and refusing to socialise with men who did not volunteer.

Others set out to help the war effort in any way they could – as nurses and Red Cross volunteers, or by forming organisations to help women suffering financial woes because of the war. Thousands wrote to the defence department offering their services, in any capacity. None was successful: the department rejected all offers to admit women as workers, even to replace men in uniform doing clerical work in Australia. There was no Women's Australian National Service, as there would be in the Second World War.

That did not stop one girl from attempting the ultimate deception. Maud Butler had grown up in Kurri Kurri, New South Wales. When she tried to join the war as a nurse, the Red Cross rejected her. She moved to Sydney and acquired a khaki uniform, piece by piece. In December 1915, unable to wait any longer, she went to a barber and had her hair cut short. She then walked to Woolloomooloo docks and waited. When a sentry was distracted, she climbed a mooring rope onto the troopship *Suevic*, hiding in a lifeboat. The next day she mingled with soldiers on deck, who suspected nothing. She was discovered by an officer who noticed that her boots were the wrong colour. He demanded to see her ID tags, so she confessed to being a stowaway. He still did not suspect that she was a girl, let alone aged fifteen. Maud Butler was off-loaded when the ship docked in Melbourne, but she tried again a few months later – in March 1916. This time she pretended to be drunk, joining a line of similarly inebriated soldiers returning from shore leave. By now she had the proper boots and a home-made identity disc. She was discovered the next morning and handed to the Water Police.

The newspapers loved her story, as they did any story of under-age daring. In a recruiting speech in Newcastle in 1916, Colonel WC Markwell told the crowd that he had discovered an eleven-year-old boy stowaway during his most recent voyage to Europe. Markwell claimed the boy had been training in Western Australia for four or

The taller of the two lads is "Corporal" John Smith, of Port Melbourne. The other is "Private" Frank Day, of West Australia. Smith stowed himself on a troopship by climbing up the life line as the vessel was leaving, and made a temporary hiding-place on top of the boilers. Day spent the whole journey in a military kit bag.

JOHN SMITH and **FRANK DAY** stowed away to Egypt in 1915, and are pictured here on their return to Australia. Smith was fourteen and Day was just eleven.

five months and had marched himself aboard. 'My duty was to send him ashore but the little fellow was brought aboard again the next day rolled up in the blankets. I took him to Egypt and the child cried bitterly because I would not allow him to go to the front. He is now safely back at home and I had a letter from his mother recently, stating that the boy was quite well.'

This boy was 'an example for many', said Markwell. 'That young chap wanted to fight for his country and his Empire. Surely there are a few here who could be induced to come forward ... You are wanted, and wanted badly.'

The newspapers carried another stowaway story in December 1915, when John Smith and Frank Day were returned to Australia from Egypt. Smith stowed away at fourteen, hoping to get to Gallipoli, but Day was still only eleven, and most likely the boy mentioned by Colonel Markwell. Smith had shimmied up the rope of a troopship leaving Port Melbourne and got as far as the army camp at Zeitoun, outside Cairo, where he was given a uniform and put to work in the mess. 'I thought I would like to have a trip with the boys as a lot of my cobbers had gone,' he told the Melbourne *Herald*. 'I knew I was too young to enlist, for I was not a turnip altogether, but when the troops were being sent I made up my mind I would go as far as I could with them ...'

Reports like this point to a stark difference in attitudes between then and now. The idea of adulthood has changed, along with the age at which the young achieve it. In a sense, the concept of 'teenager' barely existed in 1914. There was childhood up to the age of eleven or twelve, then adulthood. Many boys, especially those who were poor and working class, left school at twelve or earlier to learn a trade. Frank Day had already spent a year in the workforce when he stowed away at eleven. In New South Wales, children were supposed to stay at school until fourteen. If a boy tried to enlist from school, his absence would have been noticed. A 'young man' of sixteen might have had four years experience of hard work as a carpenter or miner or boot-maker: he was used to earning a living, making decisions, courting girls and drinking alcohol, if he could get hold of it.

There was also a common belief that boys and girls 'in the colonies' grew up faster and were more physically developed than their counterparts in Britain.

War correspondent Charles Bean, born in Australia but schooled in England, wrote that the young Australian learned something of the arts of soldiering before he was ten years old, from time spent in the Australian bush. He was 'half a soldier before the war.'

This is Bean at his most romantic, but there is also a darker reading. If boys of ten are 'half a soldier', it is easier to accept that boys of fifteen, sixteen and seventeen are ready to become full soldiers.

Despite all these forces exhorting the young to take up arms, the doors were hardly flung open for under-age recruits. There had to be a lot of connivance for boys to gain entry – and there was. Some doctors turned a blind eye to boys as young as fourteen. By 1915, cunning boys exploited the fact that recruiters were different at every major town: if you failed in Sydney, you could always try Melbourne or Goulburn or Narrabri, where you might find a more sympathetic medical officer. In the middle of 1915, the government relaxed standards because casualties needed to be replaced. Australia had by now offered to send every man it could muster – not just the original 20,000. Boys who failed at age fourteen six months earlier might now succeed.

There was also a loophole. An order from late August 1914 stipulated that youths under nineteen could be enlisted as buglers provided they had the written consent of their parents. This explains the number of under-age boys listed as buglers – often in their death notices. The bugle did not save these minstrel boys.

Later in the war, official indifference changed, perhaps in step with public disquiet about casualty lists. The government began in late 1917 to crack down on the numbers of boys still in the ranks. In 1918, some ships were bringing back

> No-one knows how many under-age boys joined the Australian and New Zealand forces, nor how many came back. They fought in every major battle in which the Anzacs took part, but left little trace.

thirty or more under-age boys at a time, rounded up and scolded for their service, their pay docked for inconveniencing the army and country they had served for up to four years. This was perhaps the final indignity – to be ostracised by those who had let them go.

No-one knows how many under-age boys joined the Australian and New Zealand forces, nor how many came back. They fought in every major battle in which the Anzacs took part, but left little trace. Most of their letters are gone, if they wrote them. Few kept a diary, probably because teenage boys are less inclined to do so, and it was forbidden anyway. Some of them have no known photograph and no known grave. It's as if they never existed: all the more reason to tell some of their stories.

None could know what they were letting themselves in for. Neither did their (mostly) British generals, who thought that cavalry charges and stout hearts could still win wars against a new industrialised form of war, dominated by big guns. Families and recruiting officers didn't know either: many thought the war would be over by

Christmas, when the great powers came to their senses. It's easy to forget that almost no-one, in any of the countries involved, had clear sight of how monstrous this war would become. And all of them sent under-age boys to war, not just Australia and New Zealand.

In the end, the stories of the under-age Anzacs lead more to pity than glory. Some died in battle, some in hospitals and casualty clearing stations, or months later in vast war hospitals in England. Some were wounded, healed and wounded again before they were killed. Some were patched up and sent home minus an arm or a leg, or with lungs damaged by gas. Some were sent home because they were under-age. Some have graves, many do not. Some just disappeared into the ground, victims of the pitiless and unprecedented slaughter by artillery on the Western Front in France and Belgium from 1916 onwards.

After the war, those who had survived faded back into Australian society, like their older comrades, with all the same legacies of illness, debility, alcoholism and shell-shock, or what we now call

In the end, the stories of the under-age Anzacs lead more to pity than glory. Some died in battle, some in hospitals and casualty clearing stations, or months later in vast war hospitals in England. Some were wounded, healed and wounded again before they were killed.

post-traumatic stress disorder (PTSD). The survivors often got into trouble, getting drunk and raving in the streets before the police locked them up or charged them with vagrancy. A few died soon after they got back, in accidents that make you wonder if they were suicides. A few managed to live long lives, into the 1980s and 1990s. Some even became famous, like Alec Campbell and Jim Martin, whose stories have been told in earlier books.

No-one apologised for letting them go, but no-one asked for an apology. Even if there was an official failure in what we now call the duty of care, it was a shared failure. Many families allowed their sons to go. I have not found any boy who was forced to go. In a very real sense these boys wanted to become men and they did so, if they lived long enough.

For the others, the traces of grief they left behind are still visible, a hundred years later. War cemeteries in Turkey, France and Belgium carry reminders that families still visit these lost boys. Some carry an Australian or New Zealand or British flag; some leave personal messages in plastic sleeves on graves lovingly tended by the Commonwealth War Graves Commission, which was formed after the war to look after the graves of almost a million British and colonial war dead.

These cemeteries are beautiful places, as peaceful and tranquil as their deaths were not. At least for those who have a grave, there is a kind of camaraderie here. Man and boy have become equal at last, in memoriam. ❀

TURKEY
1915

ALBERT SCOTT, JOHN LYONS & HUGHIE O'DONNELL

OUR THREE SONS

ALBERT SCOTT, a Queensland cane-cutter, was 'thoroughly anxious to serve' in the First World War when he was seventeen.

When war broke out, Andrew Fisher was about to become prime minister of Australia for the third time in six years. He was a quietly spoken Scot, a miner who had migrated to Australia in 1885. He had led the Australian Labor Party since 1907, guided by firm socialist principles and a high sense of humanity. The idea of war appalled him but his loyalty to Great Britain was firm, even if his belief in its greatness was qualified.

At the end of July 1914, as the drums beat their loudest in Europe, Fisher pledged Australian support for the Mother Country if war should come. Fisher won the election on 5 September 1914, a month into the war. On 7 September he gave a speech from a hotel balcony in Maryborough, Queensland, in which he repeated his now famous phrase: Australia would support Britain 'to the last man and the last shilling' against its foes. The crowd cheered lustily.

A few kilometres from this hotel balcony, Albert Stanley Scott 'heard the call'. He was the fifth son of Joseph and Eliza Scott, who had lived in Gympie in earlier years. They now grew sugar cane in a beautiful valley at Mount Bauple, halfway between Gympie and Maryborough. Before they met and married in Brisbane, Joe Scott had followed the same path as Andrew Fisher – leaving Britain for a better future. The Scotts almost certainly knew Fisher, who had come to Gympie as a miner in 1887.

After his schooling at Mount Bauple, Albert Scott went cutting cane – back-breaking physical work. The photograph

> Older boys could go to war as heroes, with a party and cheers, and crying mothers and sisters waving handkerchiefs and flags. Boys who were under-age had to steal away and be cunning about it.

taken just after he enlisted shows he had the hands to prove it. He looks like he's wearing leather gloves. Even so, at five feet six-and-a-half inches (168 centimetres), he was just tall enough to get into the army. He was a skinny fifty-seven kilograms, with tanned face and ears that look like they could have lifted him off the ground in a high wind. With seven brothers and three sisters, those ears are bound to have attracted comment.

Recruiting began in Melbourne on 5 August and in Sydney six days later. Men had to be between nineteen and thirty-eight, at least five feet six inches tall (168 centimetres) with a chest measurement of at least thirty-four inches (eighty-six centimetres). If under twenty-one, they had to have the written consent of a parent. Albert set off for the recruiting station with a letter signed by both parents. 'We trust you will endeavour to pass him as he is thoroughly anxious to serve in some capacity.'

Enlisting at Maryborough on 23 September, he was one month past his seventeenth birthday, although he claimed to be eighteen. The recruiters sent him to Enoggera Camp in Brisbane – where the 15th Battalion was being raised.

In central Victoria, John Thomas Lyons also 'heard the call'. This was a popular patriotic phrase at the time. It's probably fair to say that each man and boy heard a different call, whatever it was – for some it was the Empire, for others it was duty or God or adventure. For some it was an escape from poverty or misery.

John Lyons was the eldest in a large Catholic family that would eventually number eleven children – same as the Scotts. They lived in South Murchison, where John Thomas senior was a 'channel overseer', working on the Goulburn Weir.

John Thomas junior was sixteen and a few months old. Older boys could go to war as heroes, with a party and cheers, and crying mothers and sisters waving handkerchiefs and flags. Boys who were under-age had to steal away and be cunning about it. John had a friend who wanted to go too. They knew the train to Melbourne would be the first place people would look, so they hopped on their bicycles in August 1914 and took the road north towards Shepparton. So began a very long ride to Sydney, more than 700 kilometres away. That they chose this path, rather than ride 170 kilometres to Melbourne, tells us something about how determined they were.

John knew it would take at least a week, maybe more. They would have to avoid the towns in daylight, in case a policeman was looking for them. They would have to sleep rough or in farm sheds, but the farmers might give them food and water, if they explained what they were doing. They would not be the only ones on this road: many men who didn't have the money for the train were walking to Sydney to join up. There were no country enlistment centres yet.

John made it to Sydney by early September. On 3 September, the Australian government offered Britain a second contingent of 6000 men, on top of the 20,000 already promised. This was the day that John Lyons signed his papers. He listed his occupation as labourer and was assigned to A Company, 3rd Battalion.

He claimed he was nineteen years and two months – adding about thirty-two months. He gave his correct birthplace – Murchison, Victoria – but put down the name of his second brother Victor as next of kin. Curiously, he did not bother to change his name. The examining doctor described John as five feet six inches tall (168 centimetres) and 149 pounds (sixty-eight kilograms), complexion fair, eyes blue, hair brown. That doctor was Captain JWB Bean, brother of the Australian journalist, Charles Bean, who was preparing to depart as Australia's first and only war correspondent of this new war.

Captain Bean had qualified in medicine at Cambridge and specialised in anaesthetics and dentistry. It tells us something about the leniency of recruiting in 1914 that a man as experienced as Bean would allow a boy of sixteen to join the battalion, but he was hardly alone. Medical officers all over the country turned a blind eye to those under nineteen. In the case of John Lyons, they even took him when there were many older men trying to find a place in the new forces.

John's plan worked. He spent the next six weeks hiding in plain sight, as the unit received equipment and stores in dribs and drabs. They were camped at Kensington Racecourse, a pony track now long gone, where the training was as primitive as the facilities. The men of the first contingent could march in step, but few knew one end of a rifle from the other, and discipline was sometimes optional. Colonel Henry MacLaurin, commander of the 1st Brigade, complained that the hurried recruitment had drawn 'all the wastrels of the city'. The September arrivals from the country, like John, were considered much more suitable. They were bigger, stronger, fitter and most of them already knew how to shoot.

John left Sydney on the *Euripides*, on 20 October 1914. He hit the jackpot in terms of vessel: *Euripides* was the largest passenger and cargo ship in the Aberdeen White Star Line, built to carry 1200 paying passengers. After a lightning refit in Brisbane, she could now carry twenty-nine officers, 2202 other ranks (and fifteen horses). The great danger on these ships, with so many men packed in, was infectious disease. Steaming away from Sydney, the *Euripides* already had eight men in the sick bay with gonorrhoea, and one case of measles.

Euripides arrived in King George's Sound, off Albany in Western Australia, on 26 October, joining thirty-six other transport ships in the first Anzac convoy. They sailed on 1 November – 30,000 men and 8000 horses, on twenty-six Australian and ten New Zealand ships, guarded by three escorts: HMS *Minotaur*, HMAS *Melbourne* and HMAS *Sydney*. The Japanese armoured cruiser *Ibuki* joined them two days later with two more transport ships out of Fremantle. This convoy, twenty-four kilometres long and nineteen kilometres wide, was the largest ever to leave Australia.

None of the soldiers on board knew where they were going, but they all knew it was going to be big – the most wonderful and terrible adventure. The

terrible started immediately: thousands were seasick. The smell of vomit and horse shit must have been overpowering.

Ten days after John Lyons sailed, Hugh Brian O'Donnell presented himself for medical examination at the Kalgoorlie recruiting office. Dr Samuel Mathews looked him over and saw a splendid lad, five feet eleven inches (180 centimetres) tall, weighing 126 pounds (fifty-seven kilograms), with blue eyes and fair hair. Hughie said he was a miner from nearby Kanowna, where his parents ran a pub. He claimed to be nineteen years old, and Mathews did not argue. Hundreds of miners from Kalgoorlie, Kanowna and Boulder were already on their way to war in the first convoy. Hughie arrived at Blackboy Hill in Perth two days later and was allocated to C Company, 11th Battalion. Hughie had not lied about anything except his age on his forms, which suggests he had his parents' blessing. He put his mother Lily as next of kin. His real age was sixteen and two months.

After basic training at Blackboy Hill, he shipped out in late February on the transport ship *Itonus* from Fremantle, bound for Egypt.

While John Lyons was on a ship heading north, cane-cutter Albert Scott was on a train heading south for Melbourne. The 15th Battalion was comprised mostly of Queenslanders but a quarter were from Tasmania. The two groups were about to meet at Broadmeadows Camp.

They were now part of the 4th Brigade, a dinkum coalition of men from every state, under John Monash, a portly and ambitious civil engineer from Melbourne. The 13th Battalion was from New South Wales, the 14th

---

PRIVATE HUGHIE O'DONNELL, from Kanowna, Western Australia, is likely to have had his parents' permission when he enlisted at sixteen years and two months old.

from Victoria and the 16th from South Australia and Western Australia. This was the first fully national brigade in the AIF. Some were meeting men from other states for the first time. Rumours were rife. Indeed, there were so many untruths in the air they soon attracted a nickname – 'furphies'. A Shepparton firm called Furphy provided the wagons that hauled away the human waste from the Broadmeadows latrines.

Albert was not perhaps the most natural soldier. On 18 December, he was absent from a roll call. Two days later, he was found in bed after the buglers sounded 'Reveille'. He may have decided, like hundreds of other men, to have a night on the town before departure. He was fined a day's pay and admonished. Three days later, Albert's unit embarked on the White Star Line's SS *Ceramic*. They too were bound for Egypt. By early February, they were at Zeitoun Camp outside Cairo, wondering what was next.

The only person who could have told them was Winston Churchill, First Lord of the Admiralty. The British and French armies were deadlocked on the Western Front in France and Belgium, mired in trench warfare after seven months of attrition. Churchill wanted to take the pressure off the Russian army, so that they might break through against the German forces in the east. Turkey had entered the war on the German side at the end of October. Churchill was determined to force the Dardanelles by sea and knock the Ottoman Empire out of the war. When the British navy failed to do so in March, Churchill convinced the War Cabinet to mount an amphibious landing on the Turkish Aegean coast. They would rout the Turkish guns that protected the straits, then storm on to Constantinople. The Australians and New Zealanders in Egypt were keen to fight. The British, French and Indians would join them for a landing in late April.

The fate of Albert Scott – and that of every Australian and New Zealand soldier then in Egypt – was now set. The Australians would join this European war at the point where Europe begins – the Bosphorus. None of them knew the plan yet, and very few would have known the name of the Gallipoli peninsula.

None of the soldiers on board knew where they were going, but they all knew it was going to be big – the most wonderful and terrible adventure.

In Egypt in December, as Albert was still on the high seas, the NZ Expeditionary Force (NZEF) and the first three brigades of the AIF were combined to become the Australian and New Zealand Army Corps, which clerks quickly shortened to 'ANZAC'. This crew was motley: it also included the Indian Mounted Artillery and the 29th Indian Brigade, the Ceylon Planters Rifle Corps, two British divisions and the Zion Mule Corps, consisting of 650 Jews recruited in Egypt.

Hundreds of ships had gathered for the assault.

The Turks knew they were coming, just not quite where or when. They had reinforced defences all along the peninsula, digging in on the high ridges to wait. They were commanded by experienced officers, both Turkish and German.

The British commander Sir Ian Hamilton decided to confuse them by seeming to land everywhere at once. Ships lined up all around the peninsula and feigned landing preparations. The real landings were to be on several beaches at Cape Helles, on the tip of the peninsula, by British forces, while French forces landed on the Asian side as a diversion. The Australians and New Zealanders would go in to the north of Cape Helles, on a five kilometre stretch of the Aegean coast largely guarded by harsh cliffs and ravines. They were to come ashore at the lowest part, between the Gaba Tepe headland and an old fisherman's hut.

Historians still argue about why the 30,000 Australian and New Zealand forces landed in the wrong place, 1.6 kilometres north of where they intended. The terrain here was much steeper and rougher, making the advance inland much harder. Blame has been laid variously on the currents and the inexperience of the British sailors commanding the landing boats, but this rougher spot was also less heavily guarded. The mistake may have reduced the casualties.

In truth, the campaign was a debacle: badly planned, badly resourced and badly led. The British, from a firm sense of superiority, assumed the Turkish troops to be inferior and demoralised: they would dissolve and run. Some did, but most fought like lions for a cause they believed in: defence of their country. The Turks thought they were fighting 'the British'. When they realised they were also fighting Australians and New Zealanders, they were as confused as some of their opponents. God is great, but where is New Zealand?

✦

Albert Scott's 15th Battalion came ashore at what we now call Anzac Cove in the evening of 25 April 1915, twelve hours after the initial landing. Its companies were sent up the ridges to plug gaps in a patchy Australian line. Like everyone else, they became hopelessly fragmented. The Turks, by now reinforced, counter-attacked in several places. The Anzacs clung to a series of outposts and ridges on the heights, short of their objectives and in danger of being over-run.

Albert would not have slept much in the first seventy-two hours. The 15th were concentrated on Pope's Hill, Courtney's Post and Quinn's Post – high ridges above the beach. The Turkish trenches were just a few metres away, which meant that bombs could be thrown by hand. The Turks were masters at this and they had plentiful supplies of what the Australians called 'cricket ball bombs'. The Anzacs had to make their own. They set up a factory on the beach, filling jam tins with nails and explosives.

We know the names of at least twenty under-age boys who fought on Gallipoli, but the real number is much higher – almost certainly in the hundreds. No-one has compiled a list of those who lived through it, only those who did not. Albert Scott, the smiling cane-cutter, has the sad distinction of being the first Anzac boy soldier to die on Gallipoli.

There is no record of where he died, simply a date, 28 April. That means he experienced at most three days of fighting, but those three days were merciless. The continual sniping made the rudimentary trenches of Quinn's Post ridiculously dangerous; it was little better at Courtney's Post and Pope's Hill.

Albert was buried at Pope's Hill Cemetery, so we know he died nearby.

His parents were notified of his death by telegram. In the early years of the war, these were usually delivered by a local clergyman. Albert's name was then wrongly included in a list of wounded published in the *Sydney Mail* in mid-June, raising hopes that he was still alive. Albert's father wrote to see if it could be true. The army wrote back that, as far as they knew, he was dead.

In 1923, his remains were reinterred at Quinn's Post Cemetery, Pope's Hill plot. His inscription, decided by his parents Joseph and Eliza, says:

'Dearest son, thou has left us, we thy loss most deeply feel.'

In September 1919, Albert's brother Walter, aged ten, took part in a tree-planting ceremony for Arbor Day at the Rossendale State School, in honour of boys of the district who had died in the war. Walter planted a camphor laurel for Albert, the brother he had barely had time to get to know.

Hughie O'Donnell's 11th Battalion was among the first ashore at Gallipoli on 25 April, but Hughie was not with them. He had been struggling to catch up since he enlisted, always one step behind. While a battalion was at full strength of about 1000 men, it had no need to call up reinforcements, except to replace men who were sick or absent. Once the 11th Battalion went into action at Gallipoli, things moved quickly, because of the casualties. On 5 May, the battalion had lost thirty-eight men killed and 200 wounded since the landing, and another 197 were still missing. The battalion was effectively at half strength after ten days.

Hughie finally arrived on Gallipoli on 7 May in a group of 214 reinforcements. He went into C Company under Captain Raymond Leane, who had already distinguished himself as a leader during the first weeks. Ray Leane had been a successful merchant in Kalgoorlie before the war, and a resident of Boulder. As in many battalions, men from the same town or district were kept together, as much as possible. Hughie's C Company was largely made up of men from the West Australian goldfields. He had friends among them, like David Crisp, who had worked at the post office in Kanowna when Hughie was a boy. Crisp was ten years older, and an Anglican like Hughie.

Soon after Hughie arrived, the 11th Battalion was sent to hold a section of the line at Bolton's Ridge, with the 2nd and 3rd Battalions on their left. Hughie and John Lyons – a long-distance cyclist – were now within coo-ee of each other's positions, in a line of trenches that ran from the beach near Gaba Tepe to the hill known as Baby 700, where the Turks could see most of their positions.

John, the sixteen-year-old from Murchison, came ashore in the second or third wave on the first day of the landing. He survived those first terrible

This memorial holds the only known photograph of **JOHN LYONS**, a long-distance bike rider from South Murchison, Victoria.

weeks, while many around him in the 3rd Battalion did not. Colonel MacLaurin, his brigade commander, was one of the dead.

After three weeks, a stalemate had set in. The British and French had failed in an attack at Krithia on 8 May, but kept up the pressure on Turkish battalions at Cape Helles. The Anzacs clung to the heights above Anzac Cove, opposite determined Turkish defences, caught between the Aegean Sea and razor-backed ridges.

The German commander of the Turks, General Otto Liman von Sanders, wanted to drive the Anzacs back into the sea with a wide frontal assault, starting early on 19 May. New battalions arrived from Constantinople, including young officers straight from the academy. The plan was simple and blunt: 42,000 Turkish infantry would fling themselves at 17,000 Anzacs and overwhelm their positions with sheer numbers. The Anzacs could tell something was about to start, and made ready to repel the attack.

Until this point, the Anzacs had rarely seen their enemy, concealed as he usually was in well-prepared trenches. Now he came at them out of the pre-dawn, thousands of voices crying 'Allah', bayonets glinting in the moonlight. The attack was sheer madness and over the next ten hours, it became a bloodbath. On Johnston's Jolly, where John was firing, the initial waves of Turkish troops were mown down by machine guns. They kept coming and dying. The men of the 3rd Battalion climbed up on the parapet to continue firing, as dazed and wounded Turks tried again and again to rush forward, against all odds. Anzacs fought each other for the best positions, their guns overheating as dawn broke. And with the light, the Turks could see the Australians sitting cockily on the parapets – and took careful aim.

Ten thousand Turks fell in that assault, for no gain. Charles Bean, witnessing the slaughter, wrote that the Australians' attitude to the Turkish soldier changed that day. A fierce hatred had motivated the Anzacs since the landing. That now disappeared, as the Turkish soldiers displayed a sobering discipline and bravery, refusing to surrender or retreat.

These three boys were among the first casualties of the war for Australia, their families among the first to experience the grief that would hit so many others over the next four years.

Anzac losses amounted to 160 men killed and 468 wounded. Unfortunately for one family in South Murchison and another in Kanowna, those numbers included their sons, Private John Lyons and Private Hughie O'Donnell.

Hughie was killed by a shrapnel blast. Captain Leane wrote to Jack and Lily O'Donnell soon after to say that although he had not known their son long, Hughie had impressed him as a lad who would fearlessly do his duty. 'He lived but a few minutes and his last words were addressed to Private Crisp also from Kanowna,' wrote Leane. A chaplain also wrote to the family, telling them that Hughie's last words had been: 'Tell my mother I died fighting'. He was one of nine men in the 11th Battalion killed that day.

We know less about John Lyons' death, except that he fell nearby on the same day. Both boys died during the greatest firefight that the Anzacs had yet seen – and during the greatest victory they would have on Gallipoli.

The tactics used there are hard now to understand. Frontal assaults against machine guns were doomed to failure, and still, both sides attempted them. The Anzacs would use the same tactics a few weeks later on a smaller scale in the August offensive, with huge losses. To some extent, 19 May was a turning point in the fight for Gallipoli. The Turks gave up the idea of winning by offence and settled in to win by implacable defence, knowing that winter would eventually be on their side. The Anzacs, in turn, now knew the determination of the men they were facing, if they had not already.

The *Murchison Advertiser* of 25 June 1915 acknowledged that John Lyons,

> The tactics used at Gallipoli are hard now to understand. Frontal assaults against machine guns were doomed to failure, and still, both sides attempted them.

now seventeen, was the first soldier from the district to die in the First World War. They mentioned his age without using the words 'under-age'. John's father would enlist in February 1916 and follow in his late son's footsteps to Europe. He was luckier: at forty-two, he developed rheumatism soon after arriving in France and was invalided back to Australia. Hughie O'Donnell is thought to be the youngest West Australian to die on Gallipoli, aged sixteen years and eight months.

These three boys were among the first casualties of the war for Australia, their families among the first to experience the grief that would hit so many others over the next four years. Albert Scott's siblings had many children. There are now at least 300 descendants of that large family, according to Adrian Scott, who grew up on the same farm at Mount Bauple. A number of them have been to visit Albert's grave on Gallipoli.

In October 1915, Prime Minister Andrew Fisher resigned in favour of his deputy, the belligerent London-born Welshman William Morris Hughes, who embraced the war as a holy duty and a cleansing fire. One of Hughes's first acts was to promise 50,000 more Australian men to the conflict. Meanwhile, in South Murchison, Mount Bauple and Kanowna, three mothers and three fathers wept for three sons. 🌸

BILLY RILEY, ARTHUR WOLSLEY & JOE HEARN

A HOUSE CALLED KRITHIA

Desperate to fight for his country, sixteen-year-old **BILLY RILEY** enlisted two weeks after war broke out in 1914.

Billy Riley, Arthur Wolsley and Joe Hearn had little in common except youth. Each was no more than sixteen when he went off to Gallipoli, with or without parental permission. Joe was from a poor family, so his pay could have made a difference. Billy had been educated at one of Melbourne's best schools, until his parents separated and his mother fell on hard times. Arthur was a gardener from Caulfield, from a family that was more financially comfortable. The sons of rich men went to war for high ideals, if they went at all; the rest had fewer choices.

William Edward Riley enlisted two weeks after war began. He was just shy of sixteen years and three months old, though he wrote nineteen on his form. That was his second lie.

The first was his new identity – Edwin Hayes, born in Sydney, clerk by trade.

> Billy Riley enlisted two weeks after war began. He was just shy of sixteen years and three months old, though he wrote nineteen on his form. That was his second lie.

He claimed to have had six months in the citizen's militia forces at Balmain, a Sydney suburb. As he enlisted in Richmond, Victoria, around the corner from where he lived with his mother, he was hoping no-one would check.

In truth, the recruitment officers had little time to check, even if they had wanted to.

The recruiting offices at the Victoria Barracks (so named in both cities) were swamped. In the first two weeks, 7000 men were accepted in Victoria and 10,000 had applied in Sydney. The recruiters had their pick of the new country's manhood – Boer war veterans, British men abroad, experienced members of the militia. That may be why Billy listed those six months in the Balmain militia; it would give him an edge. We don't know if he had ever been to Sydney, let alone the Balmain militia.

There is no signature from either parent on his attestation form. He put down his mother as next of kin, but invented a new name for her, Clara Hayes. He gave her address as 80 Glebe Road, Sydney. He got that wrong – the street is Glebe Point Road. These actions show he had not asked her permission, although she found out soon enough.

In truth, Billy was probably running away from an unhappy home life. His parents, William and Clara, had married in Perth in October 1897. Clara was twenty-one, her husband thirty-seven. Billy was born seven months later in Whittlesea, Victoria, where Clara grew up. Two sisters soon followed. William senior had been a miner in Western Australia and may have done well, because they enrolled their son at the exclusive Scotch College in Melbourne in 1907. There is a photo of young Billy in 1905, looking extremely well groomed. Billy attended Scotch for three years, but then his fortunes changed. Clara left his father in 1910. She would later cite his drinking and what she called 'family differences'. She wrote to the army in 1920 to explain her circumstances: 'During that time I have had very little assistance from my husband. I have supported myself and children to the best of my ability.'

She said that her son was always in her care, with the exception of the short time when 'my husband took him away from school unknown to me'. Her husband had told the boy he was taking him to buy him something and placed him in 'the Geelong orfornage where he took ill, then he brought him back to me'. How Clara sustained the family is unknown – but single mothers in the inner cities had few choices, other than factory work or domestic service. It may be that the two daughters were living with their father by 1914.

After Billy enlisted, Clara wrote to her estranged husband, who was now driving trains and living at a railway camp in Gippsland, to say that the boy was going to the war, 'but he failed to answer it and refused to let the girls write to him or see him before he went away …'

Billy joined the 6th Battalion, his service number a proud 316. He had no difficulty passing the physical: he was five feet eight inches tall (173 centimetres) and weighed sixty-eight kilograms, with the required thirty-four-inch chest. He was blue-eyed with dark brown hair and a fair, clear complexion. He put down his religion as Catholic. The medical officer would have also checked Billy for scars or distinctive marks. One wonders how many of the recruits understood the purpose of this record: if all else failed, it could be used to identify their body.

A studio photograph, taken before Billy left Melbourne, shows a fresh-faced young man with handsome features and a hint of a wry smile. His tunic looks overly large and uncomfortable, his pockets stuffed, his cap at the required jaunty angle. He has kind eyes and a slightly shy look.

Billy joined the river of men flowing into Broadmeadows Camp, in a field north of Melbourne, for basic training. And this did mean basic: the men lived in bell tents they erected themselves, sleeping on mattresses stuffed with straw. They washed their clothes in buckets and spent their days learning

to march, take orders and dig trenches. After some time, they were shown how to fire a rifle, but most of those who left Australia in the first contingent at the beginning of November 1914 were little more than civilians with sore feet.

By the time the 6th Battalion arrived in Egypt on 2 December 1914, Private Edwin Hayes (Billy's new name) had already been fined for being absent without leave on two occasions – on 15 September and 3 October. Both of these were before the battalion embarked from Australia on the *Suffolk*, a 7000-ton steamship. Neither absence was unusual; many soldiers took 'time off' to say goodbye to their families.

In Sydney, Alexander Joseph 'Joe' Hearn was a fifteen-year-old tailor's machinist. His family had emigrated from England in the early months of 1914, finding lodgings in Campsie, an inner-western suburb of Sydney. They were 'Geordies', from

Newcastle-Upon-Tyne, poor Catholics trying to find a better life. Morris Hearn was illiterate; his wife Margaret or one of the children handled all correspondence after the war. For Joe, as with most fifteen-year-olds of the working class, school was a memory. They worked or they starved. The Australian Army paid five shillings a day. The rate was based on what men were paid in the militia before the war. Once a soldier's unit left Australia, an extra shilling was due, but compulsorily deferred, to be paid on return. Joe allocated two of his five shillings to his family, which tells us that supporting them was a consideration. For some families, that money and one less mouth to feed was a blessed relief.

Joe joined up on 16 November 1914. He claimed he was twenty-one, so he did not have to produce consent from his parents. He had brown eyes and dark hair. Someone may have suspected he was under-age, because they sent him home for three months. He was not required at Liverpool Camp until 2 February 1915, and then they made him a bugler – one of the jobs routinely given to under-age boys. He was allocated to the 2nd reinforcements of the 4th Battalion. He was probably the youngest of those 150 men. They shipped out of Sydney on 11 February 1915, on the *Seang Bee*, bound for Egypt.

Of these three boys, Arthur Garnet Wolsley was the last to leave Australia, but he was still in time for Gallipoli. Arthur was a gardener from Caulfield, Melbourne, with three brothers and a sister. He grew up within coo-ee of Caulfield Racecourse, which may have been where he did his gardening. Arthur's father, Edward, who was born in Norfolk, England, had been an ironmonger, then a salesman. By 1905, he listed himself as a man 'of independent means'. Arthur did not allocate any of his pay to his family.

Edward Wolsley appears to have given his son a genuine letter of consent to enlist. Arthur presented himself on 29 December 1914, shortly after he turned sixteen. He was initially assigned to the 7th Battalion, 2nd reinforcements. He left Melbourne on the *Clan MacGillivray* two months later and went the same route as most of his predecessors: the dust bowl of Mena Camp, beside the Pyramids. Here he was reassigned to the 5th Battalion, on 4 April 1915. The 5th was a Victorian unit of 'originals' – raised in two weeks in August 1914. They had been kicking sand since the start of December. And, like most of the Australians now in Egypt, they were bored, restless and potentially troublesome – anxious to get to war, preferably against Germans, not Turks. What had they got against the Turks?

On the eve of the landing at Gallipoli, Sir Ian Hamilton was aboard his command ship, the *Queen Elizabeth*, in Mudros Harbour. He was about to command one of the largest amphibious military landings in history, and he was feeling the weight: 'Death grins at my elbow,' he wrote in his diary. 'I cannot get him out of my thoughts … God has started a celestial spring-cleaning, and our star is to be scrubbed bright with the blood of our bravest and our best.' God had not started any of this, but He was already getting the blame. And yet Hamilton's belief that a blood sacrifice was somehow overdue was common, and not just among the British. German and Turkish officers had similarly romantic notions: if God wants war, who are we to say no? And God – whichever god – was always *on their side*, even if he required their blood. In this way, war became not just inevitable but necessary, to wipe out the dross, as well as the bravest and best.

Some men did pray on the decks of the *Galeka*, carrying the 6th and 7th battalions. Major Gordon Bennett noted that they weren't praying so much for their own safety, but that they would not let down their unit or their country. One wonders how he knew.

Billy Riley was aboard the *Galeka*. The men ate a hot breakfast at 2.30 am. It was now Sunday 25 April. Arthur Wolsley was with 1100 men crammed into a small uncomfortable ship, the *Novian*, where the drainage from the horse decks leaked onto the mess tables below. The 'hot breakfast' here was bully beef stewed with potatoes 'and a liberal addition of water'. The 5th had endured three weeks on this dirty ship. Most couldn't wait to get off, even if someone would be shooting at them.

Joe Hearn was on the *Lake Michigan*, with the 4th Battalion. They steamed out of Mudros Harbour at 11 pm on 24 April. Colonel Astley John Onslow Thompson, commanding the 4th, addressed the troops on deck. He expected them to behave like gentlemen at all times and uphold the good name of Australia 'when they reached Constantinople'. Colonel Henry MacLaurin, commanding the 1st Brigade, sent a message affirming his confidence. He told the men to keep a cool head and listen to the fire orders of their officers. He knew they didn't have nearly enough ammunition: 'When you shoot let every bullet find its mark; when you use the bayonet see that you stick it in.' Three days later, a Turkish sniper killed him as he stood up on the hill that now bears his name. Colonel Thompson was already dead, cut down by a machine gun on the second day.

The 3rd Brigade of the AIF (9th, 10th, 11th and 12th battalions) were to land first, as a covering force, with the 12th in reserve. Their commanding officer, Colonel EG Sinclair-Maclagan, had grave doubts about the plan. He told his superior, General Sir William Bridges,

---

German and Turkish officers had similarly romantic notions: if God wants war, who are we to say no? And God – whichever god – was always *on their side*, even if he required their blood. In this way, war became not just inevitable but necessary, to wipe out the dross, as well as the bravest and best.

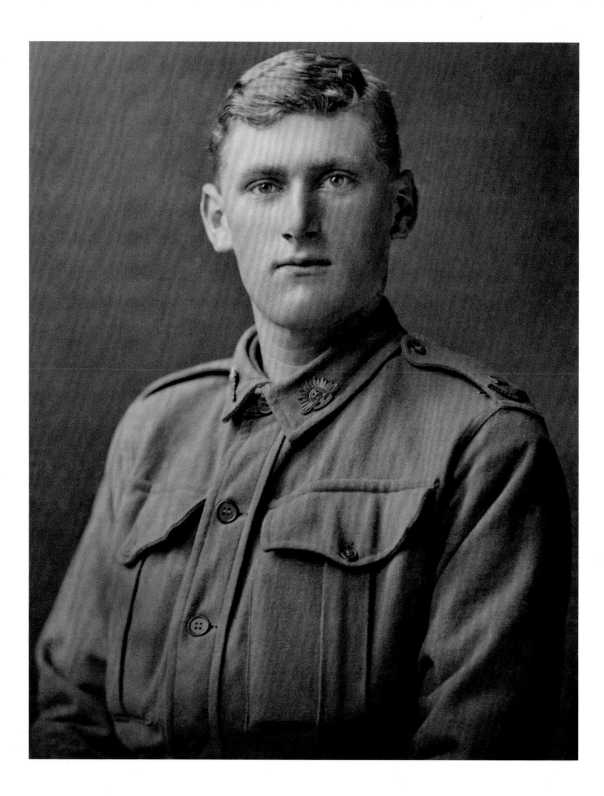

that if the Turks held the ridges in any strength, 'I honestly don't think you'll ever see the third brigade again'.

Some of the English boat crews shared their thick naval rum with the infantry they were carrying ashore – a kind gesture for doomed men. Several kilometres out, the Anzac battalions transferred from larger ships to destroyers, then into small boats to be towed to shore by steam-powered 'pinnaces'. Each man carried a pack weighing almost thirty-five kilograms.

Until just after 4 am, there was little resistance until one pinnace coughed up a thirty-second shower of sparks from its funnel. The Turks opened fire. In the boats carrying the 11th Battalion, raised in Western Australia, the rowers were all shot. They were pushed into the water to enable the rest of the men to get at the oars and row for their lives. As they got close to shore, some men jumped over the side, not realising the depth. They drowned under the weight of their packs.

Those who did get ashore dropped their sodden packs and greatcoats and fixed bayonets. No Australian had yet fired a shot, if he was following orders. They had been told to wait until after dawn.

The 12th Battalion, coming in behind, copped it in their boats, as the tiny Turkish force stepped up fire. There were at least two under-age soldiers in the 12th – Private John Erol Benson, a farmer, and Private Alfred Edwards, a blacksmith's labourer. Both were from Tasmania and aged seventeen. Both made it ashore safely. Both would be dead within a few months.

P rivate Riley, aka Edwin Hayes, the boy with the warring parents, landed at Anzac Cove shortly after 6am in the second wave. The 6th Battalion, under Geelong headmaster Walter McNicoll, had shared the *Galeka* with the 7th Battalion, commanded by

---

PRIVATE JOHN EROL BENSON, a Tasmanian farmer, was seventeen when he joined the 12th Battalion bound for Gallipoli. There, he suffered gunshot wounds that eventually killed him three months later in September 1915.

Harold 'Pompey' Elliott. The first 140 men of the 7th, in four ships' boats, were cut to pieces – 100 men killed or wounded on the way in. McNicoll's men, in faster boats, made it ashore with fewer casualties but no more clarity.

Both battalions were 1.6 kilometres north of where they should have been, making their orders meaningless. Communications were almost non-existent and maps inaccurate. In most cases, men charged up the hills, found a patch of ground and defended it, waiting for someone to tell them where to go and what to do. Over the next few days, the 6th held the 400 Plateau above Anzac Cove. Billy Riley's C Company took a position west of what would soon be called Lone Pine.

Arthur Wolsley, the Caulfield gardener, landed between 5.30 and 8am with the 5th Battalion, who, like most other units, stumbled into the heights not knowing where they were or what their objective now was. The 5th, 6th and 7th battalions became completely mingled as officers fell in droves. Men without leaders started to fall back; corporals and sergeants rallied stragglers to charge forward, some never to be seen again.

Joe Hearn, the Geordie, landed with the 4th Battalion in full daylight, shortly after 7am. The 4th were held in Shrapnel Gully for a few hours, while General Bridges waited for clear information. Late in the afternoon, with a Turkish attack threatening to swamp the Australian 2nd Brigade on 400 Plateau, the 4th went into battle for the first time, spreading out along the southern part of the plateau, plugging gaps and securing Bolton's Ridge.

The inexperience of both officers and men cost Australia dearly that day, but Billy, Joe and Arthur had survived the landing. By nightfall, cold, hungry and exhausted, their greatcoats left behind on the beach, they were huddled in shallow trenches somewhere on 400 Plateau and its flanks, wondering what would come next.

In truth, the battle for Gallipoli was already lost, and some of the commanders on the beach knew that. At their urging, Lieutenant General Sir William Birdwood, the British commander of the Anzacs, sent an urgent message to Hamilton, asking in typically opaque language about a withdrawal: 'if we are to re-embark it must be done at once'.

Hamilton was asleep on the *Queen Elizabeth*. His staff woke him to discuss withdrawal, but he could not believe things were that bad. A British admiral sealed the Anzacs' fate when he said that it would take days to get everyone off, with the likelihood of immense casualties. Hamilton wrote his famous response to Birdwood: 'You have got through the difficult business, now you only have to dig, dig, dig, until you are safe'.

What came next for Billy and Arthur was Krithia – a name that should be better known to Australians, for all the wrong reasons. It wasn't just a costly disaster: it was the third disaster in three days in the same spot.

From the distance of 100 years, it seems to defy logic but logic was starting to take strange forms on Gallipoli a week after the landing.

A string of failures could now be redefined as a sort of success, both in London and on the ships from which the generals observed the peninsula through binoculars. Careers were at stake, not just the lives of men.

Anzac Cove was now a siege, not an invasion. Australia had landed twelve battalions of 1000 men and eight of those battalions had lost half their strength, after five days. The 7th Battalion, hit so hard on the boats, had lost 524 men. Billy's 6th Battalion lost 119 officers and men killed, and hundreds more wounded. All who remained were exhausted. The men of the 5th – Arthur's Victorians – thought they were to be taken off on 5 May for a rest, but it was only a rumour. They boarded destroyers and minesweepers from Anzac Cove, wondering where they were going.

The British and French landings at Cape Helles to the south had been hideously bloody. The forces were ashore but pinned down by a determined Turkish defence in front of a tiny village – Krithia. Behind the Turks rose Achi Baba, one of four major hills that had to be taken (the other three being nearer to Anzac Cove). Hamilton had decided to send some of the colonial troops to help break through at Krithia. The Second Battle for Krithia was about to begin.

Instead of attacking an hour before dawn, as Hamilton wanted, the Allies attacked at 11 am, because Lieutenant General Aylmer Hunter-Weston, commanding the British 29th Division, feared his men would get lost in the dark. Instead they got shot in the daylight. There was no reconnaissance, so the commanders – many of them replacing wounded or dead officers – had little idea of the terrain and their orders arrived late. The British naval guns could not find the Turkish guns so their opening barrage was simply a warning to the Turks. When the attack failed on the first day, 6 May, Hunter-Weston repeated it on the second. Again, little ground was gained. On day three, Hunter-Weston decided to send the Kiwi battalions in on the left, replacing his 29th Division. Hamilton came ashore and watched it from a hill.

Three battalions of New Zealanders went forward in broad daylight across broken but open ground towards Krithia. They made it 400 yards (365 metres) and were cut to shreds, pinned down by a torrent of Turkish fire from positions the New Zealanders could not see. New orders arrived from Hunter-Weston: attack again at 5.30 pm. Hamilton could see the attack was faltering. At 4 pm, he intervened with an order that suggested desperation: the whole line – Kiwis, Australians, British and French – were to rise up at 5.30 pm with fixed bayonets and storm Krithia and Achi Baba. Just like that.

After two days of waiting, the four Australian battalions had forty minutes to reach their start line, 800 metres ahead. Charles Bean was there when McNicoll arrived with his 6th Battalion. They rested for three minutes, then McNicoll rose to blow the whistle to advance. He fell back immediately, shot through the shoulder. Bean crouched in a trench and watched the Australians go forward, despite the odds. He was in awe. His report quoted one leader as shouting, 'Come on chaps, we've got to

This is how Billy Riley and Arthur Wolsley died, in a battle that should never have happened, advancing on an enemy they could not see, under orders from men whose failures had not yet taught them any lessons. It was a day full of heartbreaking bravery and unbearable, maddening waste.

Australian dead on the plains
of Krithia, after the battle.

get it sometime'. Within thirty minutes, Turkish machine guns firing from both sides cut the Australian battalions in half. Watching from the hill, Hamilton was also awed. He wrote later that he heard a wounded British officer say it was worth 'ten years of tennis to see the Australian and New Zealanders go in'.

Since landing at Helles two weeks earlier, the British had lost 10,000 men, killed or wounded, the French, 12,000. In their one day at Krithia, the New Zealanders lost 835 men. The Australian 2nd Brigade lost 1000 men in that terrible hour, from 5 pm to 6 pm on 8 May. For Billy's 6th Battalion, this was their worst day of the war.

This is how Billy and Arthur died, in a battle that should never have happened, advancing on an enemy they could not see, under orders from men whose failures had not yet taught them any lessons.

It was a day full of heartbreaking bravery and unbearable, maddening waste.

Billy has no known grave. So many dead and dying lay on the ground around Krithia that night that no-one knows what happened to them. His name is commemorated on the Helles Memorial there. It's possible he was buried in one of two mass graves dug by two different sets of Australians.

In his memoirs, Captain Percy Lay noted that some of his 8th Battalion men buried fifty-seven men that night; Herbert Lloyd of the 5th Battalion wrote that a group of their men buried eighty-six dead in a mass grave the next morning. Many were never buried. They could not be, because the Turks still held the battlefield.

In 1919, Charles Bean walked the ground again at Krithia and found the remains of Australians 'everywhere on the plain'. He estimated that perhaps

> The Australian 2nd Brigade lost 1000 men in that terrible hour, from 5 pm to 6 pm on 8 May. For Billy's 6th Battalion, this was their worst day of the war.

200 Australians were buried there.

Arthur Wolsley's papers say he died at No 11 Clearing Hospital, Gallipoli, on 9 May, from a gunshot wound to the abdomen. What that likely means is that he was wounded in the late afternoon of 8 May with his battalion, then helped back to a dressing station where he died. An entry in red pen says he was buried at Lancashire Landing Cemetery, 600 yards north of W beach at Cape Helles.

When Arthur joined up, his parents lived at Railway Road in Caulfield. After the war, they moved to a new house just around the corner. They called their new house 'Krithia'. It takes a minute to understand what that name must have meant to them, and the pain that went with it – pain they would never allow themselves to forget.

Fifteen-year-old Joe Hearn, still on the hills above Anzac Cove with the 4th, copped a bullet the day after Riley and Wolsley at Krithia. His service record says he was wounded on 10 May, with a severe gunshot wound to the shoulder. He was taken to a hospital ship and admitted to the 17th General Hospital at Alexandria on 13 May.

A month later he was sent to England, where they tried to save him at the 4th General Hospital in London. He died of wounds there on 4 August, the records noting 'empyema', an infection of the lungs. It is a slow and extremely painful way to die. Nine days later, newspapers across Australia carried a report of his death, under variations of the same headline: 'Australia's Youngest Soldier Death in London'. We know now that he was not the youngest soldier to die, but these reports say he was wounded 'by a sniper through both collarbones, and having his right arm broken'.

'The force of the bullet striking him, spun him round and he then received five bullets in the back, the whole of them passing through his left lung,' the Sydney *Sun* informed its readers on Friday, 13 August. The article, with a photograph of Joe, was unattributed, but the information is most likely to have come

Billy Riley has no known grave. So many dead and dying lay on the ground around Krithia that night that no-one knows what happened to them.

from his parents. Joe's last journey was back to Newcastle-Upon-Tyne, where he was born. He is buried there in Byker and Heaton Cemetery, a long way from his immediate family, but close to friends. In March 1922, Joe's sister Lillian wrote to the army about her brother's grave. The family was worried that his grave would be reopened and reused, as was common practice in some parts of Britain. 'Now he has been dead about seven years, usually they open the ground and bury again, and we want to know, could we prevent that by buying the ground. Could you please delay any action if such be the case and give us time to forward the money immediately.'

The army replied that the family had the right to claim title to Joe's grave, via the newly formed Commonwealth War Graves Commission. The CWGC maintains Joe's grave to this day. He is buried beneath a simple inscription: 'R.I.P AN ANZAC'. Joe Hearn had become an Australian, if only in death.

The squabbles between Billy Riley's parents continued into the 1920s. They fought each other for every scrap of his

memory: his medals, his deferred pay, his personal effects. William Senior filled out a statutory declaration declaring that Clara was not 'a fit and proper person' to receive her son's medals. One of the daughters retaliated with a declaration that he had been a terrible father, and she considered her brother was a better father to the family than William had ever been.

Such disputes were not uncommon after the war and they were not only about medals. There were pensions at stake. Based on how many people were dependent on the late soldier before the war, these pensions could make the difference between poverty and a degree of comfort for a poor family. A mother or widow could expect one pound a week, twice that if the deceased had been a breadwinner. An Australian pound was worth 20 shillings. The basic wage in 1914 was 53 shillings.

A pound a week in pension was halfway to happiness for some families – and little or no comfort. They would still have to confront the empty bedroom of their Joe, their Billy, their Arthur, the wardrobe of his clothes, the pictures of his childhood. 🐾

LESLIE SHAW

THE KIWI THAT FLEW

If you had met Leslie Shaw in a bar in the 1930s, you would have heard some tall stories: how he had shot down four German planes in the war (not true) and broken his neck when he crashed his aeroplane in New Guinea (true). He might also have told you he was the youngest Anzac, although he could not have been sure of that. There were many who claimed that distinction: Australian newspapers carried frequent reports naming this person or that, but in Shaw's case, it really was true.

Leslie Shaw is the youngest known Anzac, based on age at enlistment. When he turned up at the New Zealand High Commission in London on 28 September 1914, ready to fight the Germans, Leslie was thirteen years, eight months and six days old. He was a bantam who wanted to be a rooster.

That morning's newspapers were filled with terrible news from the war, then in its seventh week. Three British sister ships – the *Hogue*, *Cressy* and *Aboukir* – had been torpedoed the day before, with the loss of almost 1400 men. Leslie had already made the decision that would shape the rest of his life, for better and worse.

> Leslie Shaw is the youngest known Anzac, based on age at enlistment ... thirteen years, eight months and six days old.

On that Wednesday morning in September, Captain Francis Lampen faced a difficult decision. Lampen, a former British officer, was putting together a unit of New Zealanders based in Britain. Standing before him was a mere boy. Leslie Shaw, five feet five inches (165 centimetres) tall, weighing 53.5 kilograms, was keen to go to war, but he was under-age. Recruits for the New Zealand forces at that time had to be twenty; Leslie had innocently written sixteen on his form. Lampen ignored that, perhaps because he was expecting him.

Strings had been pulled, Leslie told a reporter in Australia some years later. Lampen decided that this boy from a well-connected family in New Zealand was old enough to fight for King and Country.

☀

Leslie Shaw's desire to enlist was not unusual for the times. Boys in the far corners of the British Empire were raised in a martial spirit. Like Australia, New Zealand had compulsory cadet schemes to introduce schoolboys to basic military skills: marching, taking orders, handling a rifle.

When Leslie's parents migrated to Britain in 1912, they sent him to the historic Bedford Grammar School north of London, where his military indoctrination continued. This school's Roll of Honour lists 454 former pupils who died in the First World War. Leslie was at Bedford for eighteen months, from September 1912 until April 1914. After that, he had a private tutor, which might suggest he was not happy at Bedford. English boarding schools could be notoriously harsh and Leslie was a country kid from the far side of the world. Not that he would have really needed outside pressures to make him feel sad and angry: his family life had been in turmoil for two years. The animosity that sometimes characterised his parents' marriage in New Zealand had turned into open warfare before they arrived in Britain. There were divorce lawyers on both sides.

Leslie's father, Langley Lansdowne Shaw, came from farming gentry on the east coast of New Zealand's North Island around Hawke's Bay. In February 1900, he married Mary Reeve at St Paul's Anglican church in Auckland. Mary was twenty-five. Langley, nine years older, was more worldly. Leslie Raymond was born at Korokipo, Napier, on 17 January 1901.

LESLIE SHAW (left) is the youngest-known Anzac, having enlisted at just thirteen years old. He is pictured here on a ship with New Guinea goldfields medical officer Dr Ian Dickson in 1928.

Mary found out soon after that Leslie was not her husband's first child. Langley had fathered two children with a Maori girl, Emere Te Rito, who was seventeen when she bore a son, Manapouri Langley Shaw, around 1893. Another son, Karauria (Claude) followed in 1895.

In 1912, Langley uprooted the family and moved to Australia, where Leslie briefly attended The King's School in Sydney. They soon sailed for England, aboard the SS *Geelong*.

In the divorce papers, Langley accused Mary of adultery with George Akerman, a family friend. Mary denied it and accused her husband of cruelty, and adultery with a Maori woman named 'Gemere'.

Langley had demanded £3000 in damages and custody of the children, who now included a daughter, Doris, born 1903. The divorce was never finalised but it appears they agreed to separate the children. Mary retained custody of Doris and went to live with Akerman, with whom she had more children. Leslie stayed with his father, who gave his consent when Leslie joined the New Zealand Expeditionary Force (NZEF).

It's possible that Leslie's desire to go to war had nothing to do with the divorce, but it hardly seems likely. In his thirteenth year, his family was blown apart by ugly accusations of betrayal on both sides. He was in a new country with few friends, his mother and sister were living elsewhere, and his father was shaken and humiliated by these events. For Leslie, the war may have offered more than adventure: it might have been his chance to run away from his troubles.

Within days of enlisting, thirteen-year-old Leslie Shaw was sleeping under canvas at the freezing Bulford Camp on Salisbury Plain, in Wiltshire. The first task of the 240 men Lampen had recruited as the British Section of the NZEF was to build huts for 4000 troops – half of the New Zealand main force – who were then en route from the Antipodes. The site, called Sling Camp, was little more than a series of markers on the ground.

New Zealand had offered Britain a

force of 8000 men, to be recruited immediately. There was no shortage of volunteers. They left New Zealand in ten ships, heading for Albany in Western Australia. Here they joined the first convoy to leave Australia, an armada of thirty-eight ships carrying another 30,000 men. They sailed on 1 November 1914.

The War Office in London was worried about where to put all these troops from the dominions, who still needed to be trained and equipped for a winter in France. In late November, they ordered the convoy to disembark in Egypt, rather than sail on to England. The Australians and New Zealanders, soon to be known as Anzacs, would complete their training in the desert.

The convoy landed at Alexandria on 3 December. The New Zealanders moved into Zeitoun Camp, east of Cairo – a dusty, fly-blown stretch of desert with freezing nights and sweltering days. Infectious diseases soon spread and equipment brought from rain-soaked New Zealand failed. Wooden wagon wheels shrank so much in the heat that their steel tyres fell off. After two weeks,

eighty-eight horses had died and 240 more were unfit for use. Meanwhile, on Salisbury Plain, Leslie and the rest of the British Section of the NZEF had built a camp for men who would never come. Canadian troops moved into Sling Camp instead.

Leslie and his new comrades sailed for Egypt on the *Dunera*. They marched into Zeitoun Camp on Christmas Eve. Leslie had been in the army for three months and would celebrate his fourteenth birthday at Zeitoun. Not that he would have advertised it: Leslie had to keep his head down, in case a senior officer queried his tender age.

Major General Sir Alexander Godley, the British officer commanding the NZEF, addressed the newly arrived men on Christmas Day: they could choose the engineers or the Army Service Corps, the unit that handled transport, food and ammunition. Leslie and about 100 others joined the No. 1 New Zealand Engineers Field Company. Another 120 men transferred across from the main force. The engineers threw themselves into training, learning how to construct pontoon bridges, erect and dismantle pile drivers, and build roads, reservoirs, wells and trenches. They had to learn regular soldiering as well: route marches, musketry and drill. Leslie's commander was Major FA Ferguson, seconded from the Royal Engineers. None of them knew where they would be sent to fight. Some guessed they might be sent to defend the Suez Canal from the Turks, who were out in the desert, on the other side of the canal.

Leslie had already experienced more of the world than most boys his age. He had sailed halfway round it, seen the tropics, been educated in the manly arts at an esteemed English school and witnessed the bitter breakup of his own family. He had seen the great city of London and the dusty boulevards of Cairo, whose earthly delights were a constant temptation for Australian and New Zealand soldiers. He and his comrades could walk from Zeitoun Camp to Heliopolis, a wealthy suburb of Cairo, where the streets transformed each night into bright parades full of cafes and conjurors, pedlars and acrobats. And Leslie had seen the Pyramids, one of the engineering wonders of the world. If he had needed distraction, there was plenty to be had. He was learning how to build a bridge, shoot a gun, thrust a bayonet. He was expected to be able to kill in a variety of ways, but he had to find one first.

On 10 April, the No. 1 New Zealand Engineers Field Company marched

> The *Goslar* was a miserable tub, so unseaworthy that she needed a week of urgent repairs before casting off. German submarines were active in the Mediterranean and the *Goslar* had lifeboats for just one-third of those on board.

out of Zeitoun on to a train bound for Alexandria. They still didn't know where they were going. As they boarded a captured German coastal steamer called the *Goslar*, the news came that they were going north towards Turkey, not to France. The *Goslar* was a miserable tub, so unseaworthy that she needed a week of urgent repairs before casting off. German submarines were active in the Mediterranean and the *Goslar* had lifeboats for just one-third of those on board. Nor was there even a life jacket for each man. After three days, they arrived in Mudros Harbour on the Greek island of Lemnos, fifty kilometres from the Gallipoli peninsula.

The first of the Australians left Mudros Harbour late on 24 April, charged with landing before dawn on the beach at Gaba Tepe, halfway up the peninsula. The British would land further south at Cape Helles, and the French on the Asian side at Kum Kale. The Australians were to move in from the beach and capture three ridges that ran from the high point of Sari Bair, down to the sea. The New Zealand infantry and engineers would follow later the same day.

Leslie and the No. 1 New Zealand Engineers Field Company steamed out of Mudros at 9 am on Sunday 25 April. They could hear the big guns long before they could see the Gallipoli shore. Leslie Shaw's war was about to begin. He could not have known that he was about to become the youngest Anzac in the landing.

Ferguson led his men ashore at Anzac Cove at about 6 pm that night, carrying picks, shovels, packs and engineering supplies. They went straight to work above the beach digging trenches on Plugge's Plateau. One party built a platform for an Australian howitzer gun further down the beach. Another scraped out holes for machine-gun units, to protect the flanks. The air was full of dust and smoke and the acrid smell of different explosives, but smoke was the Anzacs' friend, concealing them from Turkish snipers. As more men arrived and moved up into the ridges, the wounded came down. Shaw and his fellow engineers could see them lined up along the beach, awaiting treatment, like an open-air hospital ward.

New Zealand and Australian soldiers
land at Anzac Cove, Turkey, in 1915.

Many of them died waiting for transport off the beach.

The No. 1 Field Company camped that night where they were digging, but no-one slept. The unit diary records that they were driven back to the beach for two hours by a fierce shrapnel bombardment. They sustained their first casualty: a man helping to survey a road off the beach was hit by a sniper.

Shaw and the other field engineers had a crucial role. If the invading force was to stay put, they had to build its camps, roads and wharves. They had to ensure water supply, construct trenches from which the infantry operated and assist the signallers to establish communication lines. Shaw's field company worked for forty-eight hours straight to secure the forward positions.

Anzac Cove is surrounded by high ridges, with gullies running down to the beach. Half of the engineers were on Walker's Ridge, a spur of First Ridge, to the north of Anzac Cove. The main route off the beach was further south, skirting around Plugge's Plateau, then up Shrapnel Gully to Monash Valley, running between First and Second Ridge.

The other half of the New Zealand engineers were sent here, to where the first troops ashore were pinned down at key points along Second Ridge. A small force of Australians clung to a series of shallow pits at Quinn's Post, on the very top of the ridge, in view of the Turks. The Kiwi sappers set to work deepening these holes and 'sapping' forward to create a network of support and fire trenches (a trench deep enough for a man to stand up in, with a firing parapet).

Quinn's was the most dangerous place on Gallipoli and would remain so for the whole campaign. Pope's Hill to the left of Quinn's, Courtney's Post and Steele's Post to the right, were hardly less dangerous. The Turks on the hill known as Baby 700 overlooked them all. Everything needed for those positions – ammunition, food, water – had to travel up the same route, through Shrapnel Gully. Leslie would tell a reporter in the 1930s that he was put to work as a runner in Shrapnel

Gully. With telephone wires constantly disrupted, runners were the only reliable means of getting messages up and down, but the gully was 'hot'. Turkish snipers picked off careless men and shrapnel was a constant problem. Leslie was literally running for his life.

The Gallipoli landings were a failure from the first day. The attack was badly prepared, badly resourced and badly led. The Australians landed in the wrong place, the British landings at Cape Helles were a bloodbath, and the Turks were a much more determined opponent than the British had predicted. A stalemate set in quickly, but to admit the attack's failure was to shame its fathers. With enough reinforcements, there was still a chance of success, the Allied commander Sir Ian Hamilton told himself and London. Hamilton and First Lord of the Admiralty Winston Churchill would both lose their jobs in coming months because of the failure at Gallipoli.

The price for the men was much higher: Australia would lose just over 8700 dead and New Zealand, 2700. Britain and Ireland counted 21,000 dead; France, almost 10,000; India, 1350. Turkey lost far more – close to 87,000 men.

A few months later, the Allies attempted to break the deadlock in a complex offensive. On 6 August, the Australians attacked at Lone Pine, a small plateau south of Quinn's Post. The Turkish trenches here were very close, but heavily defended by machine guns. This was a diversion, designed to convince the Turks that this was the main attack.

At the same time, New Zealand, British and Australian troops headed north from Anzac Cove, to attack the steep northern flanks of Sari Bair, the range on which stood the high points of Hill 971, Hill Q and Chunuk Bair. Before this, British troops attacked again at Cape Helles, where they had already sustained great losses. This was another feint, to stop the Turks from sending reinforcements north. Meanwhile, new British divisions would land at Suvla Bay, north of the Anzacs, to establish a base.

The main attack on Sari Bair began after dark on 6 August, as the New Zealand and Australian Division, the British 13th Division and an Indian brigade moved up three valleys on the northern side of Sari Bair. The New Zealand engineers were to play an important role here, and pay a heavy price.

Leslie's company went up the left and middle of these valleys before the Anzacs, clearing wire and other obstacles, consolidating positions and trying to find water. They worked all night to make a mule track up the central valley, Chailak Dere, only to have the track swamped with wounded coming down the next morning. As the sun rose, exhausted British, Australian, Indian and New Zealand troops held grimly to exposed ridges on the left and right, unable to move under deadly Turkish fire. The fight went on through the next day with terrible losses. On the morning of 10 August, the Turks counter-attacked, pouring down the ridges and over-running the Allied gains of the first three days. This was probably the most intense fight that Leslie ever encountered: when they were not digging and grubbing for water, the NZ sappers had to reinforce the firing lines. It was hard and intense fighting, all men to the fore, against a determined and resourceful enemy who came at them with blood-curdling cries of 'Allah!'. The engineers lost many men, but the British attack failed. It was to be the last major British offensive on Gallipoli.

Ten days later, Leslie reported sick and was evacuated to Lemnos Island, then to England for treatment at the 2nd Western General Hospital in Manchester. His file gives one word for his condition: febrile. In a medical context, that means feverish, but it could also lead to a seizure. He was well enough to go on leave in November 1915, and was then assigned to the NZ Base Depot at Hornchurch, London, in late January 1916. For the next six months, he remained there, until transferred to a convalescent depot at Codford, in Wiltshire. Either he was not yet fully recovered, or someone was looking after him. He had just turned fifteen, after all.

Meanwhile, the New Zealand Division had transferred to France, into the hell of

The war on the Western Front was indescribably worse: a new form of industrial slaughter, dominated by heavy guns that pounded the industrial lowlands of Belgium into an unrecognisable quagmire.

the Battle of the Somme, in the summer of 1916. Leslie eventually rejoined them on 16 January 1917 in Flanders, Belgium. Three days later, he was admitted to a military hospital with a slight case of mumps.

He returned to the front in February, one month after his sixteenth birthday. He had been in the army for almost thirty months, but for fifteen of those months he had been ill, convalescent or kept from the fray. He was now to face the battles of Messines and Passchendaele. Nothing he had seen on Gallipoli could have prepared him for this. The war on the Western Front was indescribably worse: a new form of industrial slaughter, dominated by heavy guns that pounded the industrial lowlands of Belgium into an unrecognisable quagmire. Centuries-old drainage channels were obliterated, so the trenches filled with water. The shells destroyed the roads as fast as the engineers repaired them. Trees, farms and villages turned into brick dust. Leslie spent the next nine months here, with the valiant engineers. Those who had come through the Somme in 1916 could not imagine

there could be anything worse, but in many respects Passchendaele was even more hellish. The British had more heavy guns and more shells than at the Somme, and worse weather, turning the ground the infantry had to cross into a foul bog.

At Messines, just south of Ypres, the Germans regularly used phosgene and mustard gas. Among their many tasks, the New Zealand engineers worked frantically to keep water pipes running to the front lines. German gas shells often ruptured them, which left the water around the breaks toxic to the skin. The demand for labour was so strong that 100 infantrymen were attached to each field company in the run-up to the start of the battle on 6 June 1917. The official history of the New Zealand Engineers describes the 'keen disappointment' felt by the engineers when the infantrymen they had been working with for weeks were called forward. The engineers had technical work to do behind the lines but it was hard to watch their new comrades go forward to fight and die. The engineers died too, but not at the rate of those in the front line. This may be part of the reason that Leslie Shaw was able to survive the war.

Passchendaele is a small village on a ridge east of Ypres, in Belgium. The Germans held it and could see all Allied movements in and through Ypres, the once-prosperous medieval city that had been largely turned into rubble since 1914. The Battle of Passchendaele, also known as the Third Battle of Ypres, began on 31 July and had bogged down Allies, literally, in mud, by the time the New Zealand Engineers were called up on 24 September.

All traffic to the front had to go through Ypres, travelling east through what was left of the Menin Gate, towards Hell Fire Corner and the ruined village of Zonnebeke. The road became worse closer to the front. On both sides, the debris of war machinery marked the way: field guns, trucks, wagons, ammunition boxes and spent shells beside dead horses and dead men in slimy shell holes, filled and refilled by late summer rain. This slushy, slippery road was where Leslie's company took up their shovels and picks, trying to keep it open while enemy shells rained shrapnel on their working parties. They worked wet, slept wet and worked again, laying plank roads, hauling bogged vehicles out of the mud and sometimes joining the stretcher-bearers to bring in the thousands of wounded.

Leslie endured a month here. The Canadians took over the sector on 21 October. Leslie was granted leave from 23 October, returning on 8 November. Soon after, his mother wrote to the army to say he was under-age.

> Those who had come through the Somme in 1916 could not imagine there could be anything worse, but in many respects Passchendaele was even more hellish.

That suggests he may have seen her or his sister Doris, now about fourteen, during his leave. He was sent back to England and discharged on 18 December 1917, for being under-age.

Leslie was no longer a mere boy. He had been in the army for more than three years and, for a third of that time, he was close to the action in both Turkey and the Western Front. Almost seventeen, he had become a veteran of war; his body damaged by bouts of illness, his mind full of things he could not unsee. And, like many soldiers confronted with normal life, he couldn't wait to get back to war.

Leslie spent the winter in the UK, plotting his return. As the weather turned in May, he joined the Royal Air Force. He received his commission as a 2nd Lieutenant in No. 62 Squadron on 5 November, returning to France in late 1918 as an observer. The observer sat behind the pilot, manning a gun. Leslie would later claim he shot down four enemy planes but he was probably too late to see any action. The Armistice took effect at 11 am on 11 November 1918. Leslie had survived. He was hardly unscathed, but he was unwounded and undaunted, thinking about his future.

His then commanding officer, Lieutenant-Colonel Louis Shera, wrote a glowing reference. It makes it clear that Shera knew about his age.

'About December 1917, an Army order was promulgated that all those serving who were under-age were to be sent to England for their discharge.

> Almost seventeen, he had become a veteran of war; his body damaged by bouts of illness, his mind full of things he could not unsee. And, like many soldiers confronted with normal life, he couldn't wait to get back to war.

As Shaw was then not quite seventeen years, having joined when 13½ years, and his mother claiming him as well, he was sent to England and discharged.

'During the year he served with the 1st Field Co NZ Engineers, he carried out his duties well, showed that he could be trusted, and was of a courageous nature, keen and quick in emergency, and carried out work equal to, and dangerous as the other sappers. I was personally sorry that it was necessary for him to relinquish his services with the unit. After his discharge from the New Zealand Expeditionary Force he joined up afresh in the Royal Air Force in England and received his commission …

'From my opinion formed in those years I can recommend Shaw to anyone desirous of having a trustworthy, courageous and reliable young man.'

The one word Shera left out was 'restless'. By 1920, Leslie was a tea-planter in India. Then he tried working for a glass merchant. In 1923, he rejoined the RAF and qualified as a pilot. Flying became his new passion –

it combined danger with freedom, and it was a new industry with possibilities for those who dared. Nowhere was there more danger and more money to be made than in the newly discovered goldfields in the mountains of New Guinea, north of Australia. The flying here was seat-of-the-pants. Many of the pilots were 'war birds' who loved the risks as much as the rewards.

The writer Ion Idriess met Leslie in New Guinea, noting in his book *Gold-Dust and Ashes* that Leslie 'did great work in a little Tiger Moth' and a Bristol Fighter that had belonged to the Australian air pioneer, Charles Kingsford Smith. In March 1928, Leslie crashed the Bristol while attempting an emergency landing after dark at Lae. The plane was low on fuel, the strip had no flares out, and Leslie was thrown out of the plane when it somersaulted. A few weeks later he came south to Sydney on business. After seeing several specialists for a sore neck, an X-ray showed he had broken his neck in the crash. He spent six weeks in plaster in a Sydney hospital, where he gave upbeat reports to visiting press-men. 'I don't want people to get the idea that flying is not safe,' he told the Sydney *Sun*.

Ion Idriess admired Leslie's personality. 'Shaw is as lively as a cricket and flying again. It takes a hard knock to kill a New Guinea pilot.'

In fact, hard knocks were just around the corner. The goldfields pilots of New Guinea were notorious drinkers and Leslie appears to have been no different. In February 1929, he and George McNamara, a rubber planter, pleaded guilty to having unlawfully used a motorcar at Sydney on 18 October 1928. The judge was lenient but stern: 'Let me give you warning. I know the tropics, and you keep off the drink,' he told them. The *Sydney Morning Herald* described Leslie as thirty-four, five years older than he was. The legend had become fact.

Leslie tried to straighten up and fly right. He had big dreams. By September of that year, he and a friend announced that they were planning to pilot a flying boat from Western Australia to Tokyo.

Their scheme was national news for a time and then never heard of again – perhaps because the world's stock markets crashed at the end of October.

The Depression was not kind to Leslie Shaw. In 1930, he married Theresa Josephine Morgan in Sydney. He was by now privately employed as pilot to Howard Jolley of the Queensland Probate Insurance Company. They flew all over Australia selling insurance, visiting up to 3000 outback stations each year.

Leslie was still flying in December 1935, but a year later, he was on the skids. Like many returned soldiers, he had become an alcoholic.

Over the next few years he was in trouble with the West Australian police for canvassing donations of a few shillings in support of a fake petition to reduce telephone charges, keeping the money for himself. The police alleged he was 'addicted to drink' and that most of the money he obtained went on alcohol. He was sentenced to two months imprisonment in 1937. Six months later, he was sentenced to four months jail for the same scam.

In 1939, as a new war broke out in Europe, Leslie joined the Royal Australian Air Force as a Flying Officer but was discharged in October 1939. He enlisted again in 1940 in the army, but was discharged in November 1940. In December 1940, he was fined £75 for using premises in Hay Street, Perth, as a common betting house.

Leslie Raymond Shaw died in 1947. He was forty-six years old, one of thousands of returned soldiers who died young. He appears not to have had any children with his first wife, or his second, Marian. His place in Anzac history was largely forgotten until the New Zealand historian Ian McGibbon wrote an article about him in a New Zealand newspaper in 2012. Since that article, the New Zealand War Graves Commission has erected a headstone on his grave in the Anglican section of Karrakatta Cemetery in Perth.

In a sense, Leslie was one of the lucky ones. He came home, although home is perhaps not the right word. His life after leaving for England in 1912 was restless, especially after the war. He seems never to have settled anywhere for long during the 1920s and early 1930s, until reaching Perth, where he spent the last twelve years of his life. He seems to have had a gift for blarney, for adventure, for squeezing the juice from life, until his drinking caught up with him. A man who joins up four times in one lifetime does not like to be bored. And one of the stories he told turned out to be true. He was the youngest Anzac. 🔖

> In a sense, Leslie was one of the lucky ones. He came home, although home is perhaps not the right word. His life after leaving for England in 1912 was restless, especially after the war.

JOHN HARRIS

THE LAMB OF LONE PINE

'Onward, Christian soldiers, marching as to war,
With the cross of Jesus, going on before;
Christ the royal master leads against the flow;
Forward into battle, see, His banners go.'

'Onward, Christian Soldiers',
a 19th century English hymn.

JOHN 'JACK' HARRIS was fifteen when his father signed the permission form for him to go to war. He's pictured in his cadet uniform before enlisting.

Some boys went to war for God, King and Country, and the glory of Empire. Others went for adventure and travel, or to escape a boring job or an unhappy home. We don't know which of these drove John 'Jack' Harris, a slight boy from Waverley in Sydney, but religion may have played a part. He joined the AIF on 2 June 1915. He was fifteen years and seven months old. He would not see his sixteenth birthday.

His story is one of the strangest and saddest in this book, partly because his progression from Sydney teenager to casualty on the heights of Gallipoli took little more than two months. And the one man who might have stopped him, an Anglican clergyman the boy looked up to, did nothing. In fact, he led the way to the battlefield where both were killed within minutes of each other, a few hours after arriving on the peninsula.

The Reverend Everard Digges La Touche was a fiery Anglo-Irish preacher whose sermons in Sydney before the war garnered many followers, some of whom joined up with him. There were enough of them to earn nicknames – 'Digges and

his Ironsides' and 'Digges and his Sol-dier-Saints'. Jack Harris would become one of them.

Australia in 1914 was overwhelmingly Christian, although as historian Michael McKernan has noted, many were Christian 'in name only'. Anglicans made up nearly 40 per cent of the population, Catholics just over 20 per cent. Most of the rest followed the other Protestant creeds, the largest being Methodist and Presbyterian, then Baptist, Congregational and Lutheran.

Protestants were overwhelmingly in favour of the war, Catholics slightly less so, because the Irish loyalties of many Catholics did not extend automatically to defence of the British Empire. Protestant clergymen were, almost by definition, quick to support the war. For Anglicans, the British Empire was part of their religious cosmology. Some saw the war as God's way of 'cleansing' and 'rejuvenating' a tired Europe; others saw a chance for a young country to prove its vitality and equality.

McKernan believes clergymen embraced the war as enthusiastically as the rest of the population and began immediately to surround it with religious and divine significance.

Digges La Touche came from a long line of religious warriors. The Digues de La Touche family were staunch Protestants, hounded out of Catholic France in the seventeenth century. David Digues de La Touche des Rompieres joined the forces of William of Orange in Holland, and fought at the Battle of the Boyne in Ireland. He then set himself up as a banker in Dublin and became very rich. His great-grandson Everard Neal Digges La Touche was a major in the Bengal Lancers, a British Indian Army regiment. His eldest son, who would become the Sydney preacher, was born in 1883 and graduated from Trinity College, Dublin, in 1904. As a curate in Yorkshire and Ireland, he developed a love of public speaking, intellectual contest and controversy. He married

Eva King and they had two children, although his family did not accompany him when he left for Australia around 1912, ostensibly for his health. Everard never saw them again.

Everard seems to have been too restless for mere parish work. He left his first post as vicar of Emmaville, New South Wales, after a short spell in the bush. He taught at the Sydney Anglican theological school, Moore College, for a year, battling anyone he considered a liberal, and resigned from the staff while giving a speech in the presence of the principal, with whom he was in dispute.

> He saw the British Empire as ordained by God and the battle against Germany as a 'holy war' in which he was destined to die.

He saw the British Empire as ordained by God and the battle against Germany as a 'holy war' in which he was destined to die. He told several friends that was what he wanted, even going so far as to redistribute his valuable library among friends in the Sydney clergy before he left.

'He was a born fighter', wrote the former dean of Sydney, AE Talbot, who became a chaplain at Gallipoli and buried him there. 'When the war broke out his patriotism simply possessed him. He laid aside the pen for the sword. He has often been heard to say he was coming here to die for his country.

It turned out to be a true presentiment but his death was the death of a hero and we thank God for it.'

What then does that make the death of Jack Harris, aged fifteen? Jack's father, Alfred Thomas Harris, was a chemist in Newtown around 1903, but by 1913 he and his family were living in Denison Street, Waverley. Jack was born on 6 October 1899, and given an impressive suite of names – John Auguste Emile Harris, which reflects his mother's origins in New Caledonia, a French colony. Jack's parents were married in a Roman Catholic church but Jack wrote Church of England on his attestation form in 1914. He attended Cleveland Street High School, which was not a Catholic school. That suggests he was raised Anglican. His friendship in the unit with Digges La Touche supports that.

Jack probably left Cleveland Street High School at the end of 1913, just after he turned fourteen. Most Australian children were supposed to stay at school until fourteen, but many left at twelve, to start a trade. Jack listed 'clerk' on his attestation form on 2 June 1915, but that may be only as truthful as the age he gave – eighteen years. Alfred Harris's signature appears genuine on his son's permission form, dated 25 May. The handwriting matches his later letters, held at the National Archives of Australia. We can only wonder why Alfred Harris

> 'When the war broke out his patriotism simply possessed him. He laid aside the pen for the sword. He has often been heard to say he was coming here to die for his country.'

was prepared to let a fifteen-year-old go to war, but in many similar cases, the boy threatened to run away and join up under a different name.

Jack had been a 2nd Lieutenant in the school cadets, so he had some experience of soft soldiering. If Digges La Touche knew Jack's parents, that might have reassured them that he would keep him safe. If he didn't know Jack, it becomes hard to explain the extreme speed of the boy's rise to lance corporal ten days after enlistment (on 12 June) and his departure from Australia four days after that, on the *Karoola*, in Digges La Touche's unit.

Digges La Touche had by now been in the army for about nine months. In fact, he had been in the army twice. He tried first for selection as a chaplain, but was rejected, which shows that someone in the church hierarchy did not think him suitable. He then enlisted as a private, incurring the displeasure of his archbishop, who did not believe clergymen should become soldiers. La Touche at this stage wanted to be among ordinary soldiers: 'If I obtain promotion, I want it to be that which I win by my own efforts'.

His mother Clementine later wrote that he said, 'I could not tell a man to face danger which I am not prepared to share'. He then had a change of heart. He resigned from the AIF in November and re-enlisted a month later, on 28 December. Charles Bean, in the *Official History of Australia in the War of 1914–1918*, says it was because he needed to have an operation for varicose veins. Why that would require his resignation from the army is unclear. In February 1915, Digges La Touche went to officer's training camp at Marrickville in Sydney. On 10 May, he was commissioned as a 2nd Lieutenant with the 6th reinforcements of the 2nd Battalion.

On the *Karoola*, he continued his preaching, impressing some of the men with his fervour. Others found him tiresome. Private William Bendrey complained in his diary of Digges La Touche's frequent lectures on the evils of sexual intercourse and the benefits of daily shaving. Bendrey was disciplined twice in three days by Digges La Touche; when he complained to his commanding officer, the second sentence was reduced.

Digges La Touche's desire to die was becoming clearer in his letters. The joy and anticipation of being with Christ made the peril to life 'almost delightful', he wrote to his mother.

The *Sydney Morning Herald* reporter Oliver Hogue had known Digges La Touche in Australia, and at various army camps before departure. Hogue joined the 6th Light Horse and wrote columns about army life as 'Trooper Bluegum', which were later collected into a couple of popular books. In *Trooper Bluegum at the Dardanelles*, he wrote that Digges La Touche, before his commission, was a great recruiting sergeant.

'His addresses on the war were fiery orations, inspiring men to patriotic self-sacrifice and zeal for Empire ... And though no Turk or Hun died by his hand, Dr La Touche inspired many young Australians to take their place in the firing line. Some of these were with him in the fatal charge.'

Early in August 1915, on the ship taking Digges La Touche and 136 reinforcements of the 2nd Battalion to Gallipoli, Digges La Touche wrote to Jack's mother, Camille.

'My dear Madam, Your son, L/Cpl Harris, is with me and I shall try to keep him with me throughout the campaign. He is a gallant little chap with the greatest of military virtues – faithfulness – and as such is of very great assistance to his officers. If he had a few years more to his credit, he would make a fine officer. Meanwhile he is doing his duty without a thought of self and will serve his country as an Australian gentleman should.

'I will try to keep him with me and to see after him as far as I can. Otherwise my power is very limited, but we are both in God's hands and He doeth all things well. Yours Sincerely, ED La Touche.'

Digges La Touche knew Harris well enough to judge his virtues with affection; the letter also shows he knows he's under-age and needs protecting. Given that La Touche is hoping to die once he arrives at Gallipoli, the first line 'I shall try to keep him with me' becomes more ominous.

La Touche and the 6th reinforcements arrived on Gallipoli on 5 August. That morning, the commanders of the 1st Brigade, of which the 2nd Battalion was a part, learned that they were to attack at Lone Pine at 5 pm the next day.

The Gallipoli campaign had dragged on for three months without result, except for the thousands of dead on both sides. Winston Churchill's plan, to take the straits and knock Turkey out of the war, was in tatters. The Turks, hardened by years of war, had proved much tougher than the British expected. Now, the British High Command sanctioned a new offensive, trying to end the stalemate.

The main attack was on the heights north of Anzac Cove, by British, Indian, Australian and New Zealand troops. At the same time, the British would land troops at Suvla Bay to establish a base. In order to distract the Turks, Anzac units would attack the Turkish trenches at Lone Pine, a small plateau on one

of the ridges above Anzac Cove. In military terms, it was a feint. In human terms, it was to become a disaster for both sides – an epic four-day battle that set a new standard of horror for the Australian troops. When it was over, there were more than 800 Australian dead, and 1500 more casualties. The Turks lost at least 1500 men and 4500 missing and wounded. In mathematical terms, it was an Australian victory, but what did it achieve? The trenches they won were overlooked by Turkish positions, so that for the rest of the campaign, no man could raise a hair above the parapet.

All of that was yet to come, as the three Australian battalions moved up into position on the afternoon of 6 August. The Turkish defences here were some of the strongest on the peninsula, and close enough for hand-thrown bomb battles. Three lines of Australians were to go over simultaneously – the 4th Battalion on the left, the 3rd Battalion in the centre, and the 2nd Battalion on the right, the southern flank, with the 1st Battalion in reserve. These were some of Australia's most experienced men – early joiners, mostly from Sydney, who enlisted soon after the outbreak of war in August 1914.

The ranks had been much depleted by illness. Many were weak with dysentery and enteric fever, what we now call typhoid. Gallipoli, quite apart from the bullets and bombs, was not a healthy place to be. The 2nd Battalion left Australia in 1914 with over a thousand men. By August 1915, there were fewer than 500. The 6th reinforcements brought the battalion back up to twenty-two officers and 560 other ranks.

The Turkish trenches at Lone Pine were between fifty-five and ninety metres away. Aerial photographs had been used to map their lines, but inexperienced officers did not recognise a crucial feature – many of the Turkish trenches on the southern flank had been roofed over with pine logs. This is where Jack Harris, La Touche and the 2nd Battalion were to attack.

The attack had been timed so that the setting sun would shine in the eyes of the Turks. British artillery pounded the Turks in sporadic bursts for three days leading up to the attack. This increased strongly in the hour before it, in order to cut the Turkish wire in front of their trenches.

All of the Australians had sewn white patches on the back of their tunics and each man had a white armband, to distinguish himself from the enemy.

Digges La Touche arrived the night before and begged leave to join the attack. He and his men had been on the ground for less than twelve hours; they knew nothing of the landscape or layout of their trenches or the temperaments

> On the morning of 6 August, the men sharpened their bayonets … Their final meal before the attack consisted of boiled rice, and tea flavoured with rum.

of their own commanders, let alone the Turks. He could have waited and given his men time to adjust, to learn the ropes, but Digges La Touche was in a hurry for death or glory or both. The only question now was how many he would take with him.

On the morning of 6 August, the men sharpened their bayonets. They were allowed to drink as much water as they wanted. Their final meal before the attack consisted of boiled rice, and tea flavoured with rum.

The history of the 2nd Battalion, *Nulli Secundus*, gives a vivid description of the attack. 'As the hour approached the men had forgotten their sickness and weakness in their eagerness, and when at 5.30 the three short sharp whistle blasts sounded, B and C companies immediately cleared the trenches and moved swiftly forwards towards the opposing lines, to be met at once by a withering fury of rifle, machine-gun and shrapnel fire from all directions ...'

Jack Harris was with D Company, which soon followed through the smoke and dust, carrying picks and shovels.

They could see men standing up at the Turkish trenches, others lying down. They passed many wounded and dead men who had been caught by vicious machine-gun fire. They had expected open trenches, but most of the Turkish lines were roofed over, with timbers too heavy to move. Some men jumped down through small holes and engaged the Turks hand to hand. Others ran past the first trench and dropped into the uncovered communication trenches beyond, working their way back. Some tore up the timbers using levers, while others stood beside them, firing at the Turks below. Dead and wounded men soon blocked the trenches.

Charles Bean wrote that Digges La Touche was one of the first to reach a deep trench, one of the 2nd Battalion's main objectives. 'At its first bend he and two of his men fell mortally wounded ...' Digges La Touche was shot through the intestine.

Bean says that Digges La Touche insisted he be cleared out of the way. 'It's not me you must consider, but the position.' They moved him and he died shortly afterwards.

Jack probably died in the first minutes of the charge, before La Touche. The only eyewitness report came from Private Frederick H Clarke, interviewed at No 4 General Hospital at Randwick in Sydney in May 1916, by the Red Cross Wounded and Missing Enquiry Bureau. Clarke told them that on 6 August, he saw Jack lying just outside the Turkish trenches. 'He had apparently been severely wounded. Informant [Clarke] for some time was lying near Harris and has no doubt as to his identity. Informant was himself carried back to the beach and was there told that Harris had died of his wounds. Harris was short, dark, young and was called Jack.'

Private Henry Williams, interviewed at an Australian hospital in Egypt, said Jack was never seen again after the charge. He knew Jack well. 'He was a great friend of Lt La Touche who was killed the same day. Harris was very young.'

Sergeant William Rumsey, also at Randwick, told the Red Cross that Harris was killed outright in the Turkish trenches. 'He came from near Petersham and informant saw his people recently and gave them this information. His body was left where he fell.'

Some of the wounded were rescued from No Man's Land that day; others, a few days later. Some remained there until after the war. Many were buried at Brown's Dip Cemetery, just behind Lone Pine, but if Jack was one of them, the army did not record it. A handwritten note in his file dated 17 July 1917 confirms 'no trace grave site'.

The news of Jack's death did not travel quickly. His father Alfred received a telegram on 2 September to say his son had been missing since 14 August. Then on 14 September, Jack's name appeared in a Sydney newspaper, listed as wounded. Alfred rushed to Victoria Barracks in Sydney, hoping to clarify if his son had been found, and was told that the newspaper listing was 'an error on the censor's part'. It appears that Jack's death was not confirmed until late November. His effects were then sent on almost a year later, which further prolonged the agony. Alfred wrote to the army.

'The parcel consisted of a battered hair brush, without a back, a clothes brush and a kind of safety razor which was tied up in a torn blue handkerchief with white spots. I am at a loss to understand why they have been sent to me, as they did not belong to my son ...'

Everard Digges La Touche is remembered on at least thirteen memorial plaques in Australia and Ireland. Jack is remembered on one, a 'special memorial' in the cemetery at Lone Pine, which says he is 'believed to be' buried there. Digges La Touche is buried nearby, beneath the words 'faithful unto death', which is no more than the truth. Many other 2nd Battalion reinforcements who died that day share the same ground.

There are a number of ways to interpret what happened on this day to Jack Harris and his comrades. Digges La Touche was doing his duty, as he perceived it. Every man and boy that followed him did theirs, too. With hindsight, it seems clear that this clergyman's desire for death should have impeded his promotion to lieutenant, rather than helping it. It didn't, because the senior commanders valued 'offensive spirit' ahead of preparation and judgement. Even Charles Bean looked favourably upon this man's keenness to get into action. No doubt many of Digges La Touche's men were just as keen. A cooler-headed officer might have waited, giving them time to acclimatise. Even so, none of them could have known they were heading into a bloodbath at Lone Pine.

Jack Harris's war ended in minutes, in what must have been a terrifying and painful introduction to the brutality of Gallipoli. He was fifteen years and nine months old. A 'gallant little chap', whom no-one even managed to bury. ✿

ALBERT CRAMER & FREDERICK BLACK

THE GORE STREET BOYS

Alfred Deakin, Australia's second prime minister, grew up on Gore Street in Fitzroy in its heyday. By 1914, few lived there by choice. Number 15 was a large house, built as a single residence in 1878, now operating as a boarding house. There's no record that it was anything but a boarding house, although many other houses in the street operated as brothels.

At 15 Gore Street in late 1914, two boys were growing up as neighbours and pals. Frederick 'Fred' Black and Albert 'Bert' Cramer were thick as thieves and plotting their futures.

Fred Black was eighteen and living with his sister Millie. They'd had a hard upbringing since their parents died: father in 1899, mother in 1905. The seven Black children were separated and scattered. The youngest, Millie and Fred, would have been sent to relatives, if they were lucky. If they were unlucky, they went to state-run homes or an orphanage. The older siblings, four boys, were old enough to work. Millie would tell the army after the war that she had lost contact with their eldest brother George after 1905: 'His were about I do not no'.

Before the war, Fred worked on a farm in northern Victoria near Nerang. He appears to have returned to Melbourne to live with his sister around the time war broke out. Millie had little education, so she would not have had many choices for work. One was domestic service; another was factory work. Another was the 'oldest profession', although there is no record to suggest she chose that path.

> At 15 Gore Street in late 1914, two boys were growing up as neighbours and pals. Frederick Black and Albert Cramer were thick as thieves and plotting their futures.

Bert Cramer was living with his mother, Elizabeth. He had turned fifteen on 20 July. When the war started, Fred Black told Bert he was determined to go. It appears that Bert took some persuading, but once decided, he was hard to stop.

At this time, Bert's father Charles was cutting hair in Bendigo, with his nephew Fritz. They advertised the business for sale in December of that year, and Charles moved back to Gore Street. In 1915, Charles Cramer listed himself on the electoral roll at 15 Gore Street as a 'traveller'. Elizabeth Cramer was a 'boarding house keeper', so it's likely she managed 15 Gore Street and lived on the premises. Whether Elizabeth was happy to see him remains a question, for Charles Christian Cramer was less than an ideal husband.

Elizabeth came from a large family in Yatala, South Australia. She married Charles in 1895, although she was not his first wife. She wasn't even his second, and a few years later, when he was charged with bigamy, she wasn't even sure she was legally his third.

Charles had married Martha Berry in March 1892. He claimed he was a widower, his first wife having died in 1884, but there are no records of that marriage. In any case, the new marriage lasted barely a month before Martha moved out.

Five months later, the newspapers of Melbourne erupted with a major scandal. The headlines screamed 'The Road To Ruin' and 'The Fitzroy Scandal – Shocking Disclosures – Mrs Cramer committed for Trial'. The *Weekly Times* of Saturday 10 September gave a full account of the sordid story.

Amy Cramer, aged twenty-four, had been charged with 'procuring young girls for immoral purposes' at a house in Fitzroy Street. Four girls, aged fifteen to nineteen, were charged with vagrancy or being 'neglected children'. Both Charles and Amy were charged with being the occupiers of a disorderly house, for which both received twelve months hard labour. Only one paper picked up the fact that Amy was pregnant before she went to prison. The fate of this child is unknown.

After serving his sentence, Charles returned to his trade as a hairdresser and married Elizabeth Reddaway in 1895. Just over two years later, police arrested him for bigamy. Martha Berry told the Collingwood Court he was still her husband. Charles declared in court that he married Elizabeth in good faith: Martha's sisters had told him she had returned to New South Wales and died. Charles was eventually acquitted of bigamy.

This is the family into which Albert Cramer was born in July 1899. At the very least, his father had a history of trouble with the police. At the worst, he was a pimp and procurer with a jail record and a trail of marital wreckage. Elizabeth forgave him. She believed he could change, and she may have been right.

Elizabeth and Charles had a daughter in 1895 and a son in 1897, then Albert in 1899, and two more after that. After the bigamy case, Charles's name largely disappears from the criminal record. He appears to have had enough of crime and punishment.

By the end of 1914, fifteen-year-old Bert had developed his own skills in the art of deception. His mother was adamant that he could not go to war; he was equally determined that he would. He ran away, probably in early September. Instead of trying to enlist in Melbourne, he set off on foot for Albury, 320 kilometres to the north, with ten pence in his pocket. Later newspaper reports claimed he made it to Sydney and spent seven weeks in training, where a doctor told him he needed a small operation on one eye. This did not sound like a good idea to a fifteen-year-old so he returned to Melbourne. It is more likely though that Bert was rejected in Sydney, so he came home to Fitzroy, where Fred Black persuaded him to have another crack.

This time, they went together, and with a plan. Their attestation forms are almost identical – both dated 14 December 1914, with service numbers very close to each other (Fred is 1503, Bert is 1582), both signed by the same recruiting officers, who placed them in the 3rd reinforcements for the 6th Battalion – a battalion comprised largely of Melburnians. Both have the same handwritten line added to the bottom of the first page: 'I consent to my son enlisting in the expeditionary force', written by the same hand. Millie Black may actually have signed Fred's form, since he put her as next of kin. Elizabeth Cramer's flowing hand appears to have signed her own son's form too, but this must be a forgery.

Bert went to elaborate lengths to conceal who he was on this form. He enlisted as Bert Reddaway, using his mother's maiden name. He wrote that his next of kin was his father, named 'Richard Reddaway', who resided at Centre Road, Bentleigh – which was his real father's current address. For profession, Bert put down 'printer' – like his uncle and cousin. These little lies are intriguing: there is not one mention of his real father, except an address that would not work anyway. When the army sent letters to Bentleigh in 1916, they came back as 'not traceable'.

Both boys passed the medical tests this time and were sent to a depot camp, then on to Broadmeadows in mid-January. They trained together but in different companies of the battalion. They left Melbourne on 19 February on board the *Runic*, bound for Egypt. By this time, three months after he enlisted, Elizabeth must have known that she could not stop Bert from going to war. She could have reported him, had him brought home, but he had already run away twice.

Bert was finally 'taken on strength' – an army way of keeping track of which battalion has the responsibility for which soldier – on board the *Galeka*, the ship that took the 6th Battalion to Gallipoli. He landed on the first day, 25 April, and survived for only thirteen days.

Bert was fifteen years and nine months old on 8 May 1915, the day he breathed his last. Along with hundreds of Australian and New Zealand men, and other boys like Billy Riley and Arthur Wolsley, he walked to his death across an open field at Krithia, in one of the most futile 'charges' of the Gallipoli campaign. He would have known that he was likely to die. He went anyway and fell with his comrades.

His name appears on the Cape Helles Memorial there, which means he has no known grave, although he may have been buried in one of the two mass graves dug that night by the remaining Australian troops.

Fred Black arrived at Gallipoli on 7 May, the day before Bert's death, so it's not clear whether they saw each other. Fred may have fought at Krithia and survived. He went a little off the rails in the following month and copped twenty-one days 'Field Punishment No 2' (an army form of hard labour) for 'neglect of duty when acting as telephonist', which was more serious than it sounds. He didn't have time to serve the whole sentence. He was killed on 12 July and buried in Shrapnel Gully Cemetery, next to the main supply thoroughfare from Anzac Cove. The Australian newspapers recorded Fred and Bert's deaths together, because of their friendship. The *Argus*, a major Melbourne paper, carried this sad paragraph on Friday, 20 August, in a long list of casualties.

'Private Frederick Black (killed) was 18 years of age and enlisted with his mate Albert Cramer (15), who was also killed. Both had resided at 15 Gore Street, Fitzroy. Referring to the death of his mate Cramer, Private Black said: "Poor old Bert was killed in his second engagement. I was sorry for him as he would not have enlisted only for my asking him".'

Charles and Elizabeth appear to have parted ways some time in 1915, never to reunite, which may have played a part in their son's earlier decision to enlist. Charles Cramer died in Bentleigh in 1917, aged fifty-eight. Elizabeth Reddaway lived until 1946, when she was sixty-nine.

The Gore Street boys had grown up hard, in mean streets. They were physically tough and just as determined. They had not seen much of life and the world – but they had seen Cairo and the Pyramids, and that was something. Of war, they saw very little, a few days at most. They went as friends and died because of it. ❧

Along with hundreds of Australian and New Zealand men … he walked to his death across an open field at Krithia, in one of the most futile 'charges' of the Gallipoli campaign. He would have known that he was likely to die. He went anyway and fell with his comrades.

THE FLEMMING BROTHERS

A LETTER FROM KATHLEEN

In Hobart in 1992, librarian Geoffrey Farmer found a letter among the effects of his mother Norah, who had just died, aged ninety-seven. He wrote later that she had always guarded her private feelings and carried herself with British reserve, even after seventy years in Australia. He knew she had a special interest in the First World War and especially Gallipoli, but he did know why, until he read the letter, which was dated 1917.

'Dear Miss Edwards, Your welcome letter to hand. Mother and I were very pleased to hear from you again, and we both hope that you are well and happy, although, considering the state of affairs just at present, there cannot be many people really happy …'

In 1912, near the end of her schooling in England, Norah Edwards had started writing to three pen-friends in Australia. One was a Sydney boy who joined the 13th Battalion and took part in the Gallipoli landing. Another was a South Australian, who joined the 18th field artillery battery. The third was Geoffrey Lionel Flemming, from Waverley in Sydney. By 1914, when war broke out, Norah was nineteen but Geoff was just fifteen and nine months.

Geoff was the youngest of seven children of Edward and Julia Flemming. Edward was forty-one when he married nineteen-year-old Julia. Her father had tried a year earlier to have him jailed for abducting her. The case was settled when Edward, a successful importer, agreed to pay £500 and wait nine months to marry her. During the hearing, Julia's brother got himself arrested when he whacked Edward twice on the head outside the court.

Despite this rocky start, Edward and Julia had twenty years together. Then Edward died, in 1905, leaving her with six children, including six-year-old Geoff. Julia remarried within three years to an Englishman, Alexander Cornbloom. She may not have realised that he was a small-time crook, but she must have worked it out soon after. He already had one conviction for theft, and soon had several more. In 1910, a drunken man fired shots at the North Sydney house Julia shared with Cornbloom, claiming the Englishman had swindled him. Cornbloom took to carrying a pistol. He was charged with fraud in 1913 and then declared bankrupt. For Julia and the younger children, this man had delivered them into domestic chaos. For young Geoff, war may have seemed like a good way to escape.

Geoff's brother Valentine, five years older, signed up on 12 August 1914, the second day of enlistments in Sydney. He was sent to German New Guinea to help seize it for the Empire. A township there called Rabaul was then a beautiful tropical backwater with a few German missionaries and plantation owners in white suits, sweating beneath three active volcanoes. Valentine spent six months there. He must have wondered if he had joined the wrong war.

Geoff joined up on 9 February 1915, before Valentine had returned from Rabaul. As next of kin, Geoff wrote 'Julia Flemming', so it may be that Alex Cornbloom, alias Mr E Cowan, alias Cornie Reece, had already departed the Flemming household.

Geoff was sixteen. Though assigned to the 18th Battalion, he got himself transferred to the 2nd. He was hoping to join his oldest brother Richard, who was already in Egypt training beside the Pyramids, but he was too late.

Richard was in the second wave at the Gallipoli landing on 25 April. He was wounded three days later, probably by shrapnel. On the same day, he had been promoted to 2nd Lieutenant. After having wounds to his throat and arm dressed, Richard was back in the unit the next day. He was hit again on 10 May, this time a gunshot wound to the 'abdominal region'. This could have been serious, but he was lucky. He was back in the unit on 24 May. Geoff arrived two days later, to find Richard alive but battered. They had two weeks together. On 7 June, Richard suffered a 'spinal concussion' and was invalided off Gallipoli, eventually to the 3rd General Hospital in London. On 16 June, sixteen-year-old Geoff was killed in a frontline trench near Quinn's Post.

When she heard the news in London, Norah wrote a condolence letter to the Flemming family in Waverley. Geoff's older sister Kathleen replied, in August

Geoff was sixteen.
Though assigned to
the 18th Battalion, he
got himself transferred
to the 2nd. He was
hoping to join his
oldest brother Richard,
who was already in
Egypt training beside
the Pyramids, but he
was too late.

1917. That's the letter that Norah's son discovered in Hobart many years later. In it, Kathleen tells what she knew of her brother's death.

'It was a moment just at dawn, ten minutes before relief came. Geoff was on watch with two other lads at a peep-hole as they term it. One lad had his rifle through the hole taking aim. Geoff put up his hand to fix the rifle. A sniper from the Turkish lines saw the movement and fired. The bullet struck the rifle Geoff was fixing and glanced off, entering Geoff's chest under the arm and striking the bone which pro-tects the heart, grazed the heart causing severe haemorrhage resulting in his death four hours later. After being struck he fell limply on the floor and asked them to send for the stretcher-bearers. He was hurried with all despatch to the dressing station behind lines where he put up a great fight for his life but fate was against

him, and he died, as his friend told us, with the same happy smile on his dear face. And it was at sunset that a little party of men carrying a shrouded form marched slowly up Lone Pine and as they marched, word was passed that "Chum Flemming" was dead.

'Many a lad turned and followed our dear boy for he was well liked by all, he being the young-est and brightest. Dean Talbot read the simple service while bullets struck the sand into little clouds round the open grave …

'After all was over they gathered heavy stones so that his grave would be marked all round and there he lies, on the slope of Lone Pine … Geoff's chum Cecil sent us all particulars almost as I have related them here together with a letter from the men of Geoff's Company.'

Geoff died the same day that his brother Valentine, after his adventures in

> 'After all was over they gathered heavy stones so that his grave would be marked all round and there he lies, on the slope of Lone Pine …'

Pen friends **GEOFFREY FLEMMING** and **NORAH EDWARDS**, from the dedication page of the book A *Letter to Norah*.

Rabaul, left Sydney as a reinforcement for the 4th Battalion, bound for Gallipoli. He would not learn of his brother's death for some weeks.

Geoff's mother Julia and sister Kathleen were still grieving for Geoff when news came that Valentine had been killed within three days of his arrival on Gallipoli, in the charge at Lone Pine on 6 August. Private F McCormick later reported that he had seen Valentine's dead body 'in the 2nd line of captured trenches at Lone Pine'.

'He had been shot clean through the heart and was quite dead when witness saw him,' noted the Red Cross report, compiled later in Malta. 'Cannot say if he was buried.'

Lance Corporal Watkin Hawke, who came over in the same reinforcements, said later that he saw Valentine shot in the head during the charge. 'Witness was there and actually saw him dead in the Turks' trenches.'

Such is the fog of war: two soldiers, both of whom saw him dead, from two different wounds. Both might be true.

Valentine Flemming has no known grave. There were so many bodies in those Turkish trenches after the Lone Pine charge that some were piled into side trenches to make way; these trenches were then simply filled in. Other bodies were pitched out of the trenches to make room for the men still fighting. Valentine Flemming, aged twenty, is commemorated on the Lone Pine Memorial. Geoffrey, aged sixteen and eight months, lies nearby in the Lone Pine Cemetery.

Kathleen Flemming's letter to Norah, written a year later, addresses her as 'Dear Miss Edwards', but she asks if she can call her 'dear Norah' – 'the name my dear brother loved to speak of so often?'

'Mother would have written but she cannot bear to speak of my two brothers who are lying so silently in their lonely graves at Gallipoli ... I will conclude now, Norah, as the writing of this letter has brought the tears to my eyes once more, but later I will write again. Hoping to hear from you soon.'

This letter was written at Waverley. Almost three years later, Julia Flemming had moved to a war service house in Hurstville. The name of the new house, which would go with her when she moved again a few years later, was 'Geoval', with three letters from the name of each dead son.

Norah Edwards eventually met Adelaide-born Jim Farmer in London. He had been in the 18th Field Artillery battery, so he may have been the second of her three pen-friends. Farmer was gassed while serving as an artillery horse driver. He was advised to live in a hot, dry climate. After they married, Jim and Norah lived in some of the remotest parts of Australia, including some years in Kalgoorlie. By the time she died in Hobart, she had lived in many different houses, but she never lost Kathleen's letter.

In a memoir from 1981, Norah wrote how she heard of the deaths of the Flemming boys.

'My mother undertook the task of going up to AIF Headquarters at Horseferry Road, London, to read the casualty lists there, and in June 1915, saw the name of Geoffrey Flemming … About three weeks later his brother Valentine's name was also in the list of the killed. So, although Geoffrey and I had corresponded for a few years, we had never actually met. Sixty-five years later, I visited the Australian War Museum in Canberra and found his name, and his brother Val's, on the 1914–1918 Roll of Honour in that impressive building. Geoffrey Flemming was killed just three months short of his seventeenth birthday and my letters were returned to me marked "killed in action".'

Richard Flemming survived the war and returned to live in Newcastle with his new wife Pearl. He was well known in commercial circles there until his death in 1951. Kathleen Flemming married Senator Walter L Duncan in Queanbeyan in 1923. He had stood firmly with Billy Hughes in favour of conscription in 1917. When the referendums were lost, he had joined the army and served overseas in 1918. Kathleen died in 1941.

Norah named her son Geoffrey. His book, *A Letter to Norah*, telling the story of his mother and the letter she kept for seventy-five years, was published in 1993. Geoffrey Farmer died in 2015. 🌸

LEONARD JACKSON

THE JACKSON FOUR

LEONARD WALTER JACKSON was thirteen when he enlisted in the army.
He took on the false name Richard Walter Mayhew to avoid suspicion.

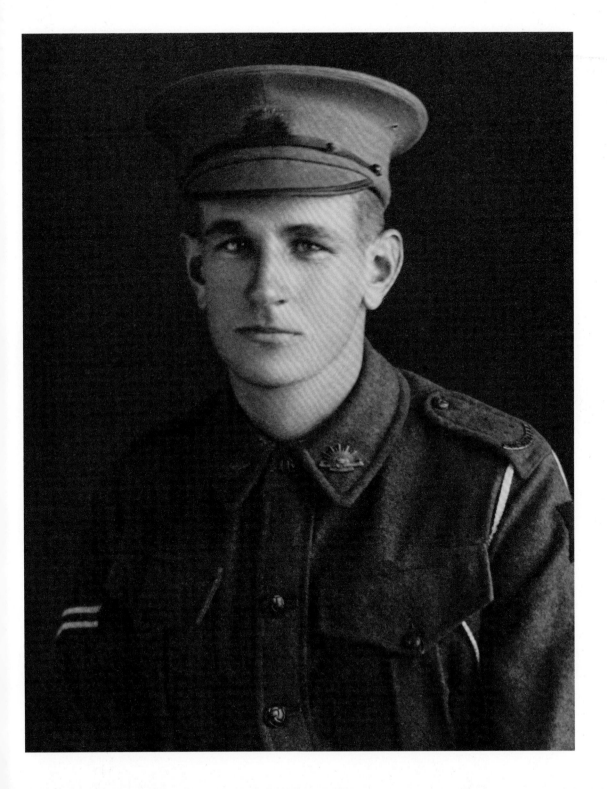

On Friday, 20 August 1915, two brothers set out for the war together, feeling they had outsmarted the system. One was under-age by almost eight years; the other had such poor eyesight that he could only read the top line of the test chart.

The elder was Dudley Jackson, aged nineteen years and ten months. He had trained in dairy science at Hawkesbury Agricultural College, before moving to the north coast of New South Wales. He tried to enlist at Lismore in late 1914, but they told him his eyesight ruled out his ever becoming a soldier. 'They said I would never be able to see a German,' he wrote later in a diary.

He failed four times in four more places, until someone told him he could bribe his way in by paying a recruiting sergeant at the new Warwick Farm Camp, on the outskirts of Sydney. Recruits were flowing in so fast after the Gallipoli landing that new camps were struggling to hold them. Dudley reported at Warwick Farm on 15 August, with the necessary funds for the sergeant. 'Much to my joy he "bit" straightaway:

£1 to him and £1 (he said) to the doctor whom I never saw. No medical exam, just "sign some papers" and get a smallpox vaccination and I was in the army.'

His younger brother Leonard signed his enlistment papers nine days before him, on 6 August, but they both took the oath of allegiance at Warwick Farm on the same day, 20 August. That suggests that Len might have used the same back-door route as Dudley. He would have needed help, since he was only thirteen years and eleven months old, one of the youngest Australians to go to the First World War.

Len was an inch taller than his brother and looked older than he was. Dudley was twenty kilograms heavier, with darker colouring, more like their father, Joseph, and older brother Harry. Len was the fairest of the three boys, all of whom were now in uniform.

When Dudley and Len reported to Warwick Farm, Harry was already on Gallipoli with the 13th Battalion. In fact, he was in the thick of the August offensive, something he wrote about in a sometimes hair-raising diary. His unit was to attack Hill 971, north of Anzac Cove, on the night of 6 August, the start of the offensive.

'All this time our warships were bombarding the Turks and keeping them occupied. Then we moved forward again. Here and there we could see heaps of stiff stark bodies of Tommies and now and again, our own chaps went down as we were under fire all the time, although we were in darkness. Cliff went first, then Dargan, then I began to lose count. The valley we thought had a river was a rough but suitable road; as we kept advancing we could hear the shouts of triumph of the Moaries [sic] and the New Zealanders on our right and the Tommies on our left. When we had gone 2 miles in, word came back enemy in strong numbers on our right. Word passed back to move round & attack. We slowly crept up the hill and they opened a fury of fire on us. SC Thompson and Paddy Boyne were killed … We rush up the hill. I bayoneted one Turk, an old chap 45 years. He had no papers on him. Captains Webber, Toohey, McGrath, Kirkwood were all wounded. Then we went down the other side and stormed a 2nd hill. An explosive bullet blew off the fore sight of my rifle. Then with a party of volunteers, I went with [illegible] to storm another hill. Somehow I got scattered from the rest and while passing a bush a gigantic Turk pounced on me and proceeded to crush me to death. However before he got any further, Tipper, a mate of mine, bayoneted him. Almost immediately afterwards, another Turk shot Tipper dead. He was revenged however as I manoeuvred round and shot his assailant dead. Soon afterwards, saw little Pocock in great pain praying. We put him on a stretcher but he died before he reached the beach.'

On 10 August, Harry was wounded in the leg by a bomb blast while working in a support trench, but stayed on through the night. 'We had a good sleep but my leg was terribly troublesome …

'August 11: My leg was twice its ordinary size this morning so I reported sick. And our battalion doctor sent me down to the beach.'

He was evacuated to Imbros Island then to Lemnos, where he developed dysentery. He noted that he was 'feeling thoroughly played out' but that the food on board was very good. Ten days after wounding, he arrived back at Alexandria in Egypt, with a septic leg. He was treated at the No 1 Australian General Hospital in what had once been the luxurious Palace Hotel at Heliopolis. His ward was the old tennis court with a temporary roof made of thatch.

Harry wrote to his mother from hospital that he had now had 'all the fighting to do me for the rest of my life'. He then told her a more violent and explicitly bloody version of the events from his diary, quoted above. The Turk that he shot in revenge for Tipper got five rounds 'full in the face'. The gigantic Turk became 'a veritable Samson'. If he was trying to soothe his mother's nerves, this was an odd way to do it, but he may also have been writing under the influence of painkillers. This was the same day that his brothers arrived at Warwick Farm.

> Harry wrote to his mother from hospital that he had now had 'all the fighting to do me for the rest of my life'.

Len had already realised his own name – Leonard Walter Jackson – was no use to him. He did not want to be easily found, so he changed his identity to Richard Walter Mayhew, draper, aged eighteen years and two months. He gave his next of kin as an aunt – Mrs Annie Blanche Jackson, of Ellalong Road, Neutral Bay. Annie was in fact his mother and that was the family home.

Len was enlisting without her consent but he didn't want to cut her off from the flow of official information: he just didn't want his parents to stop him. The problem with using a false name was that he could not now ask to be transferred into the same unit as Harry (in the 13th Battalion) or Dudley in the 20th. Len was on his own, assigned to the 6th reinforcements of the 17th Battalion.

Matters now turned serious, and quickly. On 26 August, a week after he and Dudley went into camp, the army advised Annie Jackson that Harry had been wounded on Gallipoli and sent to hospital. She wrote two days later asking if there were any more particulars. If his parents didn't already know Len had enlisted, they must have known soon after, because his father now decided to go after him. The news of Harry's wounding might have galvanised that decision.

Joseph Jackson was a former police constable from Glebe, Sydney, now in his fifty-third year. He was well known in Glebe for collaring toughs and drunks. He knew something about soldiering too. He wrote on his enlistment papers that he had served two years in the Boer War in the '2nd Bushmen'. That was a fib: he had served in the small New South Wales contingent of 750 men that went to the Sudan in 1885 to put down a native rebellion against the British. It's easy to see why he didn't mention that adventure, undertaken when he was just twenty-three. He could hardly claim that he was under forty-five, the legal limit for new recruits in 1915, if they knew he had fought in the Sudan.

Joseph had described himself as a blacksmith when he signed on in 1885. He described himself the same way when he signed on again now, thirty years later. This was on 13 September 1915, three weeks after Dudley and Len reported at Warwick Farm. Joseph wrote that he was forty-four years and eleven months, and the recruiting officers accepted that, probably with a wink. He was allocated to the 8th reinforcements of the 19th Battalion and sent to Holsworthy Camp. He was probably hoping for Warwick Farm, about ten kilometres away, but it was already at its capacity of 2000 men.

If he was trying to look after Len, he wasn't off to a good start. All four 'men' in the Jackson family were now in the army, but each in a separate unit. Harry was recovering from wounds in Egypt and the other three should not have made it past the medical test. They were too young, too old or too blind.

In Egypt, Harry wrote on September 19: 'Heard that last night a chap committed suicide rather than go to the front with his mob. Was discharged today for Helwan and went round for my complete new issue of clothes. I was examined by the doctor and told be ready to move off at 9 am.'

Helwan was a former prince's palace, then a hotel converted into a 500-bed convalescent facility for the overflowing Australian auxiliary hospitals in Cairo. Harry found it very pleasant, with its views of the Pyramids and ruins of Memphis on the opposite bank of the Nile. His dysentery had not fully cleared up, although his wounded leg had healed. On 5 October, he finally received a bundle of mail from Australia, and 'a very welcome parcel' containing tobacco and reading matter. His brother Dudley was already at sea on his way to Egypt. Len followed in November but Joseph, their father, would not sail until late January. The four would spend most of the next few months in different camps in Egypt, zigging when they should have zagged, missing each other.

Harry was the straight arrow of the three brothers. He had been a miner in Tasmania and at Newcastle. He was nearly twenty-two when he enlisted. He had been made corporal in March, before Gallipoli, and would become a sergeant in 1916. His letters show a fundamental decency and reserve. He doesn't approve of all the bad things his fellow soldiers get up to sometimes, but like almost every soldier, he calls the Egyptians 'niggers'. He wrote at least twice a week to his mother while he was away, often sending postcards and gifts for 'the little ones' – the younger Jackson children still at home: Digney, Mary, Arthur and Nellie.

If he indulged in the fleshpots of Cairo – as so many other soldiers did – he would never have said, but he probably didn't. His enjoyments were reading and picture shows and 'having a good look round' at the wonders of old Egypt. Dudley, almost three years younger, was more of a knockabout bloke. He could drink a bottle of scotch in one night and he was more forgiving of the world and its faults, except for officers and 'jacks', the military police. His diary is full of sharp insights about corrupt and stupid officers but he turned out a brave soldier,

DUDLEY JACKSON, the myopic older brother of **LEONARD**,
became an exemplary soldier.

even if he couldn't always see where he was going. His descriptions of battle are searing, contained in a number of illustrated diaries now kept at the Australian War Memorial.

Len appears to have left no written record of any sort, unlike his two older brothers. At the age of fourteen, in Egypt, he was probably more concerned that his father would catch up with him and send him home before he could experience the war. And he couldn't write to his mother using his new name, or she might tell the authorities she wanted him brought home. If he wrote to her via one of his brothers, no letters have survived.

By December, Harry was out of hospital but frustrated that no-one had yet told him what units Dudley or Len were in. A sergeant had told him that he had certain powers. 'Being the eldest brother of the three, and having already been attached to a unit, I have the power to transfer my younger brothers (either with or without their consent) to my unit. Whether this is so or not I would not like to vouch for.'

On 1 January, he wrote that he knew where Dudley was – at Abbasia Camp nearby, a walk of about four miles across the sand. He was also happy to hear that his father had joined up. 'I'm very glad to hear it. This army can do with men of his character.'

The three brothers found each other for the first time in late December 1915. Joseph had still not left Sydney. Len came down with the mumps on arrival in Egypt and Dudley followed suit, soon after visiting him. They were in hospital near Abbasia but it was a relaxed affair. Many nights, they were able to sneak out and join Harry on trips into Cairo.

Harry wrote to his mother: 'Dud, Len and I went to get our photos taken in a group. It was a poor photo but it was a group and may be interesting in the future ... We were only together for about a fortnight but still we met every night and had a good time, as much as was possible. They are both well and seem very contented. If I can I will get them transferred into my unit, but at present time our brigades and units are too far apart ... I often think that you must have a very lonely time now that you have been deserted by the four of us. Anyway, I think that the end is in sight and we'll soon all be back with you and having a good time.'

In February, Len wrote to Harry asking for help to transfer into his battalion, but Harry hesitated. He wrote to his mother that he thought it made more sense if Len transferred into his father's battalion, as transfer was easier within the same brigade. 'Then again, he is with men he knows, whereas he would be coming in with a lot of strangers here.'

As usual, events overtook these plans. In mid-February the battered post-Gallipoli AIF reorganised all battalions to absorb the large number of new recruits arriving from Australia. In effect, each existing battalion was 'doubled'. Half of the old hands went into a new sister battalion, then both were filled up with raw recruits, thus ensuring a balance of experience and youth. It was wrenching for men who had fought through Gallipoli together, but unavoidable.

The Australian and New Zealand Army Corps – the original ANZAC formation – was also split, becoming the first and second Anzac Corps (or I and II Anzac, in army parlance). Len moved from the 17th into the new 55th Battalion, where he joined the signallers. He was now part of the 14th Brigade, 5th Division, II Anzac Corps – and still no closer to either brother or his father. The 55th moved over to the huge Australian camp at Tel el Kebir, 110 kilometres north-east of Cairo. This was a tent city, spread over ten kilometres, holding 40,000 Australian troops – and far enough from Cairo to reduce the mayhem that usually followed when the Anzacs took what they called 'French leave' – meaning being absent without permission.

Many of the new recruits arriving at Tel el Kebir were so raw they had never handled a rifle. In mid-March, II Anzac Corps was sent to replace I Anzac guarding the Suez Canal, further out in the desert, at Ferry Post and Serapeum. It could have been accomplished by a simple rail journey, but the Egyptian railways were fully engaged with other troop movements. British General

Headquarters decided that II Anzac – this raw new formation that included Len's brigade – could walk to their new post on the canal. This would require a three-day route march across sixty kilometres of desert in stifling heat. The men would carry full packs. In Len's brigade they were also to carry rations and 120 rounds of ammunition.

The debacle that followed became legendary in the AIF – partly because the Australian commanders knew in advance that it would be a severe trial for the new battalions. The inexperience of the commanders put thousands of men through hell for no good reason, without enough water or medical support. Hundreds 'fell out' as the three brigades struggled on towards the canal across sandhills where the field ambulances could not follow. Many men collapsed and had to be helped in by their comrades – and by New Zealand troops already stationed on the canal, who sent out rescue parties. There were rumours that three men died in the desert, but none of the official records confirms this.

Len Jackson, aka Private Mayhew,

made it safely through his trial in the desert. His father was waiting for him at Ferry Post. Joseph's unit arrived in Egypt in late February and went into training at Zeitoun Camp, near Cairo. They had moved to Ferry Post ahead of the 14th Brigade and arrived in better shape. Joseph decided that he would seek a transfer to the 55th Battalion, to be with his son. This was accomplished by mid-April. If Len was worried that his father would send him home, he was now reassured. Joseph and Len Jackson would go to France together. They arrived at Marseille on 29 June, on the transport *Caledonian*.

Harry and Dudley were already in northern France. Both of them wrote dutifully to their mother through the early months in France, but there are no letters from Joseph or Len. Harry began to use code to date his letters, because the censors would not allow that detail, so this letter begins '73 days after my birthday', which would have meant early July. He was near Erquinghem, a village just south of Armentières, near the Belgian border.

'Dud has been over to see me a couple of times. He has not seen dad or Len. He looks in the picture of health. He is in a raiding party this week that is going out to the German trenches to raid their works.'

Harry remarks on the high quality of the local beer and wine, which is plentiful and cheap, with the result that many of his comrades are often drunk. Around 10 July, he writes to say he had not seen Joseph or Len 'since about four weeks before we left Egypt' in June, which confirms that at some point in Egypt Harry did see his father. It's also clear that the four Jackson men never got together in the same place in Egypt. They had not all been together since Harry went off to war in 1915; they would not be together in France either.

This letter is the last we have from Harry Melville Jackson. Ever positive and optimistic, he reassures his mother that he is in great condition: 'I am in a bayonet school' under a great instructor. 'Hoping you are all well at home. I must say they are all well here … give my love to all the little ones. Your loving son, Harry.'

Harry was wounded at Mouquet Farm near Pozieres a month later and taken prisoner by the Germans. He died the next day at a German dressing station near the village of Thilloy and was buried at Ehrenfriedhof cemetery north of the village. The news travelled very slowly to his family. In fact, at the end of October, the Red Cross were the first to inform Annie Jackson that Harry had died of wounds. German lists of the condition of prisoners of war went first to the Red

> Harry was wounded at Mouquet Farm near Pozieres a month later and taken prisoner by the Germans. He died the next day at a German dressing station near the village of Thilloy ...

Dudley went on to win the Military Medal in 1918, for outstanding work as a Lewis gunner during the battle for Mont St Quentin, in the last months of the war.

Cross, who passed them on to London. Annie had to bear this news alone in Neutral Bay, then write to her husband and remaining sons in France.

Again, the news did not travel fast. Dudley went to England on leave in January 1917. He only found out that his brother had been killed when he got back to France around 10 January. A few days later, he wrote to his mother that he had gone to visit his brother's battalion, as they were camped near his own in the Somme. They confirmed Harry's death.

By this time, Joseph and Len had already been through a lot together. The 55th Battalion's first major action in France was at Fromelles, which they were lucky to survive. Later news reports in Australia claimed that Len was mentioned in despatches for carrying messages during this battle; another reported that he was nominated for a Distinguished Conduct Medal. If so, neither distinction is noted in his service records. These newspaper reports also said he was sent to England in late 1916 to recover from a bayonet wound. His record says it was for 'ICT left leg'

– 'inflammation of connective tissue', which could have meant a variety of things, from suppurating skin boils to meniscus damage to the knee. Joseph was also invalided back to England late in 1916. He and Len went to Glasgow in late December on leave – just as Dudley arrived on leave in London. Again, they failed to connect.

Dudley went on to win the Military Medal in 1918, for outstanding work as a Lewis gunner during the battle for Mont St Quentin, in the last months of the war. Clearly, he didn't need to be able to see Germans to hit them with his Lewis gun. Fifty years later, he wrote to the army inquiring about specific dates of his and his brother's service. In that letter, he explained that when his father Joseph heard of Harry's death, 'he then decided in fairness to my mother to go back to Australia. He stated his right age and claimed my younger brother Len as being far too young and enlisting without his parents' consent.'

Joseph and Len went back to Australia together on the steamer *Ulysses* in February 1917, and were discharged from the army as under-age and over-age. Even then, Len could not be held back: he re-enlisted in 1918, under the same fictitious Mayhew moniker, but was not required overseas. He may have been suffering some form of post-traumatic stress.

Dudley made it back to Australia in 1919, having been wounded and decorated. He settled in Nambour in Queensland and wrote extensively about his wartime experiences.

Joseph died in Neutral Bay in 1931. Len joined the Sydney Water Board. He died in 1946, aged forty-four, a member of the Totally and Permanently Disabled Soldiers' Association. That suggests that his wounds went beyond a sore knee.

Len was probably reluctant to come home when he did. His father, in effect, saved his life. Len married Angela Cronin at Burwood in the 1930s and had three daughters: Patricia, Margaret and Annette. They lived at Penshurst in Sydney. He is buried at Woronora Cemetery.

The story of the Jackson four, full of caprice and accident, is typical of how this war acted upon the individuals who fought it. Three of them should never have been accepted, but at least one of those turned out to be a great soldier. Even when they tried to get together, they failed, but that was probably fortunate. Luck, good and bad, ruled their days as much as sickness, wounds and death in battle. But a father ultimately saved one son, while losing another, and that must have been hard to reconcile. ✽

FRANCE
1916

WILLIAM JACKSON, VC

CARRYING A CROSS

WILLIAM JACKSON had never seen a train before, let alone a city, when he left Gunbar, New South Wales, to enlist in Sydney at sixteen years old.

After the defeat of Gallipoli, the battered battalions of the AIF moved to Egypt to regroup, and then to France. They were now in the main theatre of the war – the big show. The war here was very different. Gallipoli was a lottery. There was less artillery available on both sides, but plenty of small-arms fire and hand-thrown bombs. It was no picnic but a soldier had a good chance of surviving, if he could dodge the dysentery and typhoid. The Western Front was much bigger and more brutal, because of the use of heavy artillery. It no longer mattered if men were plucky and game: the guns blew them all to pieces anyway. Those whom the shells missed were mowed down by rapid-firing machine guns, spewing forth 600 bullets a minute. The Western Front was a killing field spread along 600 kilometres from the Belgian coast to Switzerland, the like of which no-one could have foreseen.

In 1916, Billy Jackson became the first Australian to win the Victoria Cross on the Western Front. He became an instant hero at home, and for the Australian brass, the hero they dearly needed. No-one seemed to mind that he was only seventeen, and too young for the job of hero.

He was a farm boy from Gunbar, near Hay, in western New South Wales. The grazing land there is flatter than a frying pan and just as hot. The Murrumbidgee flows through Hay, making it productive and prosperous for both sheep and cattle. Gunbar to the north is sandier, drier, hotter, a bend in the road between Goolgowi and Hay. Gunbar has a Presbyterian church, a community hall and not much else. In 1914, there were four houses.

John William Alexander Jackson was born near here on 13 September 1897, the first son of Sydney-born John Jackson and his Gunbar-born bride, Adelaide Ann McFarlane. Adelaide died after her sixth child in November 1905, and the McFarlane grandparents took over raising the children. They had already raised fourteen children of their own.

John William was always known as William, or Billy, to distinguish him from his father, who worked on one of the local stations. William was educated at the one-room Gunbar School.

When war broke out, he was sixteen years and ten months old, working on 'Carlowrie' station. He was strong, fit and wiry – almost six feet tall and just over seventy-five kilograms. In February 1915, William joined a group of men drawn from all four Gunbar houses and set off to Sydney to enlist. He added a year to his age and was soon assigned to the 17th Battalion, which was raised in March, one of four new battalions from New South Wales. They would make up the new 5th Brigade of the 2nd Division.

Liverpool Camp, where the 17th headed for training, was a sea of tents and discontent. Recruits slept on the ground, with only a groundsheet and two blankets each. Men raised in the bush quickly scooped out hip holes in the earth for more comfort. They had neither hot water nor uniforms yet, and only a few rusty old rifles for training, but things were moving fast.

By May, they were encamped at Heliopolis, outside Cairo. The men trained outside in the early morning and late afternoon, to avoid the heat, but Billy was used to heat. In fact, Egypt was not that different to Gunbar, in terms of geography. What was different were the human sights: the Egyptian peddlers bearing oranges and knick-knacks, persistent boys with pet monkeys and the constant begging cry for '*Baksheesh, baksheesh*' (money). And this was a Muslim world, with grand mosques and the daily calls to prayer. Billy Jackson had never seen a city before he left Gunbar; indeed, one of his uncles later said the boy had never seen a train. Cairo was an eye-opener.

Most of the Australian units had serious problems with discipline in Egypt, but not the 17th. The commanding officer was a tall, courteous Englishman, Henry Goddard, who had come to Australia in 1899 and become a successful merchant. Lieutenant Colonel Goddard was a strict disciplinarian who punished 'to the limit'. He surrounded himself with officers who did the same, some of whom would become players in Billy's story.

The battalion history notes with pride that there were sixteen boys 'of average age 16' in the 17th, all taken on as buglers. 'Several of these lads went through every campaign with the 17th as private soldiers, being absorbed into the platoons when the use of buglers was discontinued about the time the battalion embarked for Gallipoli.'

Billy arrived on Gallipoli on 20 August with 1000 comrades who had been waiting months for the chance to fight. They were thrown into an attack on Hill 60, then into the most dangerous posts, at Pope's Hill and Quinn's Post. Billy was with them for two months before he came down with typhoid. He was shipped to a hospital in Malta then Egypt. He didn't rejoin his unit until February the next year. By then, the battalion was back in Egypt, preparing for France.

On 10 April 1916, the 5th Brigade took over a section of the trenches at Bois Grenier, south of Armentières in France. This was a quiet part of the line, used by both sides as a rest sector, a 'nursery' where new arrivals could be slowly introduced to trench life.

The terrain was dead flat and too boggy for sunken trenches, so the defences were built above ground as breastworks of heaped earth, strengthened with wood and wire and sandbags. It was cold, wet and filthy, and infested with large rats. The Australian and German lines were about 200 to 300 metres apart. Each battalion stayed in the line for three days, before being relieved.

Shelling was rare and perfunctory. Billy's B Company was the first to experience a barrage, when the Germans sent over twenty-five 'five-nines' on Good Friday, 21 April, for no casualties. On 25 April, the Germans targeted Hushi Farm, where C Company was billeted, wounding four men. Even so, the men of the 17th thought the war in France was very pleasant so far, especially when they were given leave to visit Armentières and nearby villages. They could eat and drink in *estaminets*, local cafes serving omelettes and vin blanc (which soon became known as 'plonk'). They could fraternise with French women, and more.

Everything changed on 5 May, when a small party of Germans raided the 20th Battalion's line at the Bridoux Salient, killing or wounding ninety-five men,

These raids were short, bloodthirsty and terrifying, but highly co-ordinated. In a war dominated by technology, this was a return to close-quarters old-school fighting – knives, clubs, bayonets and pistols.

taking eleven prisoners and capturing two Stokes mortars. The casualties were bad enough, especially as no Germans were killed in the raid, but the loss of the mortars was a disaster. The Stokes mortar was a new British weapon, designed for use by the infantry, rather than the artillery, at close range. It was expected to play a big role in the coming offensive on the Somme in July. For that reason, the orders were strict: it was never to be left in the line, but removed after each use. For Lieutenant General Sir William Birdwood, commander of the I Anzac Corps, the loss of the mortars was 'inexcusable'. Two officers were court-martialled and the Australian commander of the 20th Battalion was sent home.

In their first days in France, Birdwood's Australians had disgraced themselves. Charles Bean, in the official history, says it was 'most mortifying to both Australian commanders and troops'. Tommies taunted the Australians, offering to exchange gifts 'for two trench mortars'. General Douglas Haig, the British commander, upbraided Birdwood. 'You're not fighting Bashi-Bazouks now … This is serious scientific war and you are up against the most scientific and military nation in Europe.' The Australians of the 5th Brigade needed desperately to prove themselves. From early June, they began mounting raids, looking for prisoners and payback, as part of Haig's wider strategy to confuse and destabilise the enemy before the Battle of the Somme. These raids were short, bloodthirsty and terrifying, but highly coordinated. In a war dominated by technology, this was

> In their first days in France, Birdwood's Australians had disgraced themselves. Charles Bean … says it was 'most mortifying to both Australian commanders and troops'.

a return to close-quarters old-school fighting – knives, clubs, bayonets and pistols.

The 5th Brigade, commanded by General William Holmes, planned their raid for 25 June, a Sunday night. Volunteers came from all four battalions: 17th, 18th, 19th and 20th. Billy Jackson put up his hand, like most of the men in his battalion.

Major Reginald Travers of the 17th would be in command. Captain Keith Heritage of the 19th would lead the assault party. Heritage was an athletic Tasmanian, who had rowed for the victorious Australian team at Henley Regatta in 1912.

The successful volunteers – nine officers and seventy-three from other ranks – were pulled out of the line. They spent three weeks training for the raid in a back area, working in teams, each of which had a specific job. They built a replica of the German trenches they were to attack, based on aerial photographs. Billy was to be part of the scouting party, under Lieutenant Clarence Wallach, one of four brothers from Bondi, all of whom enlisted.

Wallach had represented Australia five times in rugby in 1913–14. The scouting party were to go forward before the rest and reconnoitre enemy activity in No Man's Land. They were also to knock out any enemy listening posts in front of the German positions, then lay lines of white tape along the ground to help the raiders find their way back. For most of the raid, the scouting party would be exposed in No Man's Land.

On the night, Australian artillery laid a heavy barrage on the German trenches from 11 pm, which warned the Germans that something was coming. They responded with their own barrage on the Australian lines, and with flares that periodically lit up No Man's Land like a fairground. The barrage then shifted to the German support line, to stop reinforcements from coming up. Billy's scouts reported that the Germans were out repairing the wire in front of their own trenches. That meant there was little time to lose. Two Australian attack parties entered the German trench at two points, right and left, clearing the lines for twenty-five metres in each direction.

Their job was to grab as many prisoners as they could and kill the rest. They were to be in and out in five minutes.

The raid went brilliantly, resulting in four prisoners and an estimated thirty Germans killed. The problem was then to get home safely, through the intense German shelling now raining on No Man's Land.

In 1917, Billy described what happened: 'General Holmes ... was in command of the brigade and he planned the raid. There were about 40 of us [sic]. The German trench was about 400 yards in front of us and at midnight we started out. Our object was to take a few prisoners and get back. It was information that we wanted. So we started across no man's land. It was pitch dark. It suited me. I see well in the dark. They weren't expecting us, and we got our prisoners all right, four of them, but the Germans got onto us as we were going back. Nine of our chaps went down, but some of them were able to struggle back with their wounds.

'After we got back with the prisoners, we went back to look for the wounded men and I brought one back. Then I went out for another and I was coming back with him when a shell burst and blew my right hand clean off. However, I got back with my mate. I didn't feel anything much. I saw the blood spurting but I didn't feel hurt much – just a numbing sensation. One of the officers tied it up with a string, with the aid of a little stick, and I felt all right. It struck me that there might be one or two still out there wounded and I started out again. Of course, I stood a chance of having my little finger blown off, or perhaps my head blown off, because they were firing plenty of shells then; but I didn't like leaving any wounded men out there. However, I couldn't find any more. I knew the lie of the country pretty well. I had been doing lots of scout work there before this night, and I'd have found them if they'd been there. After about half an hour I came back, and they sent me to hospital, and on to England.

'That's the whole story,' Billy told the reporter from the *Sydney Morning Herald*.

'I heard that my major had recommended me for something but I never expected to have the VC pinned on my tunic by the King, any more than anybody else ... There were rumours about something going to happen. My mates used to tell me so, and I used to laugh at them; and when they showed me the newspaper with it in, it surprised me. That was the first I knew about it, seeing it in the papers.'

Jackson was not the only one awarded for that night's work. Captain Heritage won the Military Medal and Major Travers was mentioned in despatches. Sergeant Hugh Camden, who helped Jackson to rescue men from No Man's Land, was awarded the Distinguished Conduct Medal (DCM). Some repair was thus applied to the reputation of the Australian soldier – and his officers – after the loss of the mortars.

Billy was initially awarded the DCM, but this was then upgraded. That created a controversy that dogged him for the rest of his days. His whole life changed that Sunday night in 1916. The VC made him a celebrity, one of the most famous men in Australia, but he was not prepared for fame. And the raid took away one of the things that could have

ensured a fruitful working life – his right arm. Billy would have many jobs when he got back to Australia, none of them for very long. Of troubles, he would have his share.

His return in July 1917 was a circus. After almost three years of war, the public was eager for heroes and Billy Jackson, now nineteen, and with one empty sleeve, was just the ticket. They took him to a recruiting rally in Martin Place, Sydney on 9 July, fresh off the boat. He was mobbed. The recruitment officers saw great potential in having him speak, but Billy couldn't face public speaking. The *Herald* the next day was brutally direct: 'Jackson VC Fails as a Speaker'.

'He was introduced by Lt Rickwood but when called upon to speak, and to tell the audience something of the stirring moments through which he had passed, as an inspiring example to others, he stood motionless, just as though the crowd had cast an hypnotic influence over him.'

Others tried to coax him to the podium. 'Finally, in halting words, and in practically a whisper, the big shy youth spoke, but only for a few seconds.'

A *Herald* reporter found him later at his uncle's house in Randwick, after an official reception at the Domain. 'He is no orator,' wrote the unnamed scribe. 'Proud yes, but not the sort of pride that makes him want to talk about himself.' Billy was wearing a metal ring made from a German shell, stamped with the words 'Bois Grenier'.

Billy caught the train home that night, accompanied by Sergeant Camden, who had taken part in the same raid. The train was waylaid in Hay, so the mayor and townsfolk could parade Billy through the town. Again, he could not speak, so Sergeant Camden spoke for him. This was repeated across the country for most of the next year in small towns and large cities. Slowly, Billy learned to open his throat. He became an energetic recruiter, but not always a temperate one. It may be that he was suffering from what we might now call PTSD: he lost his privacy, as well as his right arm, and he was still so young, just turned twenty.

In July 1918, during a recruitment 'March to Freedom', Jackson upset a crowd at a dance in Junee by telling those young men who had not yet joined up to leave the dance. The Tamworth *Daily Observer* said he asked 'eligibles to retire from the dance room and requested the girls not to dance with them if they remained as they would thus lose the respect of the community ... The request created quite an uproar and many of both sexes retired and said they would never enter a dance room again where there was a war function.'

Six weeks earlier, near Scone, Billy was thrown from his horse during another 'March to Freedom' procession and knocked unconscious for ten minutes. The same thing happened to him two years later at Merriwa, while helping a friend to move some stock. 'The horse

---

WILLIAM JACKSON returned to Australia a war hero, but he soon began to show signs of what might now be termed Post-Traumatic Stress Disorder.

rolled clean over Mr Jackson and from what can be gathered, injured his back severely,' noted the *Mudgee Guardian*.

Billy was struggling with his disability. At Hay, local farmers had promised to stock a farm for him if he wanted to return to farming, but he declined; how could he farm with one arm? When the war ended, he took up the lease on a pub in Wollongong. That may not have helped his state of mind either. He had begun to drink heavily, like many returned servicemen.

Things got worse through the 1920s, as he moved from job to job. He took up land at Merriwa but there followed seven years of drought. Then his house burned down. In 1927, the bench at Ivanhoe in western New South Wales issued a warrant for his arrest for non-payment of a hotel bill. The Police Gazette issued a description that ended with the words 'addicted to drink'. In 1928, he was back in Wollongong selling real estate, when he hit a publican and was fined £5 for assault. In 1929, the *Cootamundra Herald* reported that Billy had issued a writ for £5000 defamation against the *Labour Daily*. The *Herald*

also noted that Billy 'was suffering badly from the effects of his war experience' and was 'recently destitute'. Around this time, the former prime minister, Billy Hughes, sent him a telegram telling him to apply for a nightwatchman's job at a big Sydney firm and to say Hughes had sent him. Hughes had already spoken to the head of the firm. Billy Jackson still had some friends.

His luck started to turn in the 1930s, when he married Muriel Alma Morris, a dressmaker he had met while they were both in hospital in 1929. They had a daughter, Dorothea, in 1932. In 1946, he was charged with manslaughter after the car he was driving collided with a truck, killing two people. Billy was acquitted: there was no alcohol in his system. He moved to Melbourne and became a lift driver at the Town Hall. In 1956, he went to England for the celebrations around the centenary of the Victoria Cross. He died in 1959 of heart disease, aged sixty-one, and was cremated.

Billy Jackson's bravery that night in 1916 was extraordinary and worthy of the highest honours. But with hindsight, we might now ask whether he was also the hero the army brass needed – someone to boost morale and, at the same time, restore Australia's battered reputation after the loss of the Stokes mortars.

The process for awarding the VC was complicated in 1916 and it changed later in the war, specifically precluding the kind of action for which Billy Jackson won it. Many men were recommended, but few were chosen. Applications passed through many hands on their way up the chain of command, which ultimately reached the King. Any senior officer in that chain could downgrade a recommendation, if they judged the award was not merited. Billy Jackson was upgraded during that process, which was more unusual. Someone really wanted him to get the VC. We may never know who, because most of the papers relating to First World War VCs were destroyed when a bomb hit the building housing the archive in London in 1940.

The DCM Billy won for the same action was later cancelled, but he became incensed when the army asked for it back. He threatened legal action. The Australian army asked the War Office for advice. London thought it best not to press him.

Billy Jackson is a rarity among VC winners because he was decorated for an extraordinary act of valour in the service of others – going out to rescue his mates – rather than for aggression. The same act took his arm and made his post-war life a misery, at least for a while. He became a hero, then a fallen hero, and he died relatively early. As of early 2019, Australians have won 100 Victoria Crosses – but he is still the youngest. 🐾

DOUGLAS WOOD, GEORGE YENDLE, COLIN MEYERS & JOHN GORDON

BLOOD AND BONE

DOUGLAS WOOD was fifteen when he perished along with at least fourteen other under-age soldiers at Fromelles in northern France in 1916.

On 20 July 1916, the summer sun rose on a wretched, pitiless blood-soaked field in northern France that the soldiers knew as Fleurbaix. We now call it Fromelles.

During the previous twelve hours, the Australian 5th Division had endured its first major action on the Western Front and almost ceased to be. No-one knew the casualty figures yet, but those who were still breathing knew it was bad. They could even smell the blood.

We know now that there were almost 2000 dead and 3500 missing or wounded. They lay in khaki heaps in No Man's Land and the trenches on both sides. There were so many dead clogging the trenches that stretcher-bearers struggled to get the wounded away to aid posts. Nothing like this had ever happened in Australian history. Those who saw it hoped it would never happen again, but the war on the Western Front often turned hopes into ashes.

At least fifteen of the dead on that battlefield were too young to be there. At least three were only sixteen; two were fifteen. One may have been as young as fourteen and part of this chapter is an attempt to work out who that might be.

In many cases, it would be more than a year before the families knew for certain that their sons were dead. And for almost three years, hundreds of these boys lay in No Man's Land unburied, their bones bleaching in the weak northern sun. What was left of them would not be recovered until 1919, when the war was over. It's hard to think of a better illustration of the barbarity of war.

The youngest casualty we can name is Douglas Wood but he is almost certainly not the unknown fourteen-year-old. If

> At least fifteen of the dead on that battlefield were too young to be there. At least three were only sixteen; two were fifteen. One may have been as young as fourteen …

he was born on 18 January 1901 – and there are questions about that – he was fourteen years and five months old when he enlisted and fifteen years and six months when he died.

Douglas Wood's birth date was never registered. There's a clue about why on his service record, where an army bureaucrat wrote in red letters 'illegitimate son'. His father, Frank Wood, was a seaman. His mother was calling herself Christine Wood when Douglas was born, but her real name was Phoebe Jane Hutchinson. She was a woman of many names – and as far as her son was concerned, she was past tense. He wrote 'Mother dead' on his enlistment form. He lied that he was a baker of eighteen years and two months. He was short, fair-haired and blue-eyed, with a fresh complexion. His photo shows a confident boy in a rollneck sweater beneath his army tunic. He looks older than he is. This picture is mysterious: it's taken from a larger photo in which Christine stands beside her son. Clearly, she knew he had enlisted. Why then did he claim she was dead?

Frank and Christine never married. The Victorian census of 1903 shows that they lived in separate houses next door to each other at 87 and 89 Napier Street, South Melbourne. They also had a daughter, Muriel, born a year earlier than Douglas. Christine was from a prosperous family, but she was not conventional.

Christine and Frank separated before the war. She was calling herself Christine McGregor when she married Patrick Curtis in St Mary's Catholic Cathedral in Sydney in August 1915. Douglas had joined up a month earlier in Melbourne, denying that she was still alive. Was Douglas upset that his mother was remarrying?

If Douglas was angry with her, he could at least thank her for a good education. He attended Auburn State School in East Hawthorn in 1911–12, then Camberwell Grammar, one of the best private schools in Victoria, in 1913–14.

Robert Short, the head teacher at Auburn until 1926, compiled a meticulous record of every Auburn boy who had gone to war, for the Roll of Honour that still hangs in the school. He recorded

In many cases, it would be more than a year before the families knew for certain that their sons were dead. And for almost three years, hundreds of these boys lay in No Man's Land unburied, their bones bleaching in the weak northern sun.

Douglas's birth date as 18 January 1901. Short was careful about detail, recording father's name, the years each boy was at Auburn and the unit he joined. All of those are correct in the entry for Douglas Wood.

Douglas was originally assigned to the 7th reinforcements of the 12th Battalion. Once in Egypt, he was reassigned to the new 59th Battalion, which was formed by splitting off half of the old 7th Battalion and adding new arrivals. The originals were largely from rural Victoria. Douglas was a well-educated city boy among farmers and bushmen. On 18 June 1916, he embarked in Alexandria on the ship *Kinfauns Castle*. The 15th Brigade was bound for France.

Its commander was Harold 'Pompey' Elliott, a lawyer and champion athlete who would become one of the most famous Australian soldiers of the war. Brigadier General Elliott had an explosive temper and a sentimental devotion to his men. He knew some of them were not men at all, but boys.

George Yendle was on the same boat. He said he was almost nineteen, but he was barely seventeen. Still, he was a year older and wiser in the ways of war than Douglas Wood. He had joined his battalion at Lemnos near Gallipoli on 20 November, just as the Gallipoli campaign was ending. He was back in Egypt by January 1916, transferred into the 59th in February. Whether he knew Douglas or not, they were now on the same path.

The Yendle family was poor, living in the working-class Melbourne suburb of Carlton. There were six children. Their father Alfred struggled to provide. He sold furniture around St Kilda, delivering from a van pulled by notoriously skinny horses. He was fined for not feeding them and letting them wander the streets of St Kilda. He married Matilda Irons of Williamstown in 1892, but by 1914, Alfred was probably an invalid.

Matilda wrote to the army in a spidery hand to give permission for George to enlist. 'I freely give my consent should

George pass "in line" to serve his God, King and Country. His elder brothers are at present serving on the sea. May God bless and protect one & all is day and night the prayer.'

She wrote this on 19 June 1915. Two days later she wrote another letter, which included her husband's signature, barely legible at the bottom, presumably because the army wanted both parents to sign. Referring to her husband, Matilda wrote: 'His eyesight is bad so please excuse it. He does not in any way support me or my little ones. It is my dear boy who supports me and God bless him, he thinks that if he enlists, he will be serving his King and Country and also providing for me.'

George had been working at J Marsh and Sons in North Melbourne, making canisters. He can't have been earning much if the army pay of six shillings a day seemed like a better offer. Of course, George may have had other reasons. His elder brother Eric had joined the Australian Navy and the Yendle household was in mourning after the death in late 1914 of daughter Ivy, aged

just seventeen, at Melbourne Hospital. Now Matilda had to watch George go off to war. In another year, her second son, Albert Charles, would go as well. He would join the 58th Battalion, a few months after George and the 59th went up the line at Fromelles. He would not come home either. Matilda and Alfred would lose three children in three years.

A third under-age soldier, Cecil Morgan, shipped out from Egypt two days ahead of Wood and Yendle, on the SS *Hororata*, bound for Marseille. He was from Redfern in Sydney, one of five children, except their surname wasn't Morgan and he was no Cecil. Colin Vincent Meyers was born in 1899 to Emily and Reginald Meyers. He enlisted in November 1915 in Sydney, but was assigned to the 31st Battalion, which had been raised in Queensland and Victoria. 'Cecil Morgan' was clever about his next of kin – he put his real mother's name and address, but said she was his aunt. That way, his parents would still be notified if anything happened to him.

He was also brazen in the overstatement of his age: he put twenty-one years and three months, which meant the army did not require his parents' permission. In fact, he was fifteen.

He and 12,000 other Australians of the 5th Division were now heading north through France on a series of trains, enjoying the change of scenery and murdering the language in search of wine, women and good food. It was bliss after the dust and flies of Egypt. They were in high spirits: they were finally going to have their shot at the Germans.

There were many sets of brothers among them, but few with as many secrets as the two Gordon brothers, John and William. They lived in Carlton as well, with parents William and Ellen. William was sixteen and had failed on his first attempt to enlist. John was just fourteen years and ten months, but determined to go too.

The boys concocted a double ruse. Each went to a different recruiting office on the same day in July 1915, with a note purporting to be their father's written permission. In all likelihood, both notes were forged. William had used his real name the first time – William Lewis Gordon – so he changed it to John. The real John changed his name to James, after a third brother who had died in infancy. That is how two fictional Gordons entered the army – John Gordon was really William the elder; James Gordon was really John. He joined D Company of the 29th Battalion. His older brother went to the 2nd Division Signals Company and survived the war. 'James' Gordon was not so lucky.

The 5th Division was the last of the Australian divisions to arrive on the Western Front. Their commander was Temporary Brigadier General James Whiteside McCay, who was already unpopular with his men. He would soon become even more hated. He had been born in Ireland but came to Australia as a baby, growing up in Castlemaine, Victoria. At Scotch College in Melbourne, he was a year ahead of another bright boy named John Monash.

McCay was keen for battle. His British superiors thought the 5th should go into the 'nursery' sector south of Armentières to get used to trench life. McCay came under a British commander who had similarly thrusting ambitions, and no patience for planning. Lieutenant General Richard Haking, commander of XI Corps, had tried and failed at great cost a year earlier to take the Aubers Ridge, overlooking the small village of Fromelles. He wanted a win. The combination of Haking and McCay now proved fatal.

The plans for the attack had been changed, dropped, reshaped by headquarters, postponed, reworked and dropped again, before the 5th Division arrived. The Battle of the Somme had started three weeks earlier, further south. Haking persuaded his superiors, Haig and General Henry Rawlinson, that he had enough artillery to take the low-lying ground north of Fromelles, and that it would prevent the Germans from sending reinforcements to the Somme. Haig had doubts, but was always ready to give an aggressive commander his head.

Haking decided the 5th Australian Division would attack beside the 61st British division at 6 pm on 19 July, after a seven-hour artillery barrage. This was supposed to terrify the Germans and cut their defensive wire. It did neither.

It's easy to say now that the attack was doomed, but a couple of Australian and British commanders said as much before the battle. They were overruled. Five thousand men of the 5th Division and 1500 of the British 61st were about to become casualties in a battle without much purpose, for a plan that many of its commanders did not believe in. Some military historians will object: it was a feint, a 'demonstration' designed to keep the Germans occupied; it would give the Australians valuable experience. 'Pompey' Elliott, many of whose men were about to die, later called it a 'tactical abortion'.

McCay welcomed 'the honour' of having his men be the first Australians to mount a significant attack on the Western Front. He had wanted to attack the day after his division arrived. The men were keen, but unprepared. They were not used to the terrain or artillery barrages of such intensity. There had been nothing like this on Gallipoli. The old-timers knew plenty about the effects of trying to rush machine guns in a frontal attack, but half of the division was fresh off the boat.

McCay pressed ahead. The 8th Brigade were to advance on the left, the 15th Brigade on the right, and the 14th between the two. The under-strength British division would attack beside Elliott's 15th Brigade on the right.

The Germans on Aubers Ridge could see every move. Their shells rained down on the approach trenches, with deadly accuracy. On the way up, Douglas Wood, George Yendle, the Gordon brothers and Colin Meyers had to pass the bodies of men who had been blown to pieces just a few minutes ahead of them.

The attack started at 6 pm, with three hours of daylight left. Elliott's 15th had to cross 350 metres of boggy field towards the Sugarloaf Salient, where a formidable cement blockhouse protected the German lines. German machine gunners would have no problem seeing them, as they knew they were coming. They held up a sign saying 'Advance Australia – If You Can'. The inexperienced Australian artillery was late into position and their shells were already falling short. Many of those 'dropshorts' killed their own men in the 8th Brigade.

Most of Elliott's troops (battalions 57 to 60) fell on the right, cut to pieces by machine guns. The 8th Brigade (battalions 29 to 32), which included Colin Meyers, broke into the German trenches on the left. Some rushed beyond and were cut off. Others tried to hold

> The full horror only became apparent with daylight. Men writhed in No Man's Land, calling for help or their mothers, as German machine guns continued to rake the field.

The aftermath of the battle of Fromelles in 1916.

on to the old German lines, until they too were wiped out. Communications failed between commanders; orders were forgotten as men charged at the enemy guns; the soldiers could not find their objectives because aerial photographs had been misinterpreted. In every unit, Australian officers died early beside their men, leaving those who weren't dead to fend for themselves.

The full horror only became apparent with daylight. Men writhed in No Man's Land, calling for help or their mothers, as German machine guns continued to rake the field. Even if they weren't wounded, those stranded in No Man's Land could not risk trying to come back. The shell holes were full of the living and the dead, often in pieces. A number saw an Australian with no legs crawling back towards the Australian lines, calling out for others to 'make way please'. He disappeared into a shell hole. Many brave soldiers risked their lives to bring in the wounded over coming days.

Sergeant Simon Fraser and comrades in the 57th Battalion rescued a large number – up to 250 men, by their own estimate. Dragging one man in, they heard another call 'Don't forget me, cobber'. Those words inspired a famous statue by Peter Corlett at the Australian Memorial Park, which now stands in the centre of the battle site.

In front of the Sugarloaf, hundreds of men from the 15th Brigade lay in shell holes, unable to be retrieved. Douglas and George fell here. The Germans had captured 400, but another 250 were dead behind their lines – largely on the left. These were mostly from the 8th and 14th brigades; they included James and Colin. Until recently, we did not know where these men were buried.

We now know that the German commander, Major General Julius Ritter von Braun, issued strict instructions for their burial. A series of eight pits was dug at Pheasant Wood, on the edge of Fromelles village. The burial parties removed and bagged any personal items, including name tags, for return to the families. The German soldiers were warned that pilfering would be severely punished. All names were recorded, where they could be established. The burial process began with respect, the bodies laid out in orderly lines and covered with lime, but it degenerated as the day wore on. Burying 250 dead men, in all states of horror, took its toll. Berlin sent the lists of these buried men to the Swiss Red Cross later that year.

Back in Australia, the notifications sent to families were often wrong, and the army was slow to correct them. Many parents were told their son was missing or 'wounded but expected to survive'. Incompetence in London and Australia left some families hoping their loved ones had survived as prisoners. Many families only found out the truth when the tags and belongings collected by the Germans began to arrive in the mail in 1917.

None of them knew about the scandalous treatment of the bodies in No Man's Land – although the Australian war correspondent Charles Bean knew. He had visited the site the day after the battle and saw the horror for himself – not that he could have written the truth about it. The army censors would never have allowed a full account of what happened at Fromelles. On 11 November 1918, the day the Armistice was signed, Bean went back, to see where the bodies lay, before anyone could disturb them. He wanted to determine how close the Australians came to taking their objectives.

'We found the old No man's land simply full of our dead,' he wrote in his diary. '... East of the corner of the sugarloaf salient the skulls and bones and torn uniforms were lying about everywhere.'

'We found the old No man's land simply full of our dead,' he wrote in his diary. '... East of the corner of the sugarloaf salient the skulls and bones and torn uniforms were lying about everywhere. I found a bit of Australian kit lying 50 yds from the corner of the salient; and the bones of an Australian officer and several men within 100 yds of it.'

Fifteen-year-old Douglas Wood, the boy in the rollneck sweater, was almost certainly among the dead here. George Yendle, who had survived Gallipoli, was probably close by. In April 1917, the Red Cross Wounded and Missing Enquiry Bureau contacted Sergeant Harold Weston of the 57th Battalion, who had known Douglas. Weston confirmed that he had seen Douglas's body lying dead on the battlefield that night. He said he had written to Douglas's family and received confirmation that they received his letter – so at least they knew he was dead.

After the war, an Australian war graves team cleaned up the bones, placing them in pits in what became VC Corner Cemetery, a Commonwealth War Graves site. After almost three years in the open, none of the 410 men they recovered could be identified. That makes VC Corner unusual for two reasons: it's the only all-Australian war cemetery in France, and it has no individual graves. Instead, the names of almost 1299 Australians who were missing after the bat-

tle are inscribed on a wall at the back.

Retired Melbourne art teacher Lambis Englezos and a dedicated group of amateur historians spent years poring over old maps, eyewitness testimonies and photographs to try and discover where the Germans buried the enemy dead that day. New documents came to light in Germany, pinpointing the mass-grave site as directly south of Pheasant Wood. A team from Oxford Archaeology has now exhumed the remains of 250 soldiers from these burial pits and determined that one of them was about fourteen years old at the time of death.

That might be John (who signed up as James) Gordon. He was fifteen, not fourteen, but he died in the area behind German lines. Tim Lycett, an ex-policeman from the Gold Coast, and genealogist Sandra Playle, have spent years working to identify the 250 bodies. As of early 2019, 166 of the 250 have been identified, all of them Australian. Some of the 250 may never be identified: there may not be living relatives to provide DNA.

The bodies of Douglas Wood and George Yendle probably lie among the

410 reclaimed from No Man's Land after the war. Both names are on the wall at VC Corner. Colin Meyers, the 15-year-old from Redfern who called himself Cecil Morgan, is not with them. He was identified and reburied at the new Fromelles (Pheasant Wood) Military Cemetery in 2010, with full honours. If John (James) Gordon is among those exhumed, a DNA match has still to be found.

Our attitudes to these bodies have changed. One hundred years ago, the immediate families of some of these men and boys waited more than a year for confirmation of death. The bones of the 410 weren't even buried, let alone honoured, until years later. The army's base records section in Melbourne, suddenly overwhelmed with casualty reports, did their best to unravel the details, but they were often wrong. There were so many tangled stories, based on false names and incomplete records, so little concrete information. So many Johns and Williams who were not who they said they were.

The exhumations and reburials have now restored some of the singularity,

the right to a named grave, for some of the fallen at Fromelles, but the dead are many. The majority of the soldiers who died in the First World War, numbering in the millions on both sides, have no known grave. Those 410 at VC Corner are also in mass graves. The difference is that they are within a walled and tended Commonwealth War Graves Cemetery, with their names on the wall. Under CWGC rules, they can never be disturbed. Once buried within the walls, they will always rest in peace.

The debacle at Fromelles is often called the worst night in Australian history and it's hard to disagree. There were worse battles to come. Pozieres, which started four days later, lasted seven weeks and incurred 23,000 casualties. And more Australians died in 1917 than in any other year of this war, most of them in Belgium. But the 5533 Australian casualties at Fromelles occurred in less than twelve hours, for no gain and even less purpose. Fromelles was a sign of things to come, none of them good. 🏵

JAMES & WILLIAM DALY; ALFRED, FREDERICK & CLARENCE MATHIESON

BROTHERS-IN-ARMS

JAMES FITZGIBBON DALY was a native of Ballarat, Victoria, who enlisted shortly after the first casualty lists from Gallipoli were published.

On a blustery afternoon in June 1906, the North Melbourne football team came to Richmond and gave them a flogging. The mighty Tigers went down by six goals, and the Richmond supporters didn't like it. About 500 people stormed the railway station after the game to see the North Melbourne supporters off – with sticks and stones. Alf Mathieson weighed in and got arrested. Four boys appeared before a magistrate the following Monday and were fined twenty shillings each – worth half a week's basic wage. The Melbourne *Age* called it a 'disgraceful disturbance', with a headline that would soon take on a different meaning: 'A Fight for the Colours'.

Australian Rules football was a war between suburbs. Richmond boys played for Richmond, Carlton boys played for Carlton. The inner suburbs were tough places. Richmond was known as Struggletown. Rivalries between inner-city clubs were more than strong; they were potentially volcanic.

Alfred Mathieson never paid the fine. He was about seventeen and this arrest seems to have solidified his path. The eldest of six kids from Cubitt Street, Richmond, he would soon have a number of convictions for theft and housebreaking. He had served at least two stretches of hard labour by the time war broke out. The Police Gazette published a photo of him after each incarceration. His defiance is palpable.

Alfred's family was poor, but they weren't all rebels. Two of his younger brothers, Frederick and Clarence, worked as 'maltsters', almost certainly at the malt mills in Church Street, around the corner. In a few years, these three brothers would be marching in the same battalion.

Alfred went first in February 1915. Fred, well-known around Richmond as 'Dosser', signed up on 16 July. Clarence, known as 'Charlie', had gone four days earlier. That may have galvanised Fred: Charlie was still only fifteen. Fred was nineteen, Alfred about twenty-five.

WILLIAM WARREN DALY was James's brother. Together, they'd fight in the doomed Fromelles campaign for the 58th Battalion.

The tribalism that saw half of Melbourne turn out every Saturday to watch their team carried over into the recruitment of soldiers. The Richmond boys wanted to stay together, and the army was happy to oblige. That's how D Company of the 60th Battalion ended up being a Richmond stronghold. By 1918, the *Richmond Guardian* newspaper reported that at least 100 men from Richmond were in that one company. They took turns writing to the *Guardian* about their adventures.

The same localism held true in the country, where the 5th, 6th, 7th and 8th battalions were drawn from every town and hamlet in Victoria, including a number that only Victorians could pronounce, like Warracknabeal, Yackandandah and Whanregarwen. By early 1916, more than 50,000 Australian reinforcements were en route to Egypt.

James Fitzgibbon Daly was a mild Ballarat teenager. He enlisted on 7 July 1915, not long after the first casualty lists from Gallipoli were published. His picture makes him look like he's barely out of knee-breeches, but he claimed he had worked for three years for Beath Schiess and Co, a long-established clothing manufacturer. He was a warehouseman, then an apprentice salesman. He was sixteen when he enlisted.

His brother, William Warren Daly, enlisted seven weeks later, stating that he was a labourer, aged twenty-three years and one month. They were assigned to different units – Bill to the 8th Battalion and James to the 31st, the same unit as Colin Meyers, who would die at Fromelles. Both brothers transferred into the 58th in Egypt on 1 April 1916. They were now going to face the war together, literally as brothers-in-arms – like Alf, Fred and Charlie Mathieson in the 60th. Their first taste of war would be at Fromelles in northern France. For three of them, it was also their last.

The Dalys and the Mathiesons had no idea they were on a hiding to nothing. They had just arrived in France, keen to have a go at 'Fritz'. They didn't know that the attack in which they were to be used had no clear purpose. They had faith in their charismatic leader, Harold 'Pompey' Elliott of the 15th Brigade.

They were to take a German blockhouse across 350 metres of open ground – a virtual impossibility with modern machine guns trained on them.

The Australian soldiers had never seen anything like the artillery barrage that rained down on the German positions for seven hours before the attack. 'Pompey' Elliott told his men that they wouldn't find a German in the lines when they got there. But none of his men got there.

All three of the Mathieson brothers were wounded in the attack. Alf copped a bullet in the right arm that fractured his humerus bone. Fred was evacuated to an aid post, with a wound to his scalp. Both were lucky that night in being able to walk back to their lines. Neither would have known that Charlie was still out there in No Man's Land.

The Daly brothers were less fortunate. The British 61st Division had failed to take the blockhouse in the first phase of the attack; they now asked Elliott for assistance while they renewed their attack. Elliott called on his reserves from the 58th Battalion, who had been kept back to carry up ammunition and water. Meanwhile, the British commanders found out how badly their men had failed and cancelled their 9 pm attack. No-one told Elliott until it was too late.

Two companies of men of the 58th, including Bill and James Daly, went out to assist an attack that never came. In fading twilight, they rushed out past the bodies of their comrades from the 59th and 60th with what Charles Bean would later call 'splendid dash'. As they advanced, survivors of the earlier attack came out of shell holes to join them. The Germans waited until they were two-thirds of the way across No Man's Land, then hit them with a blizzard of machine-gun fire, shattering their line. Their 21-year-old leader, Major

> Bean called it 'one of the bravest and most hopeless assaults ever undertaken by the Australian Imperial Force'.

Arthur Hutchinson, fell near the German parapet, riddled with bullets. James Daly, by now aged seventeen, died in that attack. His older brother Bill was wounded in the back and arms. Bean called it 'one of the bravest and most hopeless assaults ever undertaken by the Australian Imperial Force'.

Those are dignified words for a gross failure of command. Two hundred men of the 58th went out – after most of the 59th and 60th had been butchered – and half of them were soon dead. Most of the rest were wounded and had to crawl back in during that longest night. We can only hope that Bill Daly, with a back wound, fell not far from his own lines. He was sent to the No 1 Canadian Casualty Clearing Station, where he died three days later. By then, his younger brother James was already buried with comrades at Rue du Bois Cemetery, a few hundred metres behind the battlefield. Bill was buried at what became the Bailleul Communal Cemetery Extension, about twenty kilometres north-west of the battlefield, near the hospital.

Back in Ballarat, Christina and William Daly Senior heard about Bill's death first. Christina was inconsolable. At this stage, the army was still using local pastors and priests to deliver the bad news telegrams, which explains how the Reverend Joseph Snell, a Methodist minister, was first to hear that seventeen-year-old James had also died that night. He wrote immediately to Colonel Hawker at Victoria Barracks in Melbourne, asking him to withhold the announcement from the press.

'Their mother has been laid up, ever since she was informed of the death from wounds of her other son, Private WW Daly, and it is feared that in her present condition of health, the shock would prove fatal to her.' Snell went on to say that he had told the Daly

> No-one ever wrote to Christina to apologise for both her sons being killed …

daughters of James's death, 'and it is in accordance with their desires that I now write to you'.

The army failed to stop the publication of notice of James's death, so Christina heard about it soon after. In September, the officer in charge of base records in Melbourne wrote to Snell to apologise. No-one ever wrote to Christina to apologise for both her sons being killed. That was part of the deal, although the way in which they died, in a botched and unnecessary attack, was not.

Christina survived the terrible news. The Ballarat *Courier* paid tribute to her boys, noting that Bill had once been a member of the *Courier* staff, and that James had been well liked by his workmates. After the war, the people of Ballarat planted an avenue of trees to commemorate their soldiers. It runs for twenty-two kilometres. Both James and William Daly have a tree in that beautiful Avenue of Honour.

Both Fred and Alfred Mathieson returned to Australia, but in diminished states after many medical complications. Fred had done well in the army, finishing as a sergeant, but his body was broken by shell shock. He became a carpenter and died in 1935, around the age of forty. Alfred became a lift attendant, and died in 1961. Their brother, Clarence, was declared MIA and it's assumed he died in battle in France.

Until Fromelles, the tribalism of Australian society had worked in the army's favour because it encouraged men to join up with their pals, so they could fight together. The problem was they could also die together. The effect on small communities could be catastrophic.

In the months following Fromelles, families across the country received the death-knell visits of pastors and priests. In all, twenty-five sets of brothers died at Fromelles, and two sets of fathers and sons.

Nothing would be the same for the Australian troops after Fromelles. Nothing would be the same for the families at home either. ❀

CHARLES CHURCH

'A HAPPY YOUNG CHAP'

CHARLES FRANK CHURCH holds his numbers in the
Darge studio at Broadmeadows in 1916.

Everyone at Broadmeadows Camp knew Algernon Darge. He was hard to miss: an eccentric dresser with a large black beard, driving a souped-up open-top car with a skull and crossbones on the hood. Darge knew the value of publicity, promotion and location. His office in Melbourne was at 175 Collins Street, in the same building as two daily newspapers – the *Herald* and the *Argus* – his ready market. He was one of the city's first commercial photographers.

As soon as war recruiting began in 1914, Darge set up a mobile tent studio at Broadmeadows, just north of Melbourne. There were other photographers, but Darge was the most proficient. His pictures were well composed and subtly lit, the work of a skilled portraitist.

At Broadmeadows, he was quickly overwhelmed with customers. He employed other photographers and they were soon shooting hundreds of images per day, both in the studio – against a choice of backdrops – or in the alleys of the tented camp. The backdrops usually featured painted tents, which is odd,

given there were so many just outside, if he wanted to use them. The crucial difference was that in the studio, he could control the light.

The soldier paid nothing to be photographed – only for prints. Darge had an ingenious way of keeping track. Each customer was allocated a number. The studio carried a set of small blocks with numbers on each facet – like dice. The photographer would line up the blocks and shoot the picture with the numbers visible in the shot. The Australian War Memorial purchased about 19,000 Darge negatives in the 1930s – just under half of the 40,000 pictures he made during the war – and those block numbers identify many of the soldiers in the pictures.

Charles Frank Church took his first turn in the Darge tent in late January 1916, customer number 13633. His picture is unusual, in that Charles sits before a simple white background. He looks placid, perhaps a little uncomfortable in his new uniform. His collar badges are crooked. His eyes are limpid and innocent, as if they have not seen much to upset him, but that would be wrong. Charles had seen enough.

Most soldiers had their picture taken to send home to family or friends, but it's unlikely that Charles was doing that. He wrote 'Parents deceased – no guardian in Australia' in black ink on his attestation form in November 1915, and signed his real name. He gave his birthplace as Dorking in 'Surry' (the English county is Surrey) and his next of kin as an uncle in Dorking, James Edward Cole. As far as the army was concerned, Charles was an eighteen-year-old orphan from the old country, a labourer who resided at Russ Street in Port Melbourne. In fact, he was a kid from South Australia, both parents were alive and he was just fifteen years and two months old.

Many under-age boys ran away from home to join the AIF, giving false names and addresses, but few tried to pretend that their parents were dead. If Charles was wounded, the army would try to contact James Edward Cole – who may not have existed (the initials, JEC, were also those of his real father in Adelaide). If he died overseas, his parents would be entitled to a pension, but the army would not know where to send it. Charles Church was doing more than covering his tracks; he seemed to want to annul his connection with his parents. At least in the case of his father, that is understandable.

As far as the army was concerned, Charles was an eighteen-year-old orphan from the old country, a labourer who resided at Russ Street in Port Melbourne. In fact, he was a kid from South Australia, both parents were alive and he was just fifteen years and two months old.

13550

Dora Hall married John Church, a motor mechanic, on 20 March 1900. Their son, Charles William Edward Frank, arrived six months later, on 15 September, inconveniently early. Charles grew up in Adelaide, liked to read, and was close to his maternal grandmother, Johanna Marie Hall. He wrote letters to her once he joined up, which tells us he did not want to sever all family ties – just some of them.

Charles's father was a drinker. It appears to have been the ruling passion of his life and the cause of his many troubles. He was often in trouble with the police before the war, usually when drunk. Even so, when war broke out, he was quick to respond. He enlisted on 22 December 1914, at Oaklands in Adelaide, giving his age as thirty-four years and nine months.

He joined the 11th Light Horse regiment, although it's a wonder he was able to sit on a horse. His service record is littered with fines for drunkenness,

the first on 19 February the next year, while still at Oaklands. He was also charged with being absent without leave. On 25 February, he was charged again: AWOL and being drunk in camp. In May, having transferred to Enoggera Camp in Queensland, the charge was breaking out of camp and being AWOL. The next month, he went on a three-day bender: he broke out of camp again and was found drunk in the city. By now, the army had had enough. John Church was discharged on 10 June, for being of 'bad character', a few days before the regiment sailed for the war.

Charles was still only fourteen when his father returned in disgrace to Adelaide, probably in late June of 1915. Charles turned fifteen in September. By November, he was in Ballarat, Victoria, signing his papers. It's possible that Charles wanted to go to war all along. Plenty of boys his age did. It's just as likely that the return of his drunken father spurred his decision to run away

---

CHARLES was photographed again at the Darge studio a day later with some pals: he sits (left) with **PRIVATE ALFRED WILLIAM GUEST** (centre) and an unknown friend (right).

and join up in another state, to disavow his parents and perhaps regain some sense of family honour. His grandmother, Johanna, either knew what he intended or found out soon enough, when he started to write to her.

Private Church disembarked at Marseille on 4 June 1916. It was more than a month before he was 'marched in' to a base depot at Etaples, in northern France, and another three weeks before he reached his unit, the 8th Battalion, as part of its 15th reinforcements. The 8th was full of farm boys from Ballarat, miners from Gippsland, and men from the outskirts of Melbourne.

By the time Charles arrived, the battalion had been cut to pieces at Pozieres, in the Battle of the Somme. Australians did not take part in the legendary first day of that battle, when the British lost 60,000 men – killed, wounded or missing – before lunch. Three weeks later, the attack had stalled. British units had failed

to take the two German strongpoints at Pozieres, a tiny village on the straight Roman road between Albert and Bapaume. The ground here rises slowly to a barely perceptible high point at Pozieres. Two solid German fortifications, at either end of the village, known as Gibraltar and the Windmill, protected the approaches to even stronger German positions at Thiepval and Mouquet Farm, a few kilometres to the west. Pozieres had to fall if the British were ever to threaten Thiepval.

The Australian 1st Division moved into position on 23 July and took what was left of the village that night, almost with ease. The German artillery then opened up on the Australians and did not stop for the next seven weeks. After four days, the 1st Division, of which the 8th Battalion was part, had sustained 5285 casualties. The 8th itself lost eighty-one men killed, 266 wounded and twenty-three missing (most of whom were already dead). 'Our boys are in a pitiable state,' wrote Captain Percy Lay in his diary.

Pozieres was the first major action on the Western Front for the 8th. It was much worse than anything they had seen at Gallipoli, where artillery was less common. These men had been longing for a year for 'a crack at the Germans', as they wrote in letters and diaries before the battle, but they could barely see the enemy during those first four days. The Germans, having occupied the village before, knew exactly where to range their guns. Their heavy artillery destroyed the trenches faster than the Australians could repair them, forcing them to shelter in shallow holes.

Many men went mad under the strain. Some were buried by shells, dug out by their mates, and buried again by the next shell. When the 2nd Division relieved the 1st on 27 July, they approached along roads strewn with bodies and body parts, amid the cries of the wounded, some of whom had been lying in No Man's Land for days. Pozieres was already a place of unimaginable horror but the battle had only just begun.

This is where the fifteen-year-old Private Church would join the war. He arrived on 29 July as the battalion was resting at Canaples, west of Pozieres. The senior brass came and congratulated the men on their achievement, and appointed ten new 2nd lieutenants to replace those who were gone.

After two weeks of training and long route marches, designed to bring the men back to fitness, they were sent to Vadencourt, then Brickfields, a holding area just north of the town of Albert. Here, a couple of shells fell close to their bivouac

> The Germans, having occupied the village before, knew exactly where to range their guns. Their heavy artillery destroyed the trenches faster than the Australians could repair them, forcing them to shelter in shallow holes.

during the evening of 14 August, fired from a German gun mounted on a train, without casualty. Charles now knew what they sounded like and he was close enough to hear the roar of what was happening day and night at Pozieres.

The men learned to identify the size of different shells by sound – the high-velocity 'whizz-bangs' from a 77-millimetre light field gun, which came in low and fast without much warning, and the 5.9-inch heavy field howitzer shells that shook the earth itself (the men called them 'Jack Johnsons' after the heavyweight American boxer). There was nowhere to escape. Charles Church was about to experience the worst that this war had to offer.

The next day, Charles and the 8th Battalion moved up into reserve trenches at Sausage Valley, just south of Pozieres, and set to digging a new 'jumping off trench', in preparation for an attack. They were shelled all day, as the Germans watched them dig. On the night of 18 August, A and C companies, with about 200 men in each, were ordered to attack north and east of the Windmill, at the far end of the village. The aim was to clear out German trenches protecting Mouquet Farm, a heavily fortified farmhouse. Church was in C Company, under Lieutenant Fox, on the left.

They were to advance behind a creeping barrage, a new technique in which the guns would move their rain of fire forward at set times by set distances, with the infantry close behind. The barrage was supposed to cut the barbed wire and keep the Germans in their deep dugouts; when the barrage moved forward, the infantry would rush in on top of the Germans as they emerged. It was a very successful tactic later, but this was only the second time it was used, and timing was crucial. If the infantry advanced too quickly, they would run into their own shells. If the barrage was not intense enough, the Germans would be ready. It's unlikely that Charles had ever had a chance to practise such an advance.

Almost inevitably, the attack failed. The orders arrived late, so the 8th Battalion set off without knowing the precise timing of the barrage. The Germans hit both A and

When the 2nd Division relieved the 1st on 27 July, they approached along roads strewn with bodies and body parts, amid the cries of the wounded, some of whom had been lying in No Man's Land for days. Pozieres was already a place of unimaginable horror but the battle had only just begun.

C companies with heavy machine-gun fire and hand-thrown bombs. Three times, these two companies retired and regrouped, to attack again. Three times they were repulsed, with heavy losses.

This was one of the worst nights of the war for the 8th Battalion. The initial count was twenty-five men killed, 154 wounded, thirty-two missing. When final numbers were known, fifty-one men had died that night, including this boy of fifteen years and eleven months. His first major stoush was also his last. He was initially listed among the missing. It would take the army until March 1918 to convene a court of inquiry to declare him dead. Armies were more concerned with counting the living.

A number of Charles's comrades later gave their recollections to the Red Cross, which usually made inquiries on behalf of parents. Inevitably, the recollections don't quite match.

Private GS Boden, writing ten months later, said: 'He was about 5'6" fairly stout and had a fair complexion. He was about eighteen years of age and a happy young chap. He was with the battalion three or four weeks up to 18.8.16.'

Lance Corporal A Morris, company clerk of C Company, said a relative of Church's came looking for news of him about five or six weeks later, and Morris took him to meet two men who knew him, Privates Boden and Lawton, 'who told him they had seen Church killed right on the parapet as they "hopped over" the second time at Pozieres on 18th August last'.

Private Kells of C Company told the Red Cross 'he was killed straight out at night in our trenches in Pozieres by machine gun bullets. He was buried on the spot just behind our line. I do not think his grave was marked.'

Private J Hawkins, writing from a war hospital in Epson, thought the action was at Bullecourt – but the main Australian actions there were not till later. Hawkins was right about the date and time of the advance at Pozieres. 'At August 18th at 9 pm we made a raid on the German trenches at Bullecourt [?]. Church, Johnson and myself were in a shell hole together at one time during the raid. When we got back Johnson told me that Church was killed by a machine gun bullet before he got to the German trench.'

The Red Cross wrote twice to Johnson but got no reply.

In February 1918, John S Johnson wrote to the officer in charge of base records in Melbourne. He mentions reports about Charles's death from some of the same people. He then mentions that Private AR Muirhead, of one of the 8th Battalion machine-gun companies, had visited camp 'where Sergeant Weeks took Muirhead to Church's mates, who told him Church was killed on the parapet. The last named [Muirhead] used to write often to Church's people but has lately ceased to do so, and probably has himself made the supreme sacrifice.'

In fact, Alexander Russell Muirhead, a Glasgow-born seaman, survived the war and returned to Australia in 1919.

In due course, Charles Church's family was able to prove their relationship to Charles, despite his attempts to erase them, and a war pension was duly paid

to Dora Church. Her husband continued to be troubled by alcohol. They both died in the late 1940s.

Charles Church is buried at a very beautiful small cemetery on a hillside at Ovillers, just outside Pozieres. The site looks back towards Sausage Valley, which Charles came up for the first time on the day before he died. Very few Commonwealth War Graves headstones acknowledge when someone was under-age. Charles's headstone says he was sixteen, which is just one month short of being true. 🌐

BERNARD HAINES & ROWLAND LORDING

WOUNDS THAT NEVER HEALED

BERNARD 'BABY' HAINES weighed barely forty-five kilograms
when he left Australia to fight in France.

On 21 February 1917, Bernard 'Baby' Haines entered a crimson river of casualties flowing through France towards Britain. He was seventeen years old and barely forty-five kilograms, one of the reasons his comrades in the 29th Battalion called him 'Babe' and 'Baby'. He would soon weigh a little less.

Bernard's older brother Royal was already at the war, and his father Frederick would try to follow a few months later, without success. Bernard most likely went in secret and certainly without permission. He wrote on his forms that he was Charlie Haines from Richmond and he did not know his parents' address. That was a harsh thing to do, since it cut his parents off from information when he was wounded.

He gave as his next of kin one Harry Kalwig, of Albert Park. It's possible that Bernard had already left home when he joined up and asked Kalwig to be his go-between if anything happened.

Bernard was wounded in the Somme Valley, eight months after one of the worst battles in history. He entered a medical system that was by now well-honed, partly because of the terrible casualties in 1916 on the Somme.

The flow of wounded grew faster and wider on its way to the coast, like a river.

Casualties were initially carried to an aid post where they were bandaged and loaded onto a field ambulance – usually a lorry or even a horse-drawn cart. These flowed to a casualty clearing station (CCS) – a series of small mobile army hospitals, located next to a railhead. If a major action was occurring, tens of casualties would become hundreds. The CCS surgeons would operate to save those they thought had a chance and smooth the path for those who didn't. That's why there are so many cemeteries in places where CCS hospitals were positioned. Those who needed specialist treatment and long-term care were loaded onto a casualty train and sent down the line to a major hospital near the coast. If the number of casualties reaching here was too great, even those with minor wounds were sent straight to England, to relieve pressure on beds.

Once they reached the French coast a soldier's chances of survival were much better, although that is a relative term. Some of the biggest war cemeteries in France are next to the sites of those general hospitals, simply because of the sheer volume of casualties. By now, hundreds had become thousands – men in all states of pain and suffering.

Bernard was among them, after less than a month with his unit, in the bitter winter of 1916–17. He was unlucky to be wounded. His 29th Battalion was out of the front line near Montauban when the enemy shelled them from afar. Bernard was hit in the left thigh by a fragment from a high explosive shell. Stretcher-bearers took him to the 15th Australian Field Ambulance, where his leg was dressed. They sent him on to the 45th Casualty Clearing Station at Edgehill, near Dernancourt, where his leg was amputated above the knee by British surgeons. Three days later, he arrived at the 9th General Hospital at Rouen, which designated him 'seriously ill'. In fact, he was struggling for his life. On 6 March, they shipped him across the Channel on the *St David*, a converted passenger ship from the Irish run. By 8 March, he was in the Royal Victoria Hospital at Netley, Southampton, and in a bad way.

None who passed through Netley had ever seen anything like it. It was the largest building in Britain, several hundred metres long, a vast hospital city built seventy years earlier during the Crimean War. It was beside Southampton Water, the main thoroughfare for troops leaving Britain for the front. Those going out could see the wounded coming in, up to three trains a day. The wounded were now a tide, overwhelming even this hospital's

> Haines was unlucky to be wounded. His 29th Battalion was out of the front line near Montauban when the enemy shelled them from afar.

vast resources. The whole British Empire was here – Sikhs and South Africans, Maoris and Aboriginals, West Indians and Canadians, most of them in pain. Half of all shell-shock victims were cleared through Netley. One whole floor was allocated to Indians, a million of whom were fighting in France and Belgium. The hospital built a special 'ghat' in the grounds for their cremations. Bernard arrived with a septic stump and every chance that he would soon be with the angels of his own creed – which was Baptist.

'On admission Netley – general condition very poor,' reads a card in his medical record. 'Stump of left thigh very septic, is necrosed, end of femur projecting from wound.'

Even for a non-medical reader, that sentence is horrific. The bone of his left leg was dying from infection and jutting from the wound. The Netley doctors sent him for reamputation, effectively taking more of the leg in order to save him from the raging infection.

For the first few months of 1917, the army kept sending letters to Harry Kalwig, whom Bernard had put down as his next of kin, detailing the condition of young 'Charlie' Haines. It seems likely that Kalwig wasn't quick to tell the family that their son was now on death's door because it wasn't until 9 April – seven weeks after he was wounded – that his mother Mabel wrote to the army to inquire what hospital he was in.

Bernard had survived thus far because he was young – still just seventeen. In early 1917, there were roughly 10,000 other Australians in British hospitals, and another 2000 to 3000 in Australian auxiliary hospitals in Britain. Over the three years of Australian involvement on the Western Front, 155,000 Australian casualties made the trip across the Channel from France.

BERNARD 'BABY' HAINES (left) and his brother, ROYAL. Bernard stands behind him to conceal his missing leg.

Lording experienced just nine days of this 'great war'. Haines got even less time. Both copped serious wounds in their first major action. And neither of them should have been there in the first place.

One of them was Rowland 'Rowley' Lording, from Burwood in Sydney. He and Bernard never met, but they had much in common. More than they would ever have wanted, in fact.

They were only seven weeks apart in age. Bernard enlisted in Melbourne in February 1916. Rowley joined up in Sydney in July 1915, seven months earlier. Both wrote that they were eighteen years and one month old. Both boys were bantams: Rowley weighed fifty-eight kilograms to Bernard's mere forty-five, and they were about the same height.

One difference was that Rowley enlisted with permission, perhaps after a little blackmail. He had already tried and failed twice. On his sixteenth birthday, 20 June 1915, his parents agreed to sign the papers if he became a signaller: they thought the training would take at least twelve months and by that time the war would be over. And they were afraid he would run away to another state and join under another name. He already had a taste for adventure: he had left school at fourteen to work in his father's bicycle factory. On weekends, he would take himself off on epic bike rides, sleeping under the stars with a few provisions in a pack. He could cover up to 550 kilometres in three days.

His parents were almost right. Rowley became a signaller in the 30th Battalion, but he was in Egypt by December and northern France, near Hazebrouck, by the end of June 1916 – almost a year since they let him go. He had not yet heard a shot fired in anger. As he climbed down from the train, after a three-day journey from Marseille, he could hear thunder. It wasn't thunder, but heavy guns. He estimated they were about thirty kilometres away. 'So we are getting near the Big Smoke at last,' he wrote in his diary.

Rowley experienced just nine days of this 'great war'. Bernard got even less time. Both copped serious wounds in their first major action. And neither of them should have been there in the first place.

Rowley later wrote one of the most vivid descriptions of the attack at

Fromelles, which took place on 19 July 1916. It's one of the only first-hand descriptions, since most of the men who took part were killed or did not have his literary talent. *There and Back* was published in 1935 under an odd pseudonym: A. Tiveychoc. The commander of the 8th Brigade, which contained the 30th Battalion, was Major General Edwin Tivey, a Melbourne stockbroker who was popular with his men. In Egypt, the 8th Brigade became known as 'Tivey's chocolate soldiers'. Rowley, whose middle name was Edward, called himself 'Ted Rowland' in the book. Here he is, moving up the Australian lines to Fromelles under heavy shell fire. He has just seen 'a rider' – presumably of horse – coming back without his head.

'Dazed and without being conscious of their movements, Ted and his mates go on and turn to the right towards Cellar Farm Avenue, passing the military cemetery with its field of white crosses. Ahead, in the battle zone, huge geysers of earth are spouting upwards as the high-explosive shells plunge into the ground and explode, and the air above is clouded with the woolly bursts of shrapnel. How can man live in and pass through that hell?

'But forward they go, into the "avenue", a winding sap crowded with life and death. Wounded are helping wounded. A man with a shattered arm is leading out a blinded and bloody-looking figure. Some of the wounded are laughing – others, with sagging jaws, stare ahead. Here's a shaking, trembling, raving madman. The signallers push on to get away from that. There are still four hours to go to "zero". There will be no-one left!'

At 6 pm, most of his comrades go forward into the teeth of German machine guns and many die. Ted's gang of four signallers must wait until a fifth signaller lays a cable across No Man's Land. When he returns, Ted shoulders the phone he is supposed to connect to the far end of the cable and goes out into the fray.

'God! What sights they see out there. Huddled and stretched out bodies, khaki heaps that were once men – some of A Company digging a trench – others, like themselves, making short crouching runs and flinging themselves down before anything that will afford the slightest cover …

'Crump! Bang! Crash! The shells fall. Zipzipzip—zipzip! Machine-gun bullets kick up the dirt around them. A lull and off they rush again. Zipzip! Bang! Another twisted heap of khaki hits the ground.

'It is Ted. He does not move. His cobbers crawl over to his side. "Where d'you get it?" they ask him. His lips move, but they do not hear his reply. His arm is shattered and blood is gushing from his side. He cannot last much longer – they think he is going west. His eyes ask them to do something. Stan rolls him on to a ground-sheet and drags him yard by yard towards the trench. Shell splinters tear through the sheet. The ground rocks from a nearby shell-burst which almost covers them with mud. Stan drags him on. Ted is in mortal dread of being hit again. At last they come to the sally-port and he is carried on a duckboard into the trench. "You've got the wind up," was Ted's gibe to Stan at Fleurbaix; now Stan has risked his life to bring Ted in.'

"A Tiveychoc," author of "There and Back."

ROWLAND LORDING, pictured here in a later newspaper clipping, was just seventeen when he joined the First World War.

Stretcher-bearers got Rowley to an aid post within about twelve hours, where a doctor gave him a tetanus injection and morphine for the pain. He was then trucked to a casualty clearing station and onto another train where a British nurse cut away his bloody clothes, put his letters and diary into a bag and

Some of the biggest war cemeteries in France are next to the sites of those general hospitals, simply because of the sheer volume of casualties. By now, hundreds had become thousands – men in all states of pain and suffering.

washed his face. He went to sleep again, woke up choking and vomited blood, and was given oxygen. The sister held his hand all the way to Boulogne on the coast. 'She goes with the orderlies who carry him to the platform, then stoops over, kisses him, and is gone. He sees his mother – he wants to live. He will live.'

At No 13 General Hospital, housed in the old casino at Boulogne, surgeons discovered the full extent of his injuries. He had a small gunshot wound in the left chest, but lower down he had a large hole, four inches across, which had shattered and collapsed his lung. His heart could be seen through the hole. His right arm was smashed by a bullet through the elbow and there was a small piece of shrapnel embedded in his hand. He also had two open wounds on his feet that he brought with him from Egypt. He was afraid to report them in case those in charge separated him from his battalion.

Rowley developed tetanus the next day and endured ten days of racking pain and a locked jaw. He had four inches of rib removed 'without anaesthetic', because his chest was too bad to risk an anaesthetic. The changing of dressings was painful, but not the chest wound, except when they turned him on his side twice a day to drain the pus from the chest cavity. Rowley spares no details in his descriptions of that first forty-five days at Boulogne, but it includes highs and lows. The morphine made him fond of singing, and he became very close to some of the nurses and patients. They gave him champagne before he left for England. They dressed him in a borrowed English uniform with a label, like Paddington Bear.

The journey to Fort Pitt Military Hospital at Chatham put him back into delirium. He still had a large infected cavity in his side that had to be mopped out daily.

'This does not hurt, in fact it tickles his back ribs on the inside and makes him laugh. He does not learn until later that one slip on the doctor's part and the forceps might touch his heart. A torch is kept on the locker so that interested visiting doctors may have a look at Ted's works; the youngster hears much of their talk – "The pericardium, yes, quite distinct, it has moved, yes, to the right and a little higher up, the shock, the explosion ..." Anyhow, it keeps on beating and, as Ted once said, "The open-air life agrees with it." He tells one of them that he can account for it being a little higher up, because it jumped into his mouth when he got cracked. One day he asked for a mirror to be held near the hole, and when he saw his heart he remarked that it looked like a piece of meat. Maybe he expected it to be of gold. At one time there was some talk of putting a silver plate in his side, so he asked that it be engraved with the date and name of the battle, but the idea was later abandoned.'

On 13 October, Sir Frederick Treves – 'the King's surgeon' – performed a long and rare operation in which he removed part of six ribs in order to reinflate what was left of Rowley's lung. Even Rowley is stuck for words to describe his agonising recovery, during which the staff were sure he would die. He did recover and kept the ribs in a bottle beside his bed. They went with him on 21 February 1917, on a hospital train to Bristol, to board the ship *Karoola* for the trip home. Rowley was still a few months short of his eighteenth birthday. This was the same day that Bernard 'Baby' Haines copped his wound in France.

After his reamputation, Bernard Haines spent nearly four months at Netley, as his stump healed. At the end of June, they sent him to the Australian Auxiliary Hospital at Southall, and he was well enough to go on leave in the middle of August. On 10 September, he embarked for Australia on the *Ulysses*, one of the largest and fastest of the troopships operating to Australia. On 13 February 1918, he was discharged from the army on medical grounds.

Bernard returned to live with his family in Adelaide Street, Murrumbeena. His brother Royal came home from the war and they had their picture taken in a Melbourne photo studio. In both pictures, one with Royal and one by himself, the photographer places Bernard in a way that obscures the missing leg. It is as if he has come home intact.

Soon after, Bernard applied to the State War Council for a grant of £60 in order to buy a tea room and pastry shop near the station at Murrumbeena. He stated that he had had some experience working in a pastry cook's shop before the war, and that his two sisters, aged seventeen and twenty-one, would be helping him. The problem was that the vendor, Mrs Waters, could not produce any receipts to back her claim that the shop was bringing in £18 per month. The board sent inspectors to try to verify the shop's potential. Bernard himself withdrew the application, probably on advice that he should find a business that was more suitable. In fact, he had run out of time. He was back in hospital by the middle of 1918, after a fall on a railway ramp left him unconscious for an hour. He fell again a week later; the doctors discovered blood and pus in his urine. This was to continue for the next eight years, on and off.

Bernard had contracted an infection of the kidneys while in hospital in England. The treatments would be primitive, painful and ineffective for what would now be cured quickly with antibiotics. He spent most of those years in Caulfield Military Hospital, enduring forty operations and years of pain. His medical records are like a Latin dictionary: nephrotomy, pyelitis, faecal fistula, dyspnoea, colostomy, pulmonary oedema. By 1925, he was physically and emotionally depleted. Life in a repat hospital was one long farewell to your mates: either they got better and left or they died.

In these same years, Rowley Lording was enduring similar challenges in the repat hospital at Randwick in Sydney. He had been living on morphine before he was discharged from the AIF. In the next two years, the drug, both prescribed and illicit, took control of his life. Operations continued on his right arm and on his chest, where painful spurs grew on the end of his severed ribs. These operations took place almost weekly.

Rowley writes: 'The military hospital was a good market for the war-profiteer whose nefarious business was the selling of drugs. Morphia, heroin, atropine, barbitone, cocaine "snow", and even opium, found their way into the hospital unsuspected, while the attention of the authorities was directed towards suppressing the lesser and only apparent evil – drink. A hollow bed-post, a cake of soap, and many other things provided suitable hiding-places, and a cunningly contrived fountain-pen, more than once lent to an unsuspecting sister to write her report or mark a chart, concealed a hypodermic syringe.'

Rowley began to lose interest in anything but the drugs. His pain was so severe that ten grains of morphine, forty times the usual dose, failed to quell it. His habit was concealed by the prescribed morphine until a hospital superintendent – a former sergeant – confronted him, some weeks after his forty-eighth operation. The super put him into isolation, although he still managed to find drugs, smuggled inside a box of chocolates. It took him six months to kick his habit. He left the hospital clean, 'a boy of but 20 summers', and fired with a new ambition to rebuild his life.

Rowley eventually qualified as an accountant. He worked for some years helping his comrades find jobs in the Depression. His right arm, a wound that had never healed, was amputated in 1920 and Lording endured this operation, his forty-ninth, without morphia. He relapsed into addiction when the drug was used after his fiftieth operation; again, he overcame it. He married and had three children with

> Lording began to lose interest in anything but the drugs. His pain was so severe that ten grains of morphine, forty times the usual dose, failed to quell it.

a young woman he had met when she and her mother visited his bedside in England. They later divorced. He remarried in 1943. Rowland Edward Lording died in Callan Park Mental Hospital in 1944, having survived fifty-two operations. AG Butler, official medical historian of the AIF, considered that he deserved a special place 'among the immortals of the AIF'.

If that's true, Bernard Haines should be beside him. Bernard's post-war life was an epic of pain and endurance, lived out in the wards of Caulfield Military Hospital, where he was a popular but not always placid presence. In 1925, he was transferred out of his ward for back-chatting a nurse and doctor – he was playing cards and did not want to stop for his dressings to be changed. It would be understandable if, after forty operations, he had lost some faith in modern medicine, which had failed for eight years to cure a kidney infection contracted in an English hospital. He died on 16 March 1926, 'quite suddenly', after another operation to remove a portion of bowel.

The Melbourne papers all marked his passing, with many errors of fact. They said he had enlisted at fourteen, a mistake he had probably helped to create by consistently understating his age, even after the war. One misspelled his name, but all said he had been cheerful to the end – another comforting fantasy. He was twenty-six years and ten months old when he died. He is buried in Brighton Cemetery, not far from Major General Tivey, his commanding officer: 'Baby' was another 'Tivey Choc'. The descendants of Bernard George Haines still visit his grave, particularly Lois Comeadow, his grand-niece.

Bernard and Rowley do not appear on the Honour Roll, the list of Australian war dead, because they did not die in battle. Yet they are not forgotten. Each became famous in his own way for enduring suffering that is hard now for us to comprehend. And each was under-age, too eager to go, too young to know. 🐝

EDWARD GILES, JAMES HARRINGTON & JOHN ELLARD

THE THREE COBBERS

Fifteen-year-old **EDWARD GILES** and eighteen-year-old **JAMES HARRINGTON** were typical West Australian boys: sons of labourers, tanned and strong, they were keen to do their bit and fight the Germans, whom they called 'Fritz'.

Three young men stood in line together at Blackboy Hill, on the outskirts of Perth in Western Australia. It was Friday 21 January 1916, and they were ready to begin their great military adventure.

They were among hundreds of men who would become part of the 10th reinforcements for the 28th Battalion, one of the few units made up largely of Western Australians. The rest of the battalion was already in Egypt, after missing most of the action at Gallipoli. In March, they would be one of the first units shipped to France.

Ted, Jimmy and Jack were like most West Australian boys of the time: lean and tanned from working outdoors as the sons of miners, farmers and labourers. All of them were keen to kill Germans, whom they called 'Fritz'. Even those of German extraction – and there were many in the Australian army – wanted to kill Fritz. Some were even called Fritz.

Each new soldier was allotted a service number, usually in sequence. Private John 'Jack' Ellard became 4109. He said he was eighteen, and that his next of kin was his father, John Ellard, of Maylands, a suburb of Perth. Edward 'Ted' Chichele Giles became 4125; he said he was eighteen and six months. James 'Jimmy' William Harrington got 4128, just three numbers behind Ted. Harrington said he was nineteen and eight months, that his father was dead and his mother, Mrs Edith Bowling, lived in Maylands.

None was telling the truth about his age. Ted Giles was actually fifteen and six months; Jack Ellard was a few days shy of seventeen; Jimmy Harrington was a year younger than he said, at eighteen and eight months. None seems to have had a letter of permission from a parent. These three would become thick as thieves for the rest of their war, a band of brothers who would do everything together. Their records run in tandem, to a remarkable degree, a testament to their close friendship.

It's possible they met that day at Blackboy Hill, but not likely. One of the questions on the form asked if they had been in His Majesty's army, the militia, the navy, the Territorials or the Colonial Forces. Each wrote 'no', followed by '89c'. These figures are a reference to a scheme where boys from twelve to eighteen attended cadet camps in one of 224 training areas throughout Australia. These training areas all had a number and a letter: 89c was a mining district on the Murchison River, 650 kilometres north of Perth, inland from Geraldton. This area was hot, dry and sparsely populated. The boys had probably trained together there and decided to enlist together, as mates often did.

For these young men, 'mateship' was uncomplicated. A mate was someone who had earned your trust, through thick or thin. Mates covered for you when you were late on parade; they grabbed some 'tucker' for you if you were late back from an unofficial 'jolly' into Cairo, sometimes called 'French leave'; mates saved you a 'possie' in a tent. Mates called each other 'cobber', a word that has almost disappeared from the Australian language. You could trust a mate with your beer or your life. The army understood that mates wanted to fight together; in fact, they exploited that in enlistment propaganda.

> You could trust a mate with your beer or your life. The army understood that mates wanted to fight together; in fact, they exploited that in enlistment propaganda.

As raw recruits got deeper into the war, these friendships became even more important. For some, your mate was the only thing left that was worth fighting for after a couple of years of meaningless slaughter. None of which was likely to be on the minds of these boys on that day, except perhaps in the vague notion that if you were going off to the other side of the world to fight strangers, you might as well do it with friends.

Ted Chichele Giles was born in the picturesquely named mining town Day Dawn on 21 July 1900. He was born at home, like his many brothers and sisters, because his mother Lily did not believe in hospitals – not that there would have been much choice in Day Dawn in 1900. The town consisted of a few streets, several pubs and a number of working gold mines.

With that middle name, Ted sounds like a toff, but he wasn't. The 'Chichele' name goes back to Henry Chichele, a fourteenth-century former Archbishop of Canterbury. They were Catholics, although Ted's father, Albert Edward Giles, knew more about ploughs and railway engines than the pulpit.

Ted was Albert and Lily's fifth child. The first two boys, Bill and Nathaniel, were born in Broken Hill. By the time Ted went to war, Lily had borne twelve children, two of whom died soon after birth. Ted stated his occupation as 'teamster', someone who drove a horse team, which suggests he had left the family home in Perth by 1915. Given the '89c' on his papers, he appears to

have returned to Day Dawn, his childhood home, to find work.

Like many under-age boys who went to war, Ted was following his older brothers. Bill, the eldest, went in September 1914, one of the originals of the 16th Battalion. Nathaniel joined up a year later, in the 12th reinforcements of the 11th Battalion. Ted's uncle Frank went in January 1915. All three were in Egypt by the time Ted joined up in January 1916.

James Harrington was born in South Australia but had been living in Perth since about age five, after the death of his father. His mother Edith then married George Bowling, a boiler-maker, but she made her son aware of his distinguished military heritage. She sent him to war with a Moroccan leather pocket-book with inset pictures of himself, his father in 'Highlands uniform' and his grandfather in a Crimean War uniform. Edith had told him that his grandfather won the Victoria Cross at the Battle of the Alma, which was not quite true. Hastings Edward Harrington, a lieutenant in the Bengal Artillery, won the VC at the Siege of Lucknow in 1857.

Jack Ellard arrived in Perth in 1903, a four-year-old migrating with his parents from Erith, Kent, in England. Jack was working as a labourer when he enlisted. We don't know anything of his reasons for going, except that a lot of young men of the time had the same idea – especially if they had been born in England.

The three pals had little time for basic training at Blackboy Hill. On 7 February, about two weeks after they arrived, all three were sent to Signals School for two weeks, to learn the basic skills of army communications. These included how to send and receive messages by Morse code, wireless telegraphy, semaphore flag, ship's lamp, even carrier pigeon. Much of what they learned was about laying and repairing telephone cable in the field under fire. This was the sharp end of a signaller's duty, the reason they had a high mortality rate. A signaller might also have to run, if all else failed, carrying a message. That was one of the reasons that younger men who were light and fleet of foot were often selected as signallers.

The 10th reinforcements, numbering 200 men, embarked on April Fools' Day on the ship *Ulysses*. A month earlier, the ship had struck a rock while departing Fremantle Harbour and was immediately dubbed 'The Useless' by the men she could no longer carry away to war. That was a boon for the reinforcements: after repairs, they sailed to Egypt in more comfort than most of their comrades.

Ted's brothers and uncle were already widely dispersed when he arrived. Nathaniel left for France with the 11th Battalion on 5 April, even though he was still recovering from influenza. The oldest brother, Bill, now a corporal, had been wounded on Gallipoli and was still in Egypt. Uncle Frank had also been wounded on Gallipoli and was transferred to a hospital in Cairo – where he probably saw his sister, Bridget, a nurse with the Australian Army Nursing Service. She had moved on to a military hospital at Rouen in France by the time Ted and pals arrived.

The three cobbers were now together again, in time to celebrate Ted's sixteenth birthday on 21 July. They would have known that their first battle was going to be soon.

They followed in June, arriving at Marseille on 5 June aboard the *Tunisian*.

The three signallers were soon to see what real war looked and sounded like, but they could first marvel at what France looked like, from a train taking them north. The journey to a camp at Etaples took three days, with pre-arranged stops of a few hours for meals. French citizens turned out along the route to welcome them with flowers, gifts, kisses and cries of '*Vive l'Australie*'. The trains were carefully rerouted around Paris, to avoid temptation. The progress of these men to war had been quicker than those who joined up in 1914 – four months from Blackboy Hill to within the sound of heavy guns. This suited most of the new soldiers, even those who might have wondered why they were being moved so fast into this 'theatre' of war.

The three mates spent several dull days at Etaples – a major junction and holding camp – waiting to be sent on to their battalion. In June 1916, French trains were moving hundreds of thousands of troops and vast quantities of shells towards Amiens for the coming Allied offensive – which we now call the Battle of the Somme. Jimmy Harrington and Jack Ellard made it to the 28th Battalion on 16 June, as the battalion moved north into Belgium. Ted Giles was held back, perhaps by the return of an unspecified illness that put him in hospital in May in Egypt. He set off to find his battalion on 10 July, which was not easy. The 28th was now marching south, drawn inexorably towards the Somme, moving each day to a new billet. Ted finally caught up with them at the impressive Chateau Bertangles, a few kilometres north of Amiens on 14 July, Bastille Day.

The three cobbers were now together again, in time to celebrate Ted's sixteenth birthday on 21 July. They would have known that their first battle was going to be soon. A fortnight later, the 28th was moving into position south of Pozieres, a village that no longer existed, except as rubble. The Australian 1st Division had just seized this strategic high-point from the Germans. The cost had been appalling.

Pozieres had once been a drab farming hamlet on the straight Roman road between Amiens and Bapaume. Its misfortune was to be at the highest point in the valley, which is why the Germans had fortified both ends of the village. On the southern end, beside the road, they built a large concrete blockhouse above and below ground. The British called it Gibraltar.

At the northern end, they constructed two lines of strong trenches in front of an old windmill, which they also fortified. The Allies called these trenches OG 1 and OG 2, standing for 'Old German'. From here, the Germans could see the farmhouse at Mouquet Farm, a kilometre to the east, and beyond that the hill at Thiepval, both of which were German strongholds.

The British commander, General Haig, wanted to take Pozieres first, so he could come at Thiepval from behind.

> Those coming up the line were dismayed by the sight of their comrades in the 1st. 'They looked like men who had been in hell ...'

For the first three weeks, the Germans stubbornly repelled all attacks by British battalions. The Australian 1st Division went in on 23 July, in its first major fight on the Western Front, after Allied guns had pounded Pozieres for four days. The intensity of the shelling was unprecedented. The Australians took most of the village in one night. The Germans then opened up their big guns on the trenches they had just vacated, determined to pound the Australians into submission. The 1st Division hung on for four nights, during which it took 5285 casualties.

This was a few days after the disaster at Fromelles, seventy-five kilometres north, in which the 5th Division incurred more than 5000 casualties, but that battle was over in a few hours. Pozieres ran for seven weeks. In those first four days, 400 men of the 1st Division became shell-shocked – a new experience for Australian troops.

Those are not even counted in the 5285 casualties above.

Those coming up the line were dismayed by the sight of their comrades in the 1st. 'They looked like men who had been in hell,' wrote Sergeant Edgar Rule of the 14th Battalion, '... so dazed that they appeared to be walking in a dream ... Quite a few were silly and these were the only noisy ones in the crowd ... I have never seen men so shaken up as these.'

The 2nd Division started relieving them on 25 July, but the 28th Battalion was held in reserve near La Boisselle. On their way up, the three young signallers would have seen things they could never have imagined. The scale of this war was awe-inspiring: the roads were choked with lorries carrying thousands of shells forward to the batteries of guns, which pounded an enemy six kilometres away. Ambulances tried to crawl back down through the traffic, bringing their cargo of broken men. There were aeroplanes above and tunnellers below, grubbing forward for months so they could plant huge amounts of explosive under the enemy.

Officers on horseback, messengers on motorbikes, mule teams and horse teams dragging mobile food-wagons and yet more guns – everything but elephants.

The boys from the 28th went up through lines strewn with dead – not just Australian, but British and German dead from the earlier battle, their bodies blackening with putrefaction. There was no time to bury them: the shelling destroyed trenches as they went forward, so the living cleared the dead from their path and kept going, hoping to find a trench deep enough to give cover.

The 2nd Division battalions had seen nothing that compared to this. Their only major operation so far had been helping with the evacuation from Gallipoli. Charles Bean describes them as 'half-trained' and led by a man who had no experience of attacking on a large scale. His name was Major General James Gordon Legge. Before the war, he had been the energetic quartermaster general of the Australian army. It was part of his job to spruik the advantages of the new cadet scheme to the volunteer militia officers who would have to administer it. Since the days of 89c, in that sense, Ted, Jimmy and Jack had been Legge's boys.

Legge was a theoretically minded soldier. Born in London in 1863, he came to Australia with his family when he was fourteen, studied law at the University of Sydney, then became a teacher. He returned to law in 1891, then joined the permanent army three years later, serving in India and the Boer War. His immediate superior for the Pozieres attack was the British cavalry general Sir Hubert Gough, a man who thought preparation was over-rated. Gough had tried to pressure Major General Sir Harold Walker, Commander of the Australian 1st Division, to attack Pozieres on twenty-four hours' notice, on the night of 18 July. Walker hadn't seen the ground, so he politely refused, stalling Gough for another five days, while he prepared. Even so, the 1st Division was mauled almost beyond repair on 23 and 24 July. Now, Gough turned his pressure on Legge, whose men were to replace Walker's on 25 July. Legge was more

accommodating. Walker's men had failed to take the German trenches near the Windmill at the far end of Pozieres.

Legge's 2nd Division was to take OG 1 and OG 2. The 5th Brigade, under Brigadier General William Holmes, went in first on the right. The 6th Brigade, under Colonel John Gellibrand, moved in at the southern end of the village, near Gibraltar, on the left. The 7th Brigade, which included Ted, Jimmy and Jack in the 28th Battalion, were to go in just after midnight on 28 July as the main force, between the other two brigades; 'up the guts', as they say in Aussie Rules.

The artillery had first to throw enough shells to cut the German wire, so the Australians could get into the OG trenches. Legge's men would have to cover up to 600 metres across open ground under heavy German shellfire. Every commander knew that was too far. A prudent attack would have required jumping off trenches to be dug forward, to get the men within 200 metres, but there was no time for prudence. The German shelling was destroying trenches as soon as they were dug, burying men under mounds of earth.

As at Fromelles a week earlier, the shelling did not cut the wire. The Western Australians went forward under heavy machine-gun fire. Those who got to the wire mostly died there. Hundreds fell near the Windmill and were never seen again, their bodies buried or blown apart by the shelling. This is where our three mates went forward on that dreadful night; as signallers, they were expected to repair the telephone wires that were cut as soon as any battle began. Ted Giles and Jimmy Harrington died that night, somewhere in this carnage. Neither body was ever found.

Jack Ellard said later that he saw them killed, which means they were all together to the end. He told a soldier named Shepherd, who passed the information to a Red Cross investigator from his hospital bed in Etaples a year later. 'The three of them were cobbers,' said Shepherd. That they were – three under-age boys who joined up together, sailed together, trained together. Two of them then died together in their first battle.

Frank Giles died six days after his nephew Ted, another victim of the 'mincing-machine' of Pozieres, as Charles Bean called it. Frank's sister Bridget was nursing at the 1st Australian General Hospital at Rouen, trying to cope with the thousands of Australian and British wounded flowing from the Somme. She succumbed to nervous exhaustion on 17 August, having lost her brother and nephew in the space of three weeks. She was sent back to England to recover.

Jack Ellard was invalided to England in September with heart problems and didn't return to France until the middle of 1917. He was wounded in the lower

> Jack Ellard said later that he saw them killed, which means they were all together to the end.

Australian stretcher bearers carry in a wounded soldier under the white flag, which did not always protect them from enemy fire.

The scale of this war was awe-inspiring ... There were aeroplanes above and tunnellers below ... Officers on horseback, messengers on motorbikes, mule teams and horse teams dragging mobile food-wagons and yet more guns – everything but elephants.

jaw in October 1917 and repatriated to Australia in mid-1918. Ted's eldest brother, Bill, was sent to England in September 1916 with a gunshot wound to the right hand. He went back to France in May 1917 but was sick for much of the next year. He returned to Australia, never married, and became a farmer in outback Western Australia. His brother Nathaniel won the Military Medal for gallantry in late 1918 and returned to Australia in 1919. Bridget Giles married in England and remained there.

The night of 28–29 July remains one of the worst in the history of the AIF.

'In about 15 minutes, the 28th had ceased to exist as a battalion,' wrote FA Mauger, '… we never had a chance.'

Corporal Percy Blythe won the Military Medal that night, trying to rally the wounded, then helping them back to their lines once he received an order to withdraw: 'to our eternal sorrow we left a long line of the best and the bravest boys that Australia ever produced lying along that wire … they were glorious lads, every one of them.'

The 25th and 26th battalions had 640 casualties between them, 250 of whom were killed. The 28th had 470 casualties in total, 196 of them killed. That was more than any other battalion. They include Ted Giles and Jimmy Harrington. Many were never found. Their names are on the Australian Memorial at Villers-Bretonneux.

General Haig was displeased with the results. He blamed the arrogance and ignorance of the Australian officers, rather than his pugnacious friend Hubert Gough, and he had a point. Legge went into the battle with more optimism than preparation. It only took 3500 Australian casualties to find out that he was better at administration than battle. 🕸

CECIL THOMAS

FATHERS AND SONS

Cecil Vivian Harcourt Thomas dragged himself out of the trenches at Pozieres on 15 August 1916, after five days in hell. Cecil was fifteen, a quietly serious boy, but his nerves had taken a battering, like every man in what was left of the 13th Battalion.

They had barely slept in those five days. By day, they clung to the ruins of trenches blown apart by constant shelling. By night they went forward to try to capture enemy trenches, fighting innumerable short, brutal hand-to-hand encounters with seasoned and determined German troops. The killing had been intense and personal, like a form of madness. Some men ran amok; some ran away; some ran forward and were never seen again. Both sides shelled each other incessantly, but not always accurately. Some Australians were killed by their own shells. Many were buried by showers of earth, dug out by their mates, and buried again.

The 13th, raised in New South Wales, considered themselves a crack outfit, aiming ('but never claiming') to be the best unit in the AIF. The 13th covered themselves in glory in those hot days of August, repeatedly occupying the enemy's trenches, only to be bombed back to their own. The Germans counter-attacked during daylight on 11 August, sending 2000 men out from the fortress of Mouquet Farm, just to the west of Pozieres. Half of them were cut down by the Lewis guns of the 13th and 16th battalions, in a terrible slaughter. The Germans came at the 13th again, with a party of 250 men, led by sixty bombers. Again they were repulsed.

Cecil Thomas had come through the worst days and nights of his young life. About a third of his comrades had not. The battalion suffered 386 casualties in five days – killed, wounded, missing or taken prisoner. The survivors were shelled as they moved back to Sausage Valley, the main Allied route into Pozieres. A large-calibre German shell hit one section of eight men passing along a trench called Tom's Cut and killed seven, just as they thought they were past the worst of it.

These men, so tired they could barely stand, had now to walk back fifteen

Cecil Thomas

This photograph of **CECIL VIVIAN THOMAS** appeared in a newspaper around 1916.
He was fourteen years and eight months when he enlisted.

kilometres to the village of Warloy, west of Albert. Here they received a tremendous ovation from the rest of the 4th Brigade. Men from other battalions carried their weapons for them, cheering them along to a camp where they flopped down and slept. On 17 August, they marched north-west to La Vicogne, where they bivouacked in an orchard. Cecil Thomas had been born on an orchard near Orange, New South Wales. The smell of fruit now reminded the fifteen-year-old of poison gas, rather than of home.

Cecil's father, Arthur Cecil Coplin Thomas, known in the family as Cec, passed through this same camp at La Vicogne a week earlier, in the 1st Battalion, just as his son was going into the line at Pozieres. Cec was about to tread where his son had already been, and it would have a profound effect on both their lives.

No-one knows how many fathers and sons enlisted in the AIF, but many battalions had at least one pair. Sets of brothers were more common.

Cec and Cecil Thomas were both born at 'Hillview', a property outside Guyong, on the road between Bathurst and Orange. The family was well known in the district. Arthur Cecil was born in 1877, the fourth of nine children. In December 1899, he married Margaret Helen Roberts from Orange. Cecil Vivian arrived in December 1900. Or did he?

The New South Wales birth registry says he was born in 1901. If that is true, he was a mere thirteen years and eight months old when he enlisted, which would make him one of the youngest Australians to go to war. Other sources say Cecil Vivian was fourteen and eight months when he signed the papers in August 1915. His father appears to confirm that in a letter he wrote in September 1916, in which he said that his son would turn sixteen on 17 December. That means Cecil Vivian was born in 1900.

He appears to have been born lucky, despite the number of his battalion. How does a boy of fourteen who weighs 48.5 kilograms, is 1.5 inches short of the minimum height and an inch short of the 34-inch required chest measurement even get into the army? When he signed on at the Sydney Town Hall in August 1915, shortly after the Gallipoli landings, volunteer numbers had surged in Australia. There were many thousands of older, taller, stronger men ready to go. Either he had a very deep voice or someone helped him bypass the regulations.

Cecil Vivian shipped out of Australia on the *Osterley* in the middle of January 1916. By June, he was in northern France, making his way towards Pozieres. He was an incongruous sight in the 13th Battalion, which was already known as the Battalion of Big Men.

His father enlisted on 2 September 1915, ten days behind his son. Cec wrote on his forms that he was thirty-eight years and four months old, which would have disqualified him three

months earlier. The regulations were relaxed in June to allow men up to the age of forty-five to enlist. He was five feet five inches (165 centimetres) tall and sixty kilograms, with blue eyes and brown hair. He exceeded the chest requirements, which tells us he was probably strong.

Cec left no record of why he went to war. He may simply have been doing his duty, like other men, or he may have been trying to protect his son. The family had been through a brutal divorce case in 1913. It had been rough on Cecil, who was called to give evidence against his mother.

Divorce in Australia in 1913 was difficult and messy, often relying on evidence of adultery. The *Truth*, one of Sydney's most notorious papers, gleefully recounted that Cecil's mother Margaret had left Cec in Orange and taken the children, Cecil and Gloria, to Manly, where she took up with a man named George Champion. Later, she told Cec she loved Champion and would not give him up. Cec then took the children. A judge heard evidence of Margaret's adultery and granted a decree nisi (the first stage of a legal divorce) with costs against Champion. A version of the same facts appeared in the local Orange newspaper, in case the family did not already have enough humiliation.

Two years later, Cecil Vivian enlisted, followed a fortnight later by his father. Whatever his reasons, Cecil was in a hurry to get away to the war. His father could have got him back by telling the authorities that he was under-age.

Instead, he went after him. That suggests that Cec's initial aim was to join his son, rather than rescue him. One of Cecil's uncles, Leslie Alexander Thomas, had joined the 13th Battalion in September 1914, a year earlier. Cecil's eldest uncle, William Charles, a veteran of the Boer War, enlisted in November 1915.

Cec bounced around between the 10th and 13th battalions through late 1915, before joining the 1st Battalion in March 1916. Uncle Les stayed in the 13th, alongside Cecil. Cec's movements are puzzling: why would he transfer out of his son's battalion? It would be harder to look out for him from another unit.

One explanation might be that Cecil did not want his father in the same unit: his age was a secret, after all. Having Cec nearby would make it harder to keep that secret.

When Cec arrived at his new unit in late July, the 1st Battalion had just suffered 537 casualties in roughly sixty hours – more than half its number. The battalion retired to Halloy to lick its wounds. Cecil was nearby, camped at Warloy. A week later the 13th moved up into Sausage Valley, then into the line at

> Two years later, Cecil Vivian enlisted, followed a fortnight later by his father. Whatever his reasons, Cecil was in a hurry to get away to the war. His father could have got him back by telling the authorities that he was under-age.

The day after he reported sick, Cec wrote from his hospital bed to Lieutenant Colonel James Durrant, his son's commanding officer, informing him of his son's real age. Cec's taste of Pozieres appears to have galvanised his desire to get Cecil out of the war.

Pozieres on 9 August. Cecil and his uncle Les were the first in their family to experience the horrors of this war – but not by much.

Cec's battalion followed them into Pozieres on 18 August, taking another 103 casualties over the next four days. They endured heavy shelling throughout, which took its toll on Cec. The battalion then moved north, to quieter duties in reserve near Ypres. Here, Cec reported sick on 23 September. He was then sent to England for treatment of haemorrhoids. The day after he reported sick, Cec wrote from his hospital bed to Lieutenant Colonel James Durrant, his son's commanding officer, informing him of his son's real age. Cec's taste of Pozieres appears to have galvanised his desire to get Cecil out of the war.

'If you could obtain his discharge or failing that, some duties at the Base, you would greatly oblige,' Cec wrote. Lieutenant Colonel Durrant began the arrangements to send Cecil home. Cec probably saved his son's life with that letter.

Cecil left his unit in Belgium on 10 October. A week later he sailed from Portland in England, on the HT *Ajana*, for Australia. He arrived there on 8 December and was discharged from the army on Christmas Eve.

He returned to Manly, where his mother was staying in lodgings. Some-time after Cecil enlisted in August 1915, and before Cec shipped out of Australia in April of 1916, Margaret and Cec had patched things up and remarried. That makes it clear that Cec was probably motivated by duty or a sense of paternal care when he went to war.

Cecil reunited with his mother at New Year, but he was not the same boy she had once known. Cecil came home shell shocked, another victim of Pozieres. A reporter from the *Sun* newspaper told his story in May 1917, five months later. 'ENLISTED AT FOURTEEN … BOY-SOLDIER AT "MOO-COW" [Mouquet Farm],' the piece began.

'Beside the fire at 8 Pine-street, Manly, there sits a boy who is gradually recovering from shell-shock contracted on the historic field of Mouquet Farm in

A splendid portrait of **FRANCIS THOMAS**, the patriarch, and family, probably from 1919. The group stands before a portrait of their late mother. **CEC THOMAS,** in the middle at the back, is flanked by his brothers **WILLIAM** (left) and **LESLIE** (right). Cec enlisted just two weeks after his son Cecil to join him in battle.

France. He enlisted as a boy of fourteen and a few months, and his name is Cecil Thomas. He is fair and slight and serious-looking and as he talks, he stares into the fire, seeing, you hardly dare imagine what ghastly pictures in the glowing coals,' wrote the unnamed reporter.

The story explained that Cecil had enlisted by forging his parents' permission, 'writing backhand to disguise his boyish penmanship'.

'No-one guessed how young I was,' he said, adding that he knew of another boy only a month older still serving in France. Cecil said he had twice visited his father when he was quartered nearby – presumably just before both had gone up to Pozieres.

'Of the actual battlefield the boy is yet unable to speak fluently. There are phases of it, which touched upon ever

> Cecil told the reporter that poison gas smells like fruit. 'It smells like all the fruit you ever smelt – as if the breeze were blowing off an orchard.'

so gently, set his lips trembling with memories – memories to be pushed hastily aside as part of an evil dream that is over. His mother says that a thunderstorm makes him "restless as a kitten", and that for weeks after his return he sat listlessly with his head in his hands, hardly speaking to anyone, and showing interest in nothing about him.'

For two months, Cecil did not speak one word about his war experiences. He did tell his mother that all he wanted was to get away to the country, far from the noise of the city. She sent him to relatives on the north coast, where he found solace tinkering with an old motorbike. 'On the bike his mind rode back to normal.'

Cecil told the reporter that poison gas smells like fruit. 'It smells like all the fruit you ever smelt – as if the breeze were blowing off an orchard. It is so lovely that you could go on sniffing it and sniffing it, and all the time it would be killing you.'

The rest of the report details some of his war experiences – night patrols in No Man's Land, an intelligence officer who spoke German who would don a German uniform and spend hours in the enemy trenches, a night raid where the men got caught up on the enemy's wire. Having now turned sixteen, he said he would go back to the war when he was eighteen, to finish the job.

This report is unusual because it talks openly about the effects of shell shock, which was little understood. Shell shock could mean a number of things: someone whose brain had been damaged by proximity to an explosion or someone whose nerves had broken down under the strain of warfare. Some doctors thought the nerve-cases were merely shirkers who should be sent back to the front. The army had been reluctant to admit its existence, but the numbers of men afflicted at Pozieres changed that. The Australian Army Medical Service recorded more than

400 cases on the Somme battlefield between 19 July and 5 September 1916. The *Sun* report makes clear that the term was in common usage by mid-1917.

Cecil's father returned to France in January 1917, but was sent back to England for medical evaluation in May. He was invalided back to Australia for chronic rheumatism in August 1918. He too may have been suffering from shell shock. Both of Cec's brothers survived the war.

Cecil survived partly because his luck held through those dark days at Pozieres, and partly because his father got him out, once he saw those same terrible trenches. But neither man nor boy came home unscathed – and soon, Cecil removed himself from his family, taking off for Fiji, far from the sound of the guns. He married and had a family and moved to New Zealand in the 1950s, where he died in 1980. He is buried in Tauranga. ❀

FRANK, FREDERICK & LEWIS COLLINS

GOING HOME

On 31 August 1915, Frederick 'Freddie' Collins, aged fifteen, marched into the post office at Moora, a small town in Western Australia's wheat belt, to send a telegram to his mother in England.

Telegrams were expensive but Freddie even paid for the reply – the equivalent of a few weeks' wages. The most significant part of the telegram was just three words: 'Can I enlist'. He didn't pay for a question mark.

His mother Annie was in Witley, the village in Surrey where Freddie grew up. In May 1913, Freddie's father Lewis had come out to Australia by himself, presumably to find a job and place to live. Annie followed to Fremantle in October with the four children: Frank, aged fifteen; Frederick, fourteen; Cyril, six; and the baby Muriel, two years old.

The heat of Perth could be confronting for 'new chums'. Many English migrants went back after they experienced an Australian summer. For whatever reason, Annie had returned to England with the two youngest children by 1915. Lewis and the two older boys stayed in Western Australia. Frank, now sixteen, was working as a station hand near Geraldton, 420 kilometres north of Perth. Freddie, aged fifteen and three months, was a farm hand near Moora, 250 kilometres south of Geraldton. They appear to have coordinated their decisions to go to war.

Annie's reply to Freddie's telegram is in his army records, handwritten on a cablegram dated 2 September 1915, at the Moora Post Office. The message simply says 'Yes'. There's no similar telegram in Frank's file but that isn't unusual: army record-keeping could be unpredictable.

Frank went to the recruiting office in Geraldton on 7 September 1915. His papers were accepted the next day. The medical examiner recorded that he was five feet four inches tall (167 centimetres); weighed 63.5 kilograms; had a dark complexion, brown eyes, and black hair; was a member of the Church of England; and had a mole between his buttocks and a scar on his right breast. In other words, fit as a fiddle. Frank did not arrive at Blackboy Hill until the middle of October. There was a train from Geraldton to Perth, so he could have reported there within days. He waited almost five weeks – perhaps as a favour to the farmer who employed him.

Freddie was already at Blackboy Hill by then. He signed the papers on 11 September and went into camp on 17 September. He was the same height as his older brother, but slighter, at fifty-eight kilograms. Apart from that and Freddie's hazel eyes, everything else about them was the same. To the rest of the world, they might have looked like twins – although we have no photograph of either.

They were assigned to different units. Frank was in the 12th reinforcements for the 16th Battalion. Freddie was in the 13th reinforcements for the 11th.

In the circumstances, it's not surprising that Lewis, their father, soon enlisted. His wife and two babies were already 'back home', and his two elder boys would soon be on their way to war. Lewis had been working as a railway fettler. He signed on at Perth on 9 November. In January, at Blackboy Hill he was allocated to the same battalion as his elder son Frank – the 16th – but to a different group of reinforcements. Lewis was thirty-nine, which was within the new guidelines, allowing men up to forty-five. He was built like Freddie and Frank, but a little taller at five feet seven inches (170 centimetres) and about the same weight as Freddie at 56.5 kilograms, with blue eyes and dark brown hair. All the Collins men – except for young Cyril – were now in the army, destined for France. Their paths would converge in the Valley of the Somme in summer.

It was not unusual that Lewis and Annie agreed to their sons going to war; it was unusual that both were under-age. British-born men living in Australia flocked to the recruitment halls in the early months of the war. Many did so out of a strong sense of duty; others saw the chance for a cheap ticket home to England in a war that would be over by Christmas. Many ultimately paid a much higher price.

By March 1916, sixteen-year-old Frank Collins was at Tel el Kebir, the vast Australian camp in Egypt, in the 16th Battalion. Younger brother Freddie was

G.W.

CERTIFIED COPY.

COMMONWEALTH OF AUSTRALIA
POSTMASTER GENERAL'S DEPARTMENT, WESTERN AUSTRALIA.

446

Telegraph message transmitted subject to Post and Telegraph Act and Regulations addressed

To Mrs. A. Collins

Witley, (Surrey), England

Can I enlist

Reply paid

Number of words   11

Time lodged   12.15   From   Fred Collins

Time sent   12.30

I hereby certify that the above is a true copy

Moora   on 31st Augu

£1 8 6   was paid for its transmission.

G.W.

WEALTH OF AUSTRALIA.

GENERAL'S DEPARTMENT, WESTERN AUSTRALIA.

No. 1

CABLEGRAM.

This Message has been received subject to the Post and Telegraph Act and Regulations.
All Complaints to be addressed, in writing, to the Deputy Postmaster General.

Number and Route.   Station from, Date, and Time Lodged.   Number of Words and Official Instructions.

Fifteen-year-old **FRED COLLINS** sent a reply-paid telegram (left) to his mother in England with the three simple words 'Can I enlist'. Her reply (right) was equally succinct: 'Yes'.

about to leave Egypt for France with the 11th Battalion, and their dad had just boarded a transport ship in Fremantle, heading for Europe. Lewis was still in the 16th, but he would transfer to the 48th in France in May, in the 'doubling' of battalions.

Freddie's battalion had been in France for six weeks and the first five had been like a holiday. They were sent to billets at the small village of Sailly sur la Lys, about fifteen kilometres south-west of Armentières, near the Belgian border. This was a quiet spot, partly because the Germans did not want to goad the British into shelling nearby Lille, where they had a major troop concentration and a busy rail link.

The men from Western Australia loved France, in a way they never loved Egypt. They loved the French people, who welcomed them warmly; they loved the small cafes, *estaminets*, where they could eat fried eggs and *frites*, and drink large amounts of cheap wine and beer. They enjoyed the cool weather, green fields, and forests full of unfamiliar trees. They could hear the guns in the distance, but no-one seemed in a hurry to send them up the line.

> They enjoyed the cool weather, green fields, and forests full of unfamiliar trees. They could hear the guns in the distance, but no-one seemed in a hurry to send them up the line.

This was intentional. General Haig didn't believe the Australian troops were ready for the big show. They were too undisciplined, too rash, and led by inexperienced officers. They needed training in the methods of modern warfare – like the use of poisonous gas and Stokes mortars and grenade-throwing – and above all, in following orders. Their artillery was not yet up to scratch. Part of this was British superiority, but a lot of it was true.

By 1916, most able-bodied Frenchmen were in uniform, or already dead. At Sailly, those who were left – wives, mothers, daughters and old men – attempted to carry on as though the war wasn't happening. They milked cows and herded pigs and tilled fields with horses. Some set up little cafes in their front rooms, to cook the eggs the Australians loved. Some of the Australians, new and suspicious, watched these people carefully. There were many rumours of German spies. A single white horse in a field was considered suspect, until the Germans shelled the field.

Freddie arrived at Sailly on 25 May 1916, as a reinforcement. He had now been in the army for six months. He spoke with an English country accent.

Freddie was more used to this lush landscape than his comrades, many of whom were miners from Kalgoorlie and Coolgardie. Witley was less than 300 kilometres away as the crow flies, surrounded by picturesque English farming downs. Most of his relatives and his boyhood friends were still there. Freddie had more in common with his French hosts and their German enemies than he did with most of the men in his unit. He was a European – not that he would have called himself that.

The big, suntanned Australian miners beside him came for adventure, perhaps more than duty or Empire, but those who had been through Gallipoli knew much more than Freddie did about what was in store. They knew the holiday at Sailly wouldn't last.

Four days before he arrived, the 11th finally entered the line at Petillon, just south of Fromelles. Freddie joined D Company, led by Major JT Milner. Another officer, Lieutenant Hastings, had already earned the nickname 'the Mad Mullah' for running along the top of the parapet at night.

The ground was too sodden to dig trenches so the previous occupants had built breastworks above ground with sandbags, wood and wire. These had a parapet but no parados (the back wall of a trench), and no dugouts, just small huts constructed from more sandbags and tin roofing. The front of the breastwork was metres thick but could be knocked over by a well-aimed high-explosive shell.

On the day Freddie and the other reinforcements arrived, the Germans sent over a heavy bombardment of high-explosive shells. They killed one man and wounded four others. The Australians retaliated. The same thing happened the next day, with both sides breaching the others' breastworks. The machine gunners would then try to pick off the men repairing the damaged walls. At night, the positions came alive, as 'fatigue' parties brought up food, munitions and supplies. Both sides sent small patrols into No Man's Land to repair wire cut by shrapnel, or to search for weaknesses in the enemy wire.

The intensity increased daily. The Germans fired 400 shells on 28 May, both high-explosive and shrapnel, killing two and wounding eight. Then on the night of 30 May, all hell broke loose in this 'quiet sector'. The Germans poured in shells of every kind on A, B and C companies for ninety minutes, flattening the parapet for a stretch of about ninety metres. A German raiding party then hit B Company, killing and wounding, taking prisoners, then withdrawing. The Australians were caught offguard and did not know how to respond. The history of the 11th Battalion, *Legs-Eleven*, is unusually frank: 'Being new to the game, none of the officers or men realised that it was just a local raid, terrible though it was in intensity and effect …'

The raid killed thirty-six men and wounded another sixty-nine. Eleven went missing, some of them taken prisoner. The scene next morning was diabolical: the shelling had dug up the decomposed bodies of English dead from months before, who now mingled with the fresh dead of the 11th. The stench was indescribable.

Fifteen-year-old Freddie had been at the front less than a week. He could count himself lucky that his company was not in the forefront that night, although the shelling had penetrated more than 200 metres beyond the frontline. D Company was thrown into the repair work as the shelling continued. Many men thought they had been in a major action. It's hard to describe the loss of 118 men as a 'minor' raid, but that's what it was. Much worse was in store.

Freddie's first month on the Western Front was an education: learning how to keep his head down, to handle the fear, to cope with seeing the dead lying around in all states of disrepair. Lice were a constant problem, infecting the uniform, so hours were spent 'chatting' – trying to burn the lice out with a lighted candle run along the seams of pants and tunic. Baths were infrequent and communal. There were moments of excitement, such as the warnings of a gas attack. These were mostly false alarms, or the gas was too far away to harm them. For the first time, the Australians saw aeroplanes in dogfights and balloons being used for spotting. In the trenches at Petillon, they marvelled at the size of the trench rats – brazen and foul, grown fat on the dead.

On 9 July, Lieutenant General William Birdwood, commander of the Australian forces, told the men they were being sent south to the Somme, where they would have a chance at more 'open fighting', rather than this trench skirmishing.

That was true in one sense: the place they were going did not have such well-defined trenches, mainly because the German and Allied guns had mostly blown Pozieres apart. Birdwood's news cheered them: they were going to the big show, the great Battle of the Somme.

Freddie and the 11th went south on 11 July, in French train wagons full of horse manure. They detrained at Doullens, and, with full packs, set out on a long march to the small village of Halloy, north of the Somme River. The next day they moved to Naours, a beautiful town with a series of ancient tunnels in its chalk cliffs. Many Australians visited these tunnels during July 1916, writing their names on the walls. The names are still there. The 11th camped for three days, during which the men received their pay. Much of it was spent in local hostelries, where the recent vintages were evaluated. For many, this would be the last drink they would ever take. Naours was close enough that the men could also visit the brothels in Amiens – although most French villages had local establishments.

On 18 July, the 11th Battalion marched forward to the aptly named Forceville, where preparations for the front line began in earnest. All surplus gear was collected for storage behind the lines, and steel helmets were issued. Greatcoats and groundsheets were rolled and worn like bandoliers. Each soldier sewed a pink cloth square on the back of his tunic, to signify the 1st Australian Division. Officers changed uniforms to look the same as the 'other ranks' – meaning the lowly privates, corporals and sergeants. Each man carried 150 rounds of small arms ammunition. Some were given periscopes, others Very-light pistols (for firing flares) or wire-cutters. Most important, all were issued picks and shovels. The faster they could dig, the safer they would be. A shovel could save many lives.

On the afternoon of 19 July, the 11th moved up past Albert, the roads becoming ever more crowded with men, wagons and materiel. Each step brought them closer to the deafening boom of the heavy guns, with both sides pounding Pozieres. They passed lines of German prisoners being marched back, ambulances carrying the wounded and British soldiers coming out of the line with 'treasure' – including German Pickelhaube helmets, with a pointed spike on top.

The 11th was to relieve the Durham Light Infantry. The Australians could tell from the faces of the Tommies that they were headed for a bad place, although none could have imagined how bad. As darkness fell, the Germans sent over gas shells. Freddie and D Company moved into Black Watch Alley, past the blackened unburied corpses of British victims of the first three weeks. Some men chose to walk in the open rather than through these horrors, but the presence of German snipers soon changed their minds. When German flares popped, illuminating a moonlike wasteland, the machine guns opened up.

The 9th Battalion, which was full of Queenslanders, took up the trenches on the right; the 11th to their left. The trenches were falling apart, so the men set to digging, shoring up and digging 'possies' into the front walls of the trench for sleeping. Not that there

The scene next morning was diabolical: the shelling had dug up the decomposed bodies of English dead from months before, who now mingled with the fresh dead of the 11th. The stench was indescribable.

would be much sleeping in the next five days and nights.

When they arrived on 20 July, there were still remnants of a village at Pozieres. There were trees and orchards and visible hedges around fields. Most houses were damaged but not yet powdered into red brick dust, as they would become. The shelling was frequent but not yet heavy. On 21 July, the British guns intensified their fire on the village, which was known to have many cellars where the enemy would be hiding. German and French planes duelled overhead. A French plane crashed behind C Company. An 11th Battalion sergeant ran out and rescued the pilot. The Australians were supposed to attack that day but their action was postponed, to give time for 'jumping off' trenches to be extended. These were meant to push forward across No Man's Land, to bring the men closer to their eventual objectives. Lieutenant Nicol of D company was shot dead on the night of 22 July, while reconnoitring the ground over which his men, including Freddie, would attack.

On the afternoon of 23 July, amid crashing shells, the men shaved, wrote letters home and ate a hot meal. The portions were larger than usual, because so many men had already been killed and wounded by the shells. Captain Walter Belford, who was there, wrote in *Legs Eleven* that the officers and platoon commanders went round the men, making jokes 'as man to men'.

'In this manner those splendid lads passed the time before what was to be the most terrible battle that the 1st Australian Division was engaged in, and in which the 11th Battalion suffered more casualties than any other battalion in the division.'

German shelling increased by the hour, as the enemy realised an attack was coming. By the time the 11th Battalion went forward to attack, just after midnight on 23 July, the men had been in the line for three days, enduring a heavy strain. A and B companies were to go first, to capture the nearest German line at Pozieres Trench. C and D companies were to push forward through them to capture the light railway that ran through the village. The 12th Battalion were then to come in behind and leapfrog the 11th, pushing forward to grab the old Roman road that runs north to Bapaume.

At midnight, Freddie and D Company crept into position in No Man's Land, twenty metres behind the first wave. Almost immediately, Lieutenant Hastings, the Mad Mullah, was killed. His men stayed in position, waiting for a creeping barrage of Australian shells to be unleashed on Pozieres Trench at 12.28 am. The Australian gunners this night were spot-on. At 12.30 pm, the first two companies leapt into Pozieres Trench and captured it without much resistance. Freddie and D Company ran through them, looking for the railway. In their enthusiasm, they ran too far, even through their own barrage and beyond the third objective. That showed their inexperience. Small parties of C and D companies ran right through the village to the Windmill, way beyond where they were supposed to be. Now they waited for the 12th Battalion to arrive, but the 12th had been caught up in the congestion of Black Watch Alley, now choked with returning wounded.

Belford writes that he and his brother officers collected their men at the third objective – the road through Pozieres, and set them to digging a new line of trenches. By now, most of the 11th Battalion officers were either dead or wounded, including Major Milner, commander of D Company. When the 12th finally arrived, they dug in on the right, as dawn broke. The Australians then set about clearing out German snipers from the ruined houses and cellars in the town. German prisoners were brought in and immediately 'ratted' – stripped of all belongings: watches, knives, helmets, cigarettes, chocolate and most valued of all, German automatic pistols; all souvenired. A number of Australians died in these early hours because they were too casual about snipers – another sign of inexperience. Meanwhile, HQ issued orders and then countermanded them a few minutes later. The diplomatic Belford says this was to be expected in any battle – 'but in the battle of Pozieres, a certain want of co-ordination and confusion was very noticeable', and down to 'poor staff work'.

More inexperience. The Germans now unleashed their artillery on Pozieres, in a terrible rain of shells that lasted all through 24 July. Freddie's army record says he died on 25 July at Pozieres, but he may have been killed on the first night of the attack. No-one saw him die; nor did they find his body. Indeed, some of his comrades swore they saw him being taken back to England, among the wounded. The Australian Red Cross Wounded and Missing Enquiry Bureau in London collected testimony from two men who said they knew Freddie. Private Dawson, aboard the hospital ship *Breydel* at Boulogne, a month later, said Freddie was only sixteen, and he had left Australia on 17 January that year – both details correct. But then Private Dawson claimed Freddie was taken prisoner at Sailly, during the German raid on the 11th Battalion trenches. That was a month earlier than he disappeared, and perhaps reflects the impact of battle on Private Dawson.

In March 1917, Private W Stevens of the 11th Battalion was interviewed at a military hospital in Edgbaston, Birmingham. He said he knew Freddie well, as they were in the same reinforcements that arrived in France in April. 'Pte Collins and I were both wounded about July 23rd, 1916. I was sent to the 26th General Hospital at Etaples and Collins was sent to England. Cpl Black of C Company ... told me he had seen Private F Collins in hospital in England and that he would not be sent out to join the battalion for a time as he was not then nineteen years of age.'

The bureau wrote to Corporal Black in March but received no reply. Black was killed six months later in Belgium.

The army was by now even more confused than usual. They had at first declared Freddie missing in action. On 28 November 1916, they declared that he was absent without leave from the 4th Command Depot at Wareham, one of the places Australian soldiers went to convalesce. In December 1917, they declared that this was an error and reverted to the initial report – missing from 25 July 1916, in action. In June 1918, they declared him killed in action on that same date. The Red Cross report doesn't detail what evidence they had for this finding.

What should we make of these contradictions? Could Freddie have survived and somehow returned to Surrey, or gone AWOL in England? It's unlikely, given that no-one ever heard from him again. His brother Frank returned to Surrey near the end of the war to marry his sweetheart. If Freddie was there, Frank would surely have heard. It's also true that these Red Cross testimonies are often contradictory. One of the symptoms of shell shock is loss of memory.

On 25 July, the day that Freddie's record says he was killed, his brother Frank was marching toward the same terrible battle. The 16th Battalion, Frank's unit, arrived in France on 7 June and spent the next few weeks training in northern France. On 25 July, they marched to Warloy for another week of lessons about 'jumping off' trenches, advancing under a barrage, how to lay and cut wire, throw bombs and operate the Lewis machine gun. They moved into the line at Pozieres on 9 August, with orders to continue the attack. The battle was now two weeks old. It had already ground through more than 12,000 Australians – killed, wounded or missing – since 23 July.

At midnight, Frank and the 16th advanced under heavy machine-gun fire but managed to take all their objectives – remarkable given their inexperience. The Germans shelled them mercilessly on the 10 August, before counter-attacking the next day. Frank was already on his way back down the lines – another case of shell shock.

Lewis Collins arrived at Pozieres on 14 August in the 48th Battalion. His second son, Freddie, was in all probability lying somewhere on this same battlefield, having died two weeks earlier. His first son, Frank, was by now in Boulogne, recovering from shell shock.

> On 25 July, the day that Freddie's record says he was killed, his brother Frank was marching toward the same terrible battle.

Lewis arrived on one of the worst days of the war for the 48th. They were constantly pounded by accurate German shell fire, which blew away every attempt at rebuilding the trenches and turned some men into vapour. The battalion came out of the line the day after he arrived, so he was spared some of the worst. For the next two weeks, he marched through some of the same towns his sons had passed through – Albert, Warloy, Rubempre – much of it in torrential rain. On 30 August, the 48th went back up towards Pozieres and relieved the 12th Battalion at La Boisselle, digging new trenches by night. This was to be the last battlefield that Lewis would see. A German shell landed near him on 31 August, smashing his right leg and giving him a compound fracture of the right arm. Pozieres claimed its third victim from this one family, but at least Frank and Lewis were still alive, unlike Freddie.

On 1 September, the doctors in France took Lewis's right leg off through the knee and shipped him back to England, to the 3rd London General Hospital, Wandsworth. There, in December, they reamputated the leg higher up. The large wound to his right arm was slow to heal. Lewis spent six months at Wandsworth, after which they transferred him to the 2nd Australian Auxiliary Hospital at Southall. Here he went AWOL, a remarkable feat for a man with only one leg and a badly damaged arm.

He was absent only from 9 pm till 7 am, which suggests he had a visitor. Lewis's wife Annie was still living with the younger children in Witley about sixty kilometres away. If Annie did visit him that night, they would have had much to talk about. Freddie was still officially missing, but Frank had been sent back to his unit in September. Lewis would never again be able to provide for his family, even if he survived the war. What was to become of them now?

Frank would now be expected to provide, but he was still in the front line, and his attitude to soldiering had changed. From having no disciplinary black marks before Pozieres, he was now less willing to follow orders. On 15 October 1916, in France, he was punished for leaving his work party without permission.

He would be in trouble again in July 1918, after being sent back to Britain, for neglect of duty and then in March 1919, after the ceasefire, for insubordination to an officer and failing to comply with an order. These offences all date from after his shell shock and the disappearance of his brother.

There was more tragedy to come. In November 1917, Lewis was shipped back to Australia for treatment. In late January 1918, he was about to undergo an operation at the 8th Australian General Hospital in Fremantle. He reacted badly to chloroform, which was still the most popular form of anaesthetic at the time, and died on the operating table. He was forty-one.

The army sent a telegram to AIF headquarters in London on 1 February: 'Please inform Mrs A Collins, Fowlhouse Farm, Witley, Surrey, husband died 16th Jan, collapse during administration anaesthetic, 8th AGH Fremantle'.

A few pages on in Lewis's file there is a ruling on an application for a pension, dated 30 April 1918. The pension was sought in the name of Lewis John Collins, the newborn son of Lewis and Annie. He was born in 1917, which means he was probably conceived late in 1916 after Lewis was wounded.

Annie returned to Perth in January 1920, with the three youngest children: Cecil, Muriel and the baby, Lewis. Her eldest son Frank had been repatriated to Australia in 1919. The Battle of Pozieres had taken Annie's husband and her second son, Freddie, the fifteen-year-old who had sent her the urgent telegram in 1914. It had damaged Frank too, but he survived.

Truly, neither those who fought at Pozieres, nor those who worried at home about their menfolk, had any conception that war could be like this. Nor that it could actually be worse. ❁

WALTER EYLES

THE DIARIST

When Walter Eyles sailed from Sydney in December 1915, he carried with him a diary inscribed by his sister: 'To Toby, With Love, from Minnie'.

He didn't write in it until he had arrived in Egypt and had something to report. Walter was just over seventeen. The diary reads like a long letter to his sisters, Minnie and Alice, who were back home in Five Dock, Sydney, with their mother Ellen. Minnie was fourteen when her brother left; Alice was just ten.

Most soldiers were not great correspondents, but teenage soldiers were worse. They left almost no written records. Walter was an exception. His diary, on display at the Anzac Memorial in Hyde Park, Sydney, is one of the few by an under-age Australian soldier.

In his first entry, Walter writes that he arrived in camp in Egypt on 17 January after coming through the Suez Canal. He describes the soldiers' excitement on seeing land after such a long journey: 'when half of them seen land they fairly went mad after not seeing it for some time'.

Walter's spelling, grammar and punctuation are not unusual for boys of his age and background. He describes himself as a horse driver in his enlistment papers. He had probably been in the workforce for some years by the time he enlisted, on 13 October 1915.

Walter was a reinforcement for the 2nd Battalion. He describes how he went first to Aerodrome Camp, then to guard duty at 'Averseer' – which is probably Abbasia, a suburb of Cairo. He visited the Pyramids and his unit moved to the vast new Australian camp at Tel el Kebir. He then describes the infamous route march from this camp to Ferry Post, by the Suez Canal. Walter claims seven men died on the march but no unit diary records any deaths.

When the AIF battalions were 'doubled' in Egypt, Walter ended up in C Company of the 54th Battalion, sailing towards France in mid-June 1916. After three days on a French train, he arrived in northern France, near Sailly, moving on to Fleurbaix, which he writes as 'Fleaur-baux'. We know it by its other name, Fromelles. In his entry for 19 and 20 July, written after the battle, he describes the horror of battle where 'germans had their machine guns turned upon us and of course we was mowed down like she sheep going to Slaughter'. Walter survived because his 'luck was in' and he fell over some barbed wire when the machine guns opened up on the Australian troops. He describes lying in No Man's Land while 'I could see my mates getting cut to pieces their was fellows laying all over the place with arms off legs off and others riddled with bullets'.

Walter managed to make it back after several hours, surprising his comrades, who thought he had died in the charge. 'I never saw anything like it in all my life and I can tell you I never want to either.'

Walter managed to make it back after several hours, surprising his comrades, who thought he had died in the charge. 'I never saw anything like it in all my life and I can tell you I never want to either.'

Walter was indeed lucky. Australia suffered more than 5000 casualties on that one night, the first great 'stunt' in which the AIF was engaged on the Western Front. The 54th Battalion diary lists Fromelles casualties at 534 men – seventy-three killed, 289 wounded and 173 missing. The battalion strength was now sixteen officers and 317 men. At the beginning of June, it had been thirty-one officers and 980 men.

From August, Walter begins to write in his diary almost daily, but with few surprises. His entries discuss gas alerts, German planes overhead, the quiet between battles and the number of shells sent over by 'old Fritz'.

Walter Eyles had just turned eighteen – making him legal as a soldier under the new regulations, which allowed men from eighteen to forty-five to enlist. The 54th returned north in September and spent much of the month in trenches at

(1)   Notes from
          to Aerodr

I left Sydney on 20th Dec. an[d]
the 15th Jan. and we arrived
17th the name of the camp was
town called Heleoplos alr
Cairo. well the trip we
boat was very good only
the food was none to
of the month coming ov
at the finish it got
I can tell you. well w
land they fairly went
it for some time. when
we was exactly 13 days
it then we came acros
coast we had the coast
days then we never saw

Sydney
one Camp.
arrived in Suez canal on
at a camp in Egypt on the
aerodrome that was in a
out six mile the out from
had coming over in the
for one or two things
good and 18 days out
er we never saw land
terrible mennotinous
hen half of them seen
mad after not seeing
we lost sight of land
at first without seeing
s the South Africian
with us then for five
land again till we got

A barely seventeen-year-old **WALTER EYLES** carried a diary with him as he sailed off to war. In it, he wrote to his sisters, Minnie and Alice, home in Sydney.

Wye Farm, near Fromelles. By the end of that month, the 54th, strengthened with reinforcements, was back to thirty-three officers and 678 'other ranks' – still only two-thirds of what it had been before Fromelles.

On 12 October, Walter writes about the good news from the Italian front and the Somme – but, as ever, nothing personal. There is no record for 13 October, which was the anniversary of his joining the army a year earlier. Three days later, the battalion was on the move south to the Somme. From here his entries become more sporadic, as the battalion went into one of their hardest actions of the war, which Walter describes as 'the roughest time ever I had in all my life' probably due to the fact that 'my mates are getting mowed down all around me at this present hour ...'

His battalion was relieved on 1 November and sent back to rest near Ribemont. On 7 November, he notes that a 'Zep' came over and dropped twelve bombs on the Ribemont railway station. Allied planes then tore into the air to try to bring down the zeppelin.

On 13 November, Walter was admitted to hospital suffering from bronchitis. He spent three months there, rejoining his unit on 6 February 1917. On 23 March, he writes that he left headquarters near Bullecourt to walk to Albert, from where he took a train to Boulogne and a boat to Folkestone, landing there on 25 March. He caught the train to Victoria in London and went straight to AIF headquarters at Horseferry Road where he was given leave.

What Walter does not write here, could not bring himself to even mention, was that he was being sent home for 'family reasons'. On 13 October, the one-year anniversary of his enlistment, Walter's youngest sister, Alice, now aged eleven, returned from a school outing to the new Taronga Zoo to find her mother hanging from the bedpost in the main bedroom of their Queens Park home. She had been physically assaulted before being hung up on the bedpost with reins.

Alice ran to the police station to report it, exclaiming that her father had killed their mother. When William Graham Eyles returned to the house the next day, the police arrested him for the murder of his wife Ellen.

There is no record of when Walter heard about this tragedy, but the silence in the diary from when he went into hospital in early November with bronchitis is eloquent. That would have been almost a month later. Someone sent him two press cuttings, which he then showed to his superior officers, requesting that he be allowed to return to Sydney to look after his two sisters. None of the correspondence in his file mentions that he had an older brother, Arthur.

William Eyles was tried and convicted for his wife's murder and sentenced to death. He appealed and was granted a retrial and found guilty a second time. Again he was sentenced to death. In 1917, that sentence was commuted to life imprisonment. In 1926, he tried to break out of Goulburn Gaol with a hacksaw blade. He was released sometime in the 1930s and died in Sydney in March 1945.

Walter Eyles married Vida Cunneen from Coonamble in 1924. They had a daughter, Betty Patricia, in 1928. The family lived in Abbotsford until 1964, when Walter died. He is buried at North Ryde.

In some ways, Walter Eyles's story is one of the most tragic in this book. He survived the war but had to endure the knowledge that it was because his father had killed his mother. That must have been a terrible weight to carry. ❀

THE DAWES BROTHERS

MUDDY DEATH

This is the Dawes family of Korumburra in Gippsland, Victoria, around 1909. They are dressed in their finest for a special occasion, perhaps a birthday. There are so many Dawes children it's hard to fit them all in.

The placement in this photograph is determined by seniority, but also by symbolism. Mother and father, Richard and Mary Ann, are at the centre of everything. The three older boys are like sentinels, in their fine three-piece suits with dark piping. Their watch chains tell of prosperity and ambition. That's the eldest Charles at the far right, aged about twenty-four. William, seven years younger, is in the middle. He is the tallest member of the family, and about seventeen. George, the second eldest, stands at the far left trampling a fern. He looks like he has just been told to move in closer.

Florence stands behind her mother, one hand on her shoulder. The matriarch Mary Ann holds her youngest close – little Olive is about five. Ida, the next youngest, clutches her father's sleeve but her gaze is confident. The two beauties, Eva (left) and Isabella (right) about fourteen and seventeen years old, stand in the middle, protected on all sides.

At front and centre, sitting on a box, is the fourth son, Richard Gordon, wearing a splendidly ornate suit that he probably hated. He has shortened knickerbocker pants, a ribbon tie and the widest lapels in Gippsland, even if his boots could do with a good shine. He is still blonde, where the older boys have gone dark. He is just a kid. He is the reason for our story.

Three of the four Dawes brothers went to war but Richard Gordon, known in the family as Gordon, was the only one who was under-age. The photograph powerfully emphasises that fact: if 1909 is the right year, then Gordon is nine or ten and the war is only five years away.

If no-one is smiling, that is no indication of unhappiness. Photographs were solemn events: smiling is a later convention. It's tempting to say this is the last time they would all be happy together but that's probably not true.

The last time might have been 23 August 1914, the day before George joined up. Happiness would be a rare visitor to the Dawes household after that.

George was twenty-eight years and six months old when he signed the attestation papers at a recruiting office at Surrey Hills in Melbourne's eastern suburbs. The family had a small farm, for their own needs, and George listed his occupation as farmer.

George took the oath to 'well and truly serve our sovereign Lord the King' later that day at Broadmeadows Camp, where he was assigned to C Company of the 8th Battalion. They recorded him as five feet eight and a quarter inches tall (173 centimetres), with blue eyes and fair hair, Anglican faith.

The 2nd Brigade, comprising the 5th, 6th, 7th and 8th battalions, contained a lot of Victorian farm boys and miners. George continued his training in Egypt, not knowing where or when he was going to fight. No-one knew they were going to the Dardanelles until they were steaming towards Turkey, across the Mediterranean.

George Dawes came ashore at Anzac Cove in the second wave on 25 April and survived. He got through the bloodbath that was Krithia in May, when the 2nd Brigade lost a third of its strength. He was promoted to corporal on 12 May, probably because so many officers and non-commissioned officers had been killed. He would not survive Lone Pine on 7 August.

The news of George's death reached Korumburra on 25 August, one year to the day after he joined up. A local clergymen had to bring the telegram. People had come to hate the sight of pastors and priests on bicycles.

Gordon, the blond-headed ten-year-old in the photo, was now fifteen years and eight months old. By the time he was sixteen, early in the new year, he had decided to enlist. So had the eldest, Charles. When George enlisted, Charles had been living in Melbourne with his sweetheart, Ellen Davenport. They had a daughter, born in 1913. In this early stage, married men – even if not strictly married – were discouraged from enlisting.

Charles signed up on 31 January 1916. He said he was twenty-nine years and ten months old, but he was actually thirty years and nine months. The discrepancy is curious, given that there was no advantage in lying about his age.

Before he went off to war, Gordon gave his sister Olive, with whom he was especially close, a brooch that eventually passed to her granddaughter Jennifer Dore. She wears it often.

'The story my mum told me was that Charles signed up in Leongatha, and so when the recruiters came to Korumburra, Gordon signed up five days later. When he told his parents he had signed up, Mary Ann was devastated. Mary Ann threatened to advise the authorities that Gordon was under-age so they would not let him enlist, but Charles, having had military experience, promised he would do everything he could to look after him. Charles said that he was better off going to war with a brother than a year later by himself.'

Charles was true to his word. At Broadmeadows, he helped to have

Gordon transferred from the 6th Battalion to the 21st, so they could be together. By the middle of May, they were in England, where they trained for three months. On 5 September, they crossed the English Channel, landing at Etaples, the French port through which millions of troops had to pass to get to the Western Front. Two weeks later, they were both 'taken on strength' into the 21st Battalion, which was now in Belgium.

The war they entered was very different to the one in which their brother had fought and died at Gallipoli – more industrial, more brutal, more ruthless. The Australian divisions had been shredded in July and August at Fromelles and the Somme, trying to take Pozieres and Mouquet Farm. By the time the Dawes brothers caught up with their battalion, the 21st had lost 651 men from its initial strength of more than 1000. The battalion would never return to full strength.

Most of the major offensives on the Western Front were fought in spring and summer, because the ground became too sodden in winter. So before the armies settled down for winter, the British commander General Haig wanted to make some ground in the valley of the Somme, where he had failed so spectacularly three months earlier. The French pressed him to make another advance past the tiny village of Flers near Bapaume, in the eastern part of the valley. These attacks all failed. Shells disappeared into the mud rather than exploding on impact. Without the protection of the dust curtain that followed a bombardment in dry weather, any advance had to go forward across a quagmire in full view of enemy machine guns.

In late September, the Dawes brothers were in Toronto Camp for a month's rest and training. On 14 October, they moved back into the line at Hill 60, near Messines, in Belgium. It was a relatively quiet sector, but uncomfortable. For Charles and Gordon, their introduction to trench life was thirty-six hours of continuous rain. Five days later, they were ordered back to the Somme, 150 kilometres to the south. In the *Official History*, Charles Bean writes that the Australian divisions 'almost restored by their rest at Ypres, were now to plunge into the hardest trial that ever came to them'.

Those words are chilling, because Bean had seen what the Australians went through at Pozieres and Mouquet Farm. How could Flers be worse?

'Rumours had reached the Australians of great hardships suffered during the recent bad weather offensives,' wrote

> The Australians saw British troops falling back, bedraggled and disorderly. When they saw the battlefield, they understood why. Mud was now the enemy, as much as the Germans.

Medical staff unload the wounded from trucks at the 38th Casualty Clearing Station. **CHARLES DAWES** was taken to this hospital.

Bean. The Australians saw British troops falling back, bedraggled and disorderly. When they saw the battlefield, they understood why.

Mud was now the enemy, as much as the Germans. Mud made the trenches impassable as thoroughfares, so men were forced into the open, walking up beside the trenches, where the Germans could see them. The train lines that supplied ammunition and food could not be brought close enough, and the horse teams could not cope with the loads that had to replace the trains. Many horses had to be shot when they became bogged on the way up. Men marching up to Flers would take twelve hours or more to get through a couple of kilometres, arriving exhausted. Some units had to be pulled out as soon as they arrived, because they were no longer fit to fight.

Mud made the rifles jam and stopped hot meals from getting to the front. Standing in mud up to their thighs gave soldiers a form of frostbite known as 'trench foot', which was impossible to treat in the trenches. If left untreated, it could result in amputations. It was impossible to fight through the mud at Flers, except in the eyes of the senior commanders, who ordered an Australian advance. This is the war that Charles and Gordon Dawes were now to face.

The records say that Charles was wounded here on 6 November, with a 'GSW' to the abdomen. GSW stands for 'gun shot wound' but it could also mean shrapnel from a shell. Charles was taken back to the 38th CCS behind the lines, where he died a day later. What the records do not say is that mud made the job of the stretcher-bearers almost impossible. It could take twelve hours to get one man back to an aid post, over a distance normally covered in one hour in the dry. The Australians devised a system of sleds, pulled by horses, to try to speed up the movement across the mud. It worked, but then the wooden tracks on which the sleds ran sank into the mud too. And at least once, a commander requisitioned the ambulance horses to carry ladders forward for the attack, instead of carrying the wounded back.

Richard Gordon Dawes, the youngster, was hit in the abdomen and thigh on 7 November, the day his brother died. Almost certainly, he did not know that Charles was dead. News took time to come back from the aid posts and hospitals. Gordon never made it as far as a casualty clearing station. He died at the 15th Australian Field Ambulance the next day. Gordon was buried at Dartmoor War Cemetery, a little to the east of the town of Albert. Charles lies in the Heilly Station War Cemetery near Corbie. The two brothers are about fifteen kilometres apart.

Gordon was seventeen years and ten months at the time of his death. It is no exaggeration to say that mud killed them both, at least in part. It made their attack impossible, their rescue and treatment unmanageable. It was an echo of Fromelles. Harold 'Pompey' Elliott had warned Temporary Brigadier General Sir James McCay, commanding the 5th Division, that an attack across the bog at Flers was sheer madness. It went ahead anyway.

William Dawes, the one remaining son, did not go to the war. The family legend is that he was not allowed, but his parents could not have stopped him. Even so, if he had tried, the army probably would have rejected him. Three sons was enough.

Jennifer Dore remembers her mother talking about the grief.

'Mum always said that Mary Ann found it hard, but she thought her grandfather Richard found it harder to deal with the loss of his three sons. Mum believed his grief contributed to his illness [in his old age]. Mary Ann found it particularly hard on the anniversaries of the boys' deaths. She would withdraw to her own company …'

The meaning of that photograph from 1909 changed in 1916. What was once a family celebration, an expression of pride and hope, came to represent a terrible loss. One hundred and ten years later, it has become an eloquent expression of the cost of the war for some families. 🐝

ARTHUR HILL & LESLIE PRIOR

THE LITTLE OUTLAWS

Fifteen-year-old **ARTHUR HILL** was keen to fight for his country; he disliked the regimentation and discipline of the army and often rebelled.

On the day he embarked at the Melbourne docks, Leslie Thomas Prior had more than he could easily carry: a pack, a greatcoat, a rifle, a bedroll. Leslie was also carrying something he didn't want, something no soldier wanted. If the army had known, they would not have let him go, but it's unlikely that Leslie even knew he had it.

Syphilis was one of the great unspoken humiliations of the First World War. It was a self-inflicted wound that brought dishonour and infamy. While he was undergoing treatment, a soldier with venereal disease (VD) could not be sent to fight, so someone else had to do his fighting for him. It could cost a soldier his pay and might cause him to be sent home in disgrace, where he would have to explain to loved ones what had happened.

Leslie had another secret as well. He was one of the youngest boys to enlist in the AIF – just fourteen years and six days old when he turned up at the recruiting office in Brunswick, Melbourne, on 5 February 1916. If the army had known that he was so young,

he would have been hauled off the ship and sent home.

At the same time that he was boarding the *Armadale*, on 19 July, another young soldier was cooling his heels in detention at the Australian training camp at Lark Hill, near Salisbury, in England. Arthur Hill was seventeen months older than Leslie but still under-age. He had enlisted the previous November, aged fifteen years and five months.

Arthur was from Moonee Ponds in Melbourne. He listed his occupation as farm labourer. He was on the small side: five feet three inches in height (160 centimetres) and fifty-eight kilograms, with blue eyes and a fresh complexion. He had been raised Wesleyan.

Arthur did not have syphilis, but he and Leslie had much else in common. Both disliked authority and army discipline. Both wanted to fight but neither was that keen on marching on parade or taking orders. Both would spend a good deal of their war in punishment cells. And the army would fail both of them badly, at great cost.

Both boys came from modest homes. Arthur's parents, Thomas and Edith, were eighteen when he was conceived. Thomas was a tobacco worker and keen to serve, but he was rejected for being too short. He was more successful in July 1915, after the army relaxed the rules, to accept men of five feet two inches (157.5 centimetres). Arthur was one centimetre shorter than his father, but he had no trouble following him into the army in November. A week later, Thomas Hill shipped out from Melbourne.

Thomas was thirty-three, assigned to the 6th Battalion. He had flat feet, a condition that plagued him throughout the war, but he was hardly likely to confess that. His son was allocated to the 29th Battalion, and he too was less than robust. In December he spent eleven days in the Royal Park hospital with enlarged tonsils. He was hospitalised again at Geelong in March and at Broadmeadows Camp a week later. He sailed soon after for Egypt, where his troubles were to begin in earnest.

Neither parent tried to stop Arthur – now aged fifteen and ten months – from going. Indeed, they were most likely proud of the boy. Arthur was used to soldiering: he had been a bugler in the 58th Battalion of the Citizen's Military Force at Ascot Vale in 1913. He continued as a bugler in the AIF.

Leslie Prior came from even harder circumstances. His father, David, had emigrated from England. David worked at many jobs, including mining and chimney sweeping. He died in June 1904, aged fifty-two, leaving his 34-year-old wife, Ellen, with three of their own children and a daughter, Matilda, from Ellen's previous relationship. Leslie was not yet two and a half. The family lived in Belfast Road, Brunswick, one of the poorest parts of Melbourne.

Ellen had three more children with a new partner, George Crick. When war broke out, Ellen and George had a house full of kids, and not much else. Tragedy

struck in September 1915 when the eldest boy, Arthur, aged about seventeen, died from a heart condition. That left Leslie, now the eldest boy, to step up. He joined the army four months later. That at least would ensure an income for the family.

Bob Wills, one of Ellen's descendants, remarks: 'My mother tells me the story that Leslie was determined to join the army and saw it as an opportunity to join in the "adventure overseas". His mother Ellen refused to let him join but he told her that he would join up under a false name and if he did that and something happened to him then she would never know, so Ellen eventually relented. What I find hard to believe is how a just turned fourteen-year-old boy who was only five feet three and a half inches (161 centimetres) tall and weighed only eight stone eight pounds (54.5 kilograms) could be admitted to the army. My mother says he tried to enlist when he was thirteen years old but was rejected on medical grounds because of his chest, which is actually recorded on his enlistment form. Perhaps he had similar heart problems, like his elder brother Arthur.'

Leslie is most likely to have contracted syphilis before he left Melbourne. It was a common disease and there was no shortage of places for a soldier to buy sex, even for a boy who was still not fifteen years of age. Some soldiers contracted the disease at brothels in Melbourne, others in Fremantle or Colombo en route.

> Bob Wills, one of Ellen's descendants, remarks: 'My mother tells me the story that Leslie was determined to join the army and saw it as an opportunity to join in the "adventure overseas".'

Arthur's baby-faced father, **THOMAS HILL**, was initially unsuccessful when he tried to enlist because he was too short. He was eventually accepted in July 1915.

By 1916, venereal disease was an epidemic in the Australian forces. There were few ways to prevent it, short of abstinence, and no reliable or easy cures for syphilis or gonorrhoea. The recently formed Australian Army Medical Corps was swamped with cases once the first convoy was diverted to Egypt in late 1914. By February 1916, they were treating 1000 men a day, with a series of toxic drugs like mercury, administered in painful ways. By the end of the war, that would amount to around 60,000 cases – an appalling waste of resources for an army, given that the disease was basically self inflicted.

Once casualties started coming back to Egypt from Gallipoli in April 1915, the Australian headquarters decided to send the venereal cases home, to free up hospital beds. Hundreds of men were shipped back and placed in a primitive detention camp at Langwarrin, outside Melbourne. Some ran away rather than face the shame of telling their families what had happened. Others infected their wives and girlfriends.

Leslie has the dubious distinction of being one of the youngest VD cases in the AIF. If a soldier developed symptoms, it was an offence not to report them. There were regular inspections, both before embarkation and on board, in case anyone tried. Leslie was ordered to the isolation ward of the *Armadale* on 6 September, toward the end of its voyage.

Leslie was 'crimed' on the ship on 22 August, for 'breaking off ship'. This probably meant that he went ashore at Colombo in Ceylon (now Sri Lanka) without permission. His record says that he lost a total of eighty-eight days' pay for catching VD, which would mean he was diagnosed around the first week of September, six weeks after leaving Port Melbourne. The daily treatments, which involved insertion of a tube into the urethra of the penis for irrigation with painful drugs, had probably not improved his temper.

After docking in England, he was transferred to the 1st Australian Dermatological Hospital at Bulford on the Salisbury Plain. Most of the patients were VD cases. He was transferred again on 15 November to the military hospital at Parkhouse, nearby. In early December, he was 'marched out' to join the 6th Training Battalion at Lark Hill – which simply meant that his symptoms had disappeared, not that he was necessarily cured. Relapses were common. Leslie behaved himself here for about six weeks.

Over the next two months, Leslie was fined and confined to camp on a number of occasions for missing parades and being absent without leave. He was sent to join his unit – the 13th reinforcements to the 23rd Battalion – on 31 March. It is probably safe to say the officers at Lark Hill were happy to see him go. For most of two months, he had been in detention or confined to camp.

In his defence, none of these charges was very serious. Thousands of Australian soldiers went AWOL for hours or days at a time – sometimes to see their loved ones before they left Australia, and more often, just to let off some steam in a pub or a brothel before going to the front. Most of them viewed the punishment on return as worth it – although the brothel visits could bring a much longer-term punishment.

While Leslie's crimes appear to be partly borne out of frustration at being held up in England, Arthur Hill found trouble wherever he was. He did seven days hard labour at Tel el Kebir Camp in Egypt in March for missing a parade; he was fined and confined on the ship heading to England in mid-June for missing another parade, then fined again when he reached England for missing yet another parade. Arthur was still a bugler, but only when he wanted to be.

On 26 June, Arthur's sergeant fined him for four separate offences, which suggests that Arthur took some pleasure in goading his sergeant. For this big day out, he received eighteen days detention. On 14 July, he copped another seven days for disobeying a lawful command. These offences all occurred at Lark Hill, where Arthur was supposed to be in training for the real war. He was finally moved out on 5 September, bound for France. He reached the 29th Battalion

Australian troops board the *Armadale* in Melbourne in 1916. Fourteen-year-old **LESLIE PRIOR** went to war on this ship, aching for an 'adventure overseas'.

on 15 October 1916. He had been in the army for eleven months and not yet heard a shot fired in anger.

In fact, neither Arthur nor Leslie should have been anywhere near the war. At Lark Hill on 8 January 1917, the adjutant of the 6th Training Battalion, Lieutenant Wyeth, wrote to Prior's commanding officer. 'This man is apparently unfit for musketry and is to be sent to the MO for examination with a view to his being boarded. He is not however to be relieved from training until actually boarded and found unfit for service.' The MO was the medical officer; boarding was a medical board, which in this case, the officer expected would find the soldier unfit for service. Exactly why Leslie was unfit to learn how to shoot a gun (musketry) is unclear.

There is no record of Leslie ever facing that medical board – which might have been the one time the army had a chance not to fail him, by recognising that he was so far under-age and unfit to boot. Instead, they sent him to his unit on 31 March 1917. Leslie was

killed on 3 May at the second battle of Bullecourt, a brutal and pointless 'victory'. He was fifteen years and three months old.

Arthur Hill went through a similar test in July 1916. In the midst of his private insurrections at Lark Hill, Captain Patrick Shaw of the Australian Army Medical Corps examined him on 27 July. Shaw wrote that Arthur was only sixteen years and four months old, and of 'insufficient physique for active service'. This was unusual: even when they knew that a boy was under-age, officers rarely wrote this down. Shaw would have known this, which might be why he did it – to try to save Arthur from going to the trenches. One week later, Arthur was examined again by another doctor, Colonel Charles Ryan, AMC, Shaw's superior officer, who saw a different state of fitness: 'A very muscular strong young fellow fit for general service'.

Arthur went up the line and was killed at Flers in the Somme on 27 October 1916, thirteen days after joining his unit. He has no known grave, which means his body was never found. He is commemorated on the walls of the Australian memorial at Villers-Bretonneux. He was sixteen years and four months old.

Arthur's father Thomas survived the war and returned to Australia in 1919. He found that Edith had replaced him with another man, so he divorced her. Thomas married Alvie Spence at the end of 1922 and they had three children. Those youngsters – Glen, Muriel and David – never knew they had a half-brother who had been killed in the war. After Thomas died, aged ninety-two, David found Arthur's medals, and eventually worked out who he was.

Leslie Prior and Arthur Hill were hard to handle, no question, but their offences were frequent rather than serious, the misdemeanours of teenagers restless for action and excitement. The officers who sent them forward clearly knew they were too young and in questionable health, but sent them anyway. That was part of a medical officer's job: to get men to the front. And neither Arthur nor Leslie would have argued about going. That's

what they came for. Both of them are still there, under fields that have long ago been returned to farming. Leslie is the second-youngest Australian soldier to die in the First World War, and the youngest to be killed in action.

Leslie's relative Bob Wills and his wife Judy visited those fields near Bullecourt in 2016, to see where Leslie died.

'Whilst standing in among those gently undulating fields it was impossible not to feel the hopelessness these brave soldiers must have faced and to also feel a great sadness for the loss of life of a fifteen-year-old boy named Leslie and all of his comrades in arms … I felt a great connection whilst standing in that field where he died … I will never forget that experience and it is still very emotional to think about it now.' ❀

ALBERT ANDERSON

A WINTER'S TALE

Fifteen-year-old **ALBERT ANDERSON** adopted the alter ego James Hegarty – a combination of his parents' names – to fight for Australia in 1916.

When Peter Blaxell was growing up in Perth in the 1950s, there was a big old metal trunk in a corner of the house, covered with a 'doily', an ornamental lace mat. 'I was never allowed to look inside it. My grandmother was very insistent.'

Peter, who was born in 1945, had only dim memories of his grandfather, James Anderson, who died in 1949. 'He used to take me on his shoulders to see the trains when I was about four.'

In the early 1960s, Peter became curious about the family history so he quizzed his grandmother, Evelyn, trying to find out as much as he could before she died.

'"Where did you and Pop get married?" I asked her. "Dunedin," she said.'

Evelyn died in 1963. In her last weeks, she told her daughter on a number of occasions that there was something she needed to tell her, but she could never bring herself to do it. 'She simply flung up her hands and said "Well, it will all come out in the wash", but Mum and I had no idea what she meant.'

After her death, Peter and his mother opened the trunk. At the bottom, they found a memorial medal, commonly known as a 'Dead Man's Penny', from the First World War. It was in the name of James Hegarty. There was also an AIF scroll, the kind sent to soldiers after the war as a recognition of their service, made out to 'James Hegarty, 48th Battalion' – a name that meant nothing to Peter or his mother.

Solving the mystery of James Hegarty would take Peter on a long journey, as far as a small village in Wiltshire called Sutton Veny. It would also explain the secret Evelyn had wanted her daughter and grandson to know, but could never speak of.

In late 1916 in Perth, about 200 drunken troops went on a rampage over two nights, attacking shops with German-sounding names, pubs that ran dry (after giving them free drinks all night) and tobacconists of European heritage, whose windows they smashed to get cigars and cigarettes.

The riots were nothing new. There had been similar disturbances in Sydney and Melbourne for several months. Drunken soldiers almost inevitably turned their anger on German-run businesses – or businesses that sounded German.

A small number of soldiers were charged after the Perth riots, including one James Duncan Anderson. He was fined £1 or fourteen days imprisonment for interfering with the work of the mounted police, in effect, hooting and shouting 'boo-hoo' at them. This was Peter Blaxell's grandfather 'Pop' Anderson.

Anderson was then forty-one years old, a former ship's fireman, who had enlisted on 14 December 1916, a fortnight earlier. It was his second attempt, having been rejected until he got his teeth fixed. He nominated his wife Elizabeth Anderson as next of kin but gave her address simply as 'Newtown, Sydney, New South Wales'. He wrote that his own address was 14 Money Street, Perth.

James and Elizabeth had a fifteen-year-old son called Albert. Six days after his father, Albert filled out his own enlistment papers – nominating his father as next of kin, and giving his father's address as '39 Depot, AIF, Blackboy Hill, W. Australia'. Albert gave his correct age: fifteen years two months. He indicated that he had just resigned from the cadets. His father appears to have signed his consent.

Almost every under-age boy lied to get into the AIF, but Albert told the truth. He repeated the correct age on the medical examination part of the form, so it's hard to say the army didn't know what they were getting. Before this, Albert did another unusual thing: he went to see Lieutenant Colonel Charles Battye, the commandant at Blackboy Hill, on the outskirts of Perth. Battye had been an officer in the militia in Perth, so he may have known Albert. Battye wrote Albert a note, to show the recruiters: 'The bearer, Albert James Anderson, can be enlisted as a bugler. If medically fit. C Battye, Lt-Col'.

Battye knew his regulations. An AIF Order from August 1914 said: 'Where difficulty exists in obtaining suitable trumpeters and buglers over the age of 19 years, the special enlistment of youths under 19 years of age is authorised, provided that the written consent of parents or guardians is first obtained'.

The position of bugler was a back door into the AIF, with a minimum age that was helpfully vague for the recruiting officer. One hundred years later, it's hard to believe that any recruiting officer could have thought this meant admitting boys as young as fifteen, but Albert's records and the note from Battye show that they knew his correct age when they took him. The doctors knew too, when they judged him medically fit. Captain NB Walch of the Australian Army Medical Corps wrote that he was five feet six and a half inches tall (169 centimetres), 108 pounds (forty-nine kilograms), with a fresh complexion, grey eyes, light brown hair, scars on left cheek and left hand – and fifteen years two months old. He noted the boy's religion as Presbyterian, which was odd given that his father was recorded as Church of England.

Albert was sent to the 15th reinforcements of the 16th Battalion at Blackboy Hill, where he would be soldiering alongside his father. This appears to have been their plan all along: father and son going to war together.

Peter Blaxell believes that Elizabeth and his grandfather James had already separated. 'I think that father and son enlisted together after Elizabeth went back to Sydney. What father would go to war, leaving his fifteen-year-old son by himself in Perth?'

Albert wrote to his mother from camp, telling her where he was. She then informed the army that her son was fifteen – something they already knew. Albert was discharged on 21 March and sent home – although it's not clear that he still had one in Perth. His father shipped out from Fremantle on 1 April, on the *Ulysses*.

Albert did not take kindly to his mother's meddling. He appears to have severed all contact with her from this point. On 17 May, eight weeks later, he turned up at Midland Junction recruiting office on the outskirts of Perth, claiming to be James Hegarty, aged nineteen and two months, with address c/o the Post Office, Perth.

Where the form required the signature of a parent or guardian, he filled in 'Mrs Thomas' as his guardian. He gave his next of kin as his uncle – James Weston of Rosehill, New South Wales.

Years later the army would learn that James Weston was actually Albert's real father, James Duncan Anderson. James had lost his own father in a shipwreck off the Queensland coast in 1875, when James was one. His mother remarried ten years later and James took his stepfather's surname, Weston. He reverted to Anderson only when he married Elizabeth Hegarty in Sydney in 1899. And there is that name – the key to the Dead Man's Penny and the scroll.

So Albert Anderson, fifteen and a half, was now James Hegarty, making clever use of the names of both parents. This time, the lies worked. He was in the army again, allocated to the 22nd reinforcements of the 16th Battalion, at Belmont Camp. He was also now Church of England, not Presbyterian.

Albert may have been raring to go, but the army was in no hurry to send him. He languished in camp for five months, during which he was reallocated to reinforce the 48th Battalion (the new sister battalion of the 16th). In August, he went AWOL for two days, just as many of the older men did. He sailed from Fremantle on 20 October on the *Port Melbourne*, bound for England. He disembarked at Devonport (Plymouth) on 28 December, after two months at sea.

England was in the grip of a terrible winter – the temperature remained below zero for days on end. Large snowfalls blanketed the countryside, such as had not been seen for some years. For the troops in France, the conditions in the trenches of the Somme were even more intolerable.

After the Australians began to pull out of Egypt in March 1916, most new recruits from Australia were sent straight to England for basic training, before going to France. They were housed in a series of camps on Salisbury Plain in Wiltshire, southwest of London. These had been vacated by the British Army or newly constructed 'for the use of'. There were many thousands of Australians here at any one time from 1916 on, and they got into every conceivable kind of trouble: drunkenness, fighting in the streets, romancing of local girls, abusing of local girls, and at least one murder. Village publicans made their fortunes, as did tea-shops, restaurants, pop-up cinemas and gift shops, but they needed to be careful. If they cheated or robbed a soldier, the wrath would be swift and righteous. Disgruntled soldiers burned down a cinema at Sutton Veny when the operator refused to refund money after the projector broke down.

Albert was sent to Codford, where the 12th Training Battalion was centred in one of fifteen camps spread around two tiny villages. There is a photograph of Albert, standing proudly 'at ease', hands behind his back, in front of one of the primitive Codford huts. He looks happy and healthy, older than his years.

A few weeks earlier he had been sunning himself on the deck of a ship sailing through the tropics. Now he was in a dark, freezing camp where part of the training was to impose further hardships – to 'harden them up' for France. In the late autumn and winter of 1916, men started dropping like flies.

'… Autumn found the depots quite unprepared for a winter on the plain,' wrote AG Butler in the *Official History of the Australian Army Medical Services in the War of 1914–1918*. 'Some camps were ill-sited – exposed and bleak – in particular Larkhill, Rollestone and Perham Downs. But most important, there had not been time to build up a staff capable of rising to the occasion; living, messing, training, sick parades, were mechanical – there was no vision.'

It was worse than that: the training was making men sicker. Private Geoffrey Rose of the 30th Battalion arrived at a camp near Codford in January 1917. He wrote in his diary that overcoats were not allowed on parade and scarves had to be worn under tunics. He noted that English troops training nearby wore their greatcoats every day on parade. Australian recruits who claimed to be sick were sometimes accused of malingering. Some of them died before they could be sent to hospital.

By the time Albert arrived, there was an epidemic of respiratory disease and a line of coffins to show for it.

In February, wrote Private Rose, there was a funeral every second day, as the colds turned into pneumonia. He had heard that twenty-eight men were dying per week at Lark Hill.

These figures are probably over-stated, but not by much. Butler reports that 123 men died of pneumonia and broncho-pneumonia in the Australian depot camps in the first quarter of 1917. This was out of 158 deaths in total. The situation was bad enough that the Australian High Commissioner, Andrew Fisher (the former prime minister), demanded a report on the state of health in the camps.

Albert Anderson, aka James Hegarty, took ill soon after arriving at Codford.

He was admitted to hospital, then discharged on 23 January 1917, back to his unit. On 10 February, he was admitted again, this time to the British Military Hospital at Sutton Veny, about ten kilometres west of Codford. A doctor noted on his medical chart: 'Very severe attack of bronchitis … exhaustion setting in.' He prescribed milk and a special diet that included brandy, and small doses of strychnine. This is where Albert James Anderson died, late in the evening of 22 February 1917. He never made it to France. He never heard a shot fired. He never got to see his father, fighting in France in the 48th.

Albert was buried four days later in Sutton Veny churchyard, next to a picturesque church from the 1850s. He

> There were a million ways for a soldier to die in this war – but coughing yourself to death in an English hospital before you had even seen the coast of France has to be one of the most wasteful and infuriating of them all.

Graves at Sutton Veny,
England, shortly after
the war.

was one of the first Australians buried in this churchyard, but many were to follow, victims of an epidemic of Spanish Influenza at the end of the war. By late 1919, there were more than 140 Australian graves at Sutton Veny, making it one of the largest Australian war cemeteries in England.

Albert's story is not simply tragic; it is baffling. The army knew from the start that he was under-age and by how much. Even after he re-enlisted in May 1916, a cursory check would have revealed who 'James Hegarty' really was. Worse than that, incompetent staff work by Australian headquarters in England cost his life, and hundreds of others, because the camps were not fit for use. A soldier who caught VD was punished for a crime; not so, the officers who neglected to ensure basic living standards for thousands of newly arrived soldiers. There were a million ways for a soldier to die in this war – but coughing yourself to death in an English hospital before you had even seen the coast of France has to be one of the most wasteful and infuriating of them all.

Albert was sixteen years and three months old when he took his last painful breath.

Albert's father James was invalided back to Australia in late 1917 because of rheumatism. Elizabeth had returned to Sydney to live, so the separation stood. James married Evelyn Stahmer, from East Perth. They had a daughter in April 1919, and then two sons.

In 1933, Elizabeth Hegarty wrote to the army seeking her son's unit details, and inquiring as to who was getting his pension. She wrote that she had last heard of him at Blackboy Hill in 1916. She knew he was dead, but that suggests he did not communicate with her after he enlisted the second time. During the war, the army did not know she existed. Given that they were looking for a fictitious uncle in Rosehill, Sydney, it would have taken some months for the records office to discover that Albert's real father was Private James Duncan Anderson of the 48th Battalion, recently discharged. That means it could have taken more than a year for Albert's parents to hear of their son's fate.

His headstone at Sutton Veny says 'AJ Anderson, served as 2683 Private J Hegarty'. At the bottom of the headstone, in words that suggest they were written by his mother, it says:

'In proud and loving memory
Of my dear and only son.'

In 1937, Elizabeth wrote to the army from her home in Leichhardt in Sydney, to inquire if her husband James D Anderson was dead or alive. The reason was that she wanted to remarry. The army wrote to say he was alive, offering to forward any letter she cared to write.

In the late 1990s, Peter Blaxell obtained both his grandfather's war records and those of Private James Hegarty, which revealed that one was the father of the other. When he saw Elizabeth's 1937 letter in his grandfather's file, he realised that Elizabeth and James had never divorced. That meant that James and Evelyn could not marry, and had never done so. He believes that is what Evelyn meant in her dying days, when she spoke about things 'coming out in the wash'.

'My mother was still alive, but herself suffering from cancer when I discovered the truth in about 1998. I thought long and hard whether or not to pass this new information on to her because I knew she would be upset. I decided that I should, but when I tried to tell her that her parents had never married and that her father had had an earlier son, she did not want to hear about it. She died several months later, in February 1999, without us ever discussing the matter.'

In effect, the memory of Albert, aka James Hegarty, had been erased, except for his medals in the trunk. Peter Blaxell has twice visited the little graveyard behind the church in Sutton Veny – the first time in the year 2001, after his mother died. He went to pay his respects at the grave of Albert Anderson, the boy with two names who never made it to the war, the uncle he never knew he had. 🌸

ERNEST PINCHES

THE LITTLE DRUMMER BOY

ERNEST PINCHES was determined to go to war – even after his former teacher George Vowles made sure that he was discharged for being under-age.

George Vowles was not a man to be trifled with. As one of the most respected teachers in Queensland, he had tutored thousands of youngsters across the state, turning boys into men for almost fifty years. Now the head teacher at Petrie Terrace Boys State School in Paddington, he knew the coming war was going to take many of them, but he was determined that it wasn't going to have young Ernest Pinches.

He did not care that Ernie desperately wanted to go; it was immoral to send boys to war and he would not stand for it.

Ernest Wilson Pinches had worked at the school in the previous year, as a 'teacher pupil', a designation that was later phased out. On 3 January 1916, he presented himself at a recruiting office in Brisbane, claiming to be eighteen years and nine months of age. His real age was fifteen years and eight months, but he looked older.

Ernie had his parents' permission to enlist. At least, he had a piece of paper saying they agreed, and perhaps they had. Both Thomas and Julia Pinches were born in England and still had strong ties to the old country. They had married in Brisbane in 1893 and had two children before Ernie – Ethel Gertrude, known as Eck, then Frank Thomas. When the war started, the family was in mourning. Frank had died the previous November in a Brisbane hospital, aged just eighteen. Thomas Pinches, a fifty-year-old painter, was too old to enlist. That left Ernie as the next man of the family, but he would have been keen to go, even if his brother had lived.

Ernie loved being in uniform. For some years, in the cadets, he had been a marching drummer, tutored by his friend and superior, Rich Salisbury. Rich was eight years older and from a military family – a keen exponent of both drum and bugle.

Ernie quickly learned the drum rudiments – a set of exercises that required long hours of noisy practice at home in Kennedy Terrace, Ithaca. Ernie's cadet duties were relatively light, but in the two years before the war, he volunteered to play at parades as often as he could. Captain Frank Moran, area commander of the cadets, noticed his enthusiasm and arranged a reward. The Governor of Queensland, Sir William McGregor, presented Cadet Pinches with a 'wristlet' watch – a treasured item for any boy at the time – in recognition of his voluntary drumming.

Now Ernie watched as the men he revered went off to war. Rich enlisted in August 1914, as soon as he possibly could, and shipped out that September as a drummer/bugler in the 9th Battalion. In December, Ernie would read the reports in the Brisbane papers of Frank Moran's valiant death after fighting at Gallipoli, in the 15th Battalion. Moran had been wounded in the arm, and died leading his men up ravines in the offensive of 7 August.

Ernie enlisted a few weeks later, without difficulty, but he made one mistake. He visited his old school at Petrie Terrace, where he ran into Mr Vowles. Ernie did not hide his news: he was now a soldier, in camp at Enoggera.

'Private Pinches came to my school in February, to receive money for his services. He happened then to hear that Mr Stinson of my staff was a friend of one of the captains at Enoggera Concentration Camp. He said at once "Don't tell him my age or I'll be sent away from the camp".'

Vowles wrote these lines in a letter to Lieutenant Charles French at Enoggera, on 15 February 1916. It was his second letter, after French had replied that he had looked into the matter and the boy insisted he was over eighteen.

'I regret that the boy has not been truthful,' replied Vowles. 'His age has been given me both by his mother and by his cousin, Ltnt Wilson, drill instructor, and also by Pinches himself.'

Vowles then informed French that he was arranging to get a copy of the boy's birth certificate and would send it on.

Meanwhile, Vowles went to work more directly. A note in Ernie's army file, from an unidentified but clearly miffed officer, says that 'Mr V threatened to represent matters to the minister and altogether adopted a very dictatorial attitude'. This officer then commented that 'Pinches is a big chap. Would easily pass for nineteen and was awfully keen'.

In March, Vowles wrote to Brigadier-General Lee, state commandant for Queensland, but by then Ernie had been discharged from the army. Vowles had had his victory, at least for the moment.

The Enoggera staff officers were not unusual in thinking that a boy who looked old enough could be sent to war. Their attitude had to be fairly common for so many boys of fourteen, fifteen and sixteen years of age to gain entry to the AIF. The senior officers relented in this case only because of the resourceful and determined Vowles, who had seen action himself, as a volunteer for the Maori Wars fifty years earlier.

Ernie was not pleased by Vowles' interference. He waited two months then took the train to Sydney, where

they would have had no record of his enlistment in Queensland. This time he said his name was Eric Pinches, aged twenty-one. If he could get away with that, he would not need his parents' signature. He sailed through and was assigned to the 3rd reinforcements of the 5th Machine Gun Company. By August 1916, he was in England, training at the Australian Machine Gun School at Belton Park, Grantham, in the grounds of one of the most beautiful country houses in England.

Discipline at Grantham was strict – even off the base. The waitresses in the cafes in town told soldiers to go easy on the sugar, for the war effort. The street lights were painted black, because German zeppelins came hunting at night in convoys, dropping bombs on Nottingham and looking for Belton Park – the only machine-gun school in England. In 1917, there were around 50,000 British troops here. The Australians had their own training camp, for up to 1500 men.

The new water-cooled machine gun had already changed the way the

The street lights were painted black, because German zeppelins came hunting at night in convoys, dropping bombs on Nottingham and looking for Belton Park – the only machine-gun school in England … The Australians had their own training camp, for up to 1500 men.

war was being fought. Its destructive power at long range, especially when combined with strong wire defences in front of trenches, meant that old-style frontal assaults became futile – although it took the lives of millions of men before the generals on both sides accepted this. The new machine guns were light enough to be carried by small crews of four men, so they could be mobile, and thus harder to find. One man carried the gun barrel, another the tripod to support it, others brought ammunition boxes and replacement parts for when the barrel became hot. The British Vickers gun, adopted in 1912, could fire up to 500 rounds a minute. The German Maxim gun, on which the Vickers was based, could rain down 600 rounds a minute. For both sides, there was an arms race to see who could develop the lightest and most deadly machine

guns, and tactics to go with them. That's what Ernie was now learning at Grantham – not just how to strip, clean and repair the guns in all conditions, but where to site them for maximum effect. Being a machine gunner was one of the most exciting and demanding jobs on the battlefield – and one of the most dangerous. Knocking out the machine guns opposite was always a high priority for the enemy.

The AIF allocated one machine gun company, of sixteen guns and about 150 men, for each brigade of four battalions. In effect, that meant four machine-gun crews per battalion, each four guns under the command of a lieutenant. The machine gunners were a band apart, to some extent. They were attached to, but not part of, an infantry battalion. With roughly six men supporting each machine gun, the crews became very close-knit.

> Being a machine gunner was one of the most exciting and demanding jobs on the battlefield – and one of the most dangerous.

Ernie crossed the English Channel on 30 September. For two weeks, he had to cool his heels at the Australian base at Etaples, where every soldier was supposed to be further toned up by lengthy route marches. On 15 November, he went for further training to the machine-gun school at Camiers, a few kilometres north of Etaples, on a fine beach. This was to be his last taste of civilised life: warm beds, good meals, cafes and restaurants to sample in the nearby seaside towns. Ten days later, he joined the 5th Machine Gun Company at Ribemont in the Somme, north of Amiens. They had just come through a harrowing fortnight in the lines around Flers, where the trenches were a metre deep in mud. The company had lost nine killed and forty wounded, with two still missing and fifteen men sick – roughly one-third of the company.

Though now only sixteen and a half, 'Eric' Pinches turned out to be a very good soldier – brave, quick-witted and calm under pressure. He saw his first action on 21 December, north of Montauban in the Somme. His section,

No 2, was relieved on Christmas Eve to rejoin the unit in camp near Bernafay Wood. One of his officers, Lieutenant Clarence Dakin, noted in his diary that there was not a tree standing near the camp. An issue of Christmas puddings arrived. Each man was supposed to get half a pound but only forty-eight pounds arrived, to share between 210 men. Dakin wrote that the men in camp sent all of their allocation to the men in the front line. Six boxes of 'comforts' also arrived – containing chocolates, tea, coffee, milk and cigarettes – but again, there was not enough to go round, so the officers did without. On Christmas Day, Dakin was awoken by the heavy artillery 'sending presents to Fritz'. A freezing wind blew all day.

The war for the next few months for Ernie was cold, miserable and wet, with stints of two or three days at a time in front line trenches that hardly deserved the name. They were under frequent shelling, the mud stopped them receiving hot food and German snipers were active and accurate. This was a long way from playing drums on a Brisbane parade ground. There were very few days during that winter when he would have been warm or dry.

On 15 April 1917 the machine gunners were at Noreuil, about twenty kilometres north of where Ernie had first entered the line. The Australians had taken Noreuil and Lagnicourt to its south; now the Germans counter-attacked, breaking through in several places in the early morning. In desperate fighting, the Australians turned them back, partly through the ferocious work of the machine gunners.

This is where Ernie had his finest hour. During that morning, a German machine gun had his section pinned down in a sunken road, inflicting heavy casualties. The German gun was only about thirty metres away in a shell hole. Ernie leapt up out of the road into the open and rushed the enemy gun from the flank, armed only with two Mills bombs (a form of hand grenade). Lieutenant Henry French, one of his superiors, watched astonished, as the kid they called 'Pinch' captured the gun and its crew single-handed. Ten days later, French

recommend Ernie for the Distinguished Conduct Medal. It was approved and gazetted a few weeks later in London, but it's not clear that Ernie knew he had been nominated for this honour.

Three weeks later, Ernie took part in a charge at Bullecourt, just north of where he won the DCM. The first battle for Bullecourt on 11 April had been a costly disaster: 3000 Australians killed and wounded for no gain, and 1170 men taken prisoner. The 4th Brigade lost 2339 from its total strength of 3000. Bullecourt was like Fromelles nine months earlier – a badly planned operation led by a British general (Hubert Gough) who was anxious for a win. As at Fromelles, senior Australian officers warned that the attack would not work. As at Fromelles, they were brushed aside.

Charles Bean wrote later that First Bullecourt, more than any other battle, shook the confidence of the Australian soldiers in their British commanders. Gough, whose aggression usually exceeded his planning, shrugged off the first defeat and ordered another attack. This took place on 3 May, in what is now called Second Bullecourt. It would be led by the Australian 2nd Division.

Ernie, now seventeen, was an experienced and accomplished soldier – far beyond his years. He had endured a terrible winter, in some of the worst conditions of the war, and distinguished himself. For most of the last five months, he had not left the battlefield for more than a few days at a time. He had developed close friendships with the men beside him, in particular with Freddie Snowdon, a former iron-worker from Redfern in Sydney. Freddie was three years older, married, and had already been wounded once. Ernie was a Queenslander in a unit full of New South Welshmen. Freddie and Ernie became inseparable. They were on the same gun, with George Lamond, Fred Page and LH Dixon. Lamond was No 1 on the gun, Snowdon No 2.

Two months after the battle, the Australian Red Cross Wounded and Missing Enquiry Bureau interviewed Freddie Snowdon in a hospital bed in London. This is what he said:

'E Pinches, who was on my gun, was very badly wounded in the leg at about 4 am on the morning of May 3/17, when we were about thirty-five yards from the second German line, during the attack at Bullecourt. I got him into a shell hole after bandaging his leg, and started carrying him out at about 4.15 am but was then hit myself. We lay down together and at about 3 pm the same afternoon, he appeared to be dead as his eyes were fixed and glazed and I could feel no movement of his heart. His leg had been smashed by machine-gun fire, and I am practically certain that he had bled to death. I managed to crawl out at daybreak the next day. Cpl Lamond, in charge of the gun, was laying about ten yards off, too badly wounded to be moved. Private L Dixon and F Page were some little distance off.

> For most of the last five months, he had not left the battlefield for more than a few days at a time.

The little drummer boy's body was never found. He's still out there, in the rolling farmland between the three hamlets of Bullecourt, Riencourt and Queant.

Dixon, I see in the paper, is wounded so he must have got out. Page is in England on leave. They were on the same gun.'

Others gave similar accounts to the Red Cross, but most of them were based on hearsay. Some of Ernie's mates wrote to his parents, Julia and Thomas, giving details of his death, long before the army knew what had happened. Ernie was initially declared missing. A court of inquiry finally declared him dead from wounds on 5 May (the wrong date), eighteen months later. His DCM had been approved a week after he died.

Second Bullecourt was more successful than the first battle, but even more costly. Three Australian divisions were used to break into the Hindenburg Line, the line of 'impregnable' German defences, at a cost of 7000 men – killed, wounded or missing. This was on top of the earlier 3000. The AIF never recovered from the losses. The victory wasn't followed up. General Haig, commanding the British forces, shifted his attention to Ypres in Belgium, where he had wanted all along to concentrate his attack. This new road would lead to Passchendaele.

The little drummer boy's body was never found. He's still out there, in the rolling farmland between the three hamlets of Bullecourt, Riencourt and Queant. Only George Vowles had tried to stop him going and he would have heard of Ernie's fate from the newspapers, where the teenager was celebrated as 'this brave young Queenslander', dead at seventeen years and seventeen days old. Rich Salisbury, who taught Ernie to drum, survived the war and won the Military Cross. In 1919, he married Ernie's sister, Eck (Ethel). They had a son, whom they called Frank Ernest – after Eck's two late brothers – but the baby only lived three months. As for so many other families after the war, the sorrows just kept on coming. ✦

WILLIAM DALY

A WHITE FEATHER

A photograph of **WILL DALY** taken in Albury just before he left for war. He tried and failed to enlist when he was fifteen, but succeeded two years later, still under-age.

When Australia became a nation in 1901, it was not a crime to be born in Germanton, New South Wales.

By 1915, this small settlement on the Hume highway between Tarcutta and Albury could no longer take the shame of being named after a German sheep breeder called Johann Pabst. Anti-German feeling was so high that whole districts felt the pain of suspicion, depending on how many German settlers they had once contained. The townsfolk eventually settled on the name Holbrook. Naval officer Lieutenant Norman Holbrook had recently won the Victoria Cross for piloting a submarine through the Dardanelles during the Gallipoli campaign. That is why, when you drive through Holbrook now, you pass a decommissioned Australian submarine, the *Otway* – a ninety-metre monument to the town's patriotism, or perhaps, its sense of humour, given the distance to the sea.

William Daly was born here on 3 March 1899, the third child of Patrick and Mary Daly.

Will's grandfather Owen was a pioneer in these parts, the somewhat irascible owner of Mullengandra Station, 8000 acres of prime merino country thirty-five kilometres south of Germanton. Owen was a hard task-master – which is why Patrick moved off Mullengandra for a while to farm at nearby Mountain Creek.

The old man died in 1905, leaving Mullengandra to Patrick and his brother John. They made good fortunes before the war, producing some of the finest merino wool in the state.

Will spent most of his childhood here, in a beautiful valley that offered lots of natural adventures. It was an idyllic and happy Australian childhood. Will was high spirited, bright, mischievous and musical. He could sing and play the piano, the accordion and that great Australian instrument, the gum leaf. He had some of his grandfather's entrepreneurial side as well: he chopped up his mother's Christmas cake once and sold pieces to the shearers. He used to ride around the property on a small cart pulled by pet goats.

WILL DALY and his pet goats at his home in Holbrook. When his older brother, Jack, received a white feather – the symbol of cowardice – Will set his heart on enlisting himself.

His siblings, John (known as 'Jack') and Sara, were similarly gifted. The three children were educated at home by governesses.

Mullengandra village had a pub, a post office and churches for Anglicans and Presbyterians, but not Catholics. The Dalys were staunchly Catholic. The priest had to come from Holbrook, to say mass at the homes of the faithful.

Patrick was almost sixty when war broke out, too old to enlist. His elder son Jack was nineteen, healthy but for one badly turned eye. He passed the medical in Albury in the middle of 1915, but the army in Sydney sent him home as medically unfit. Then something unthinkable happened: Jack received a white feather, the symbol of cowardice.

The tradition of shaming men not in uniform goes back at least as far as the Crusades, but in 1914, it became a cruel pastime, mainly for young ladies and women in Britain, where conscription had not yet been adopted. It spread to Australia, causing hardship and turmoil for many men. The distributors of feathers did not usually ask why a man was not in uniform. In one famous case in London, a man was handed a feather on his way to receive the Victoria Cross. Many who were recuperating from wounds also received them.

The governments in both countries instituted a badge for men who had returned from war, or those who could not go because they were in essential services. Jack received an 'unfit for service' badge, which he never wore.

Will was incensed by the white feather. It meant that someone among their neighbours thought the Daly boys were shirking their duty.

Still only fifteen, Will ran away to enlist but was quickly found and brought home. A few months later, at sixteen, he ran away again and found a job on the railways at nearby Junee, a major junction on the line between Sydney and Melbourne. He took his preliminary medical for the army at Junee on 23 March 1916. They passed him and sent him one stop north to the Cootamundra enlistment office. He was accepted there on 4 April, one month after he turned seventeen.

He gave his address as the Railway Hotel, Junee, and his age as twenty-one and two months – so he would not require a parent's signature.

He did this in secret, but he didn't expect it to stay secret. He put his father as next of kin and gave his address at Mullengandra. Will was as tall as most of

> Will was incensed by the white feather. It meant that someone among their neighbours thought the Daly boys were shirking their duty.

the older men – five feet six inches (167 centimetres), but light, at fifty-four kilograms. He had brown hair, grey eyes and a dark complexion. He went to Liverpool for the 3rd Battalion, later assigned to the 20th reinforcements for the 4th.

In August, he came home to Mullengandra to say goodbye. They knew he was coming because they gave him a send-off party on the morning of 11 August at Mrs Shea's Mullengandra Hotel. The school teacher Mr McKean presided and Angus McDonald, who had two sons at the front, presented him with an 'illuminated wristlet watch' and everyone's wishes for a safe return. The next day's *Border Morning Mail* newspaper in Albury said that Private Daly, in returning thanks, showed that he was not just brave but a good speaker. 'He said he would do his little bit, and do it well. He hoped that the watch would survive, together with himself, all the horrors and terrors of the war.' The crowd cheered, then dispersed.

Joan Quinlan, one of Jack's daughters, believes that Will's parents, Patrick and Mary, never approved of

him going, but realised they could not stop him. Before he departed, they went to Albury and had a photograph taken. The photographer did a superb job, capturing the boy's youth and innocence and a hint of his mischievous grin.

Those entering the AIF in 1916 had fewer illusions than their predecessors. They had seen the casualty lists from Gallipoli and read about British losses on the Western Front. Those words 'horrors and terrors' tell us that Will Daly had his eyes open.

Will embarked in Sydney on 9 September on the *Euripides*, the same ship that had taken many recruits to Egypt in 1914 and 1915. This time, they sailed on to Plymouth, where Will disembarked in late October into one of the meanest winters for some years. He went through the usual training on Salisbury Plain, in one of the draughty Australian camps. The conditions were so bad that hundreds of men died of pulmonary disease that winter. That might explain why Will was moved on after seven weeks here, rather than the full fourteen weeks of basic training.

He crossed the English Channel from Folkestone on 13 December. He reached his unit on 19 December at Mametz in the Somme, in a party of 150 reinforcements. The 4th Battalion commander, Lieutenant Colonel Iven Giffard Mackay, was less than impressed. He wrote in the battalion diary that all of the men, with the exception of a few old hands, were partially trained. He decided they were not to be sent into the front line but could be used in support trenches for carrying and digging. He made no comment on why the army was sending him men before they were ready.

The 4th Battalion spent the next month in and out of the mud at Flers. Depending on the temperature, the trenches were either frozen or thawed mud, both conditions difficult. Each man in the line had a blanket, a greatcoat and a waterproof sheet to keep him warm through the long nights, at which they failed. Six or seven men per day went down with 'trench foot', from standing in water or mud all day. Will, as a new arrival, would have visited these trenches to bring food from the cooks further back. Hot rations were carried up each day by small parties at dawn and dusk, a journey of two hours through the mud. It was not much less dangerous than being in the front line when the artillery on both sides opened up for the festive season on Christmas Eve. Will at least was able to sleep in camp at Bernafay Wood during those first weeks. Mackay notes in the diary for Christmas Day that 'A small plum pudding was issued to each man'.

Will's battalion came out of the front line on 11 February, after ten days. A divisional order said there was to be no training for three days – which was unusual, and probably to do with the state of the men's feet. From 12 to 25 February, they were rotated through three different camps, ending up at Bendigo Camp, from where they were warned they were going back into the line. Positions had advanced in the last month. They were to move into trenches near Le Barque.

It's likely that Will had seen very little of the front line in his first month, but that changed on 28 February. The battalion's advance parties moved up at 4 am, the rest of the battalion by 2 pm, into Wheat and Bark trenches, in front of Le Barque. The battalion diary notes that 'Enemy put down a heavy barrage between Wheat Trench and Le Barque at 1800. Otherwise quiet day'. Except that one of those shells exploded near Will, and took off both his legs below the knee. Stretcher-bearers carried him back to an aid post of the 1st Australian Field Ambulance, where he died that night. He was buried at Singer Circus Cemetery, by Captain Peter Hayes, a Roman Catholic priest and chaplain. The cemetery, now known as Bazentin-le-Petit Military Cemetery, is three kilometres east of Pozieres, where the 4th Battalion lost hundreds of men earlier that year.

> Will, as a new arrival, would have visited these trenches to bring food from the cooks further back. Hot rations were carried up each day by small parties at dawn and dusk, a journey of two hours through the mud.

When a soldier died in the field, the army sent a telegram to the district headquarters in Australia, in this case, Victoria Barracks in Sydney. An officer then notified the appropriate denomination of clergyman in the soldier's home district, who then brought the bad news in person to the family. A Colonel Luscombe addressed his telegram to the Catholic clergyman at Mullengandra – but there was none. The postman delivered the telegram directly to Patrick Daly, Will's father.

Three weeks later, Patrick's solicitor in Albury wrote to the army on behalf of his client.

'Mr Daly is very anxious to get particulars as to how he was wounded and how long he was ill and he is very anxious to have a record of his dear son's grave so that it may easily be identified and attended to. He is very anxious to have the remains removed when the war is over if it is possible ... He is greatly distressed at his young son's early death, this boy, who was only just the age to go, wanted to go when he was sixteen,' wrote the solicitor.

The lawyer was mistaken: Will was under-age when he enlisted at seventeen years and one month. He was still under-age when he was killed, a few days short of his eighteenth birthday.

The British and Australian governments decided early on that no soldier's body would be repatriated after the war. Instead, the Commonwealth countries set up the Commonwealth War Graves Commission (CWGC) to create a series of walled cemeteries in situ, designed to look like beautiful English gardens,

in an effort to give some comfort to the families.

In due course, the Daly family received three photographs of the grave, along with their son's personal effects. These reflected his strong religious faith: as well as from an identity disc and a belt, there were two religious books, two rosaries and some religious emblems. There was no mention of the illuminated wristlet watch he was given when he left Mullengandra.

Joan Quinlan has visited Will's grave in France. The first headstone erected by the CWGC said that he was twenty-two when he died, based on the Australian War Memorial's records. Dale Hummer, a member of the family, has had the AWM records corrected. The CWGC then erected a new headstone, which says Will was seventeen when he died. 🥀

Author's note: Four of Johann Pabst's grandsons served in the AIF during the First World War.

BELGIUM
1917

WILLIAM RICHARDS

THE BIG MAN AND THE BATMAN

A grumpy-faced seventeen-year-old **WILL RICHARDS**,
probably taken in 1916 when he enlisted.

Hugh Connell was a big man in a medium-sized body. He was barrel chested, quick witted, generous of spirit, confident in his opinions and unafraid to voice them. He had what one English officer called a 'large personality', which might not have been a compliment. One of his wife's relatives would remember him for his 'very alert, deep set and humorous blue eyes', and for being agnostic, which was unusual at the time.

Connell grew up in the rough-and-tumble inner suburbs of Sydney, the son of an iron-moulder and trade unionist, from whom he learned his politics. Father and son were Labor Party men to their bootstraps. The younger Connell loved all sports – in particular, rugby league, the game that has dominated Sydney's sporting life, and much of its political life, for more than a century.

Connell was bright, but few could afford university in 1900. He became a teacher, first in remote half-time schools in western New South Wales, then at Broken Hill. Here he met Billy Dunn, another schoolteacher. Broken Hill was a cauldron of labour and union politics and both men were active. Too active, according to their superiors in the education department. Both were carpeted for their political activities in 1909.

Dunn won the New South Wales seat of Mudgee in 1910. Connell married his sweetheart, Mary Elizabeth Woods, a teacher at a girls school in Broken Hill, and moved to Newcastle around 1911, where he took up a job as sports master at Wickham Superior Public School.

One of the boys at Wickham Superior that year was twelve-year-old William Richards. He was quiet, gentle, perhaps a little shy. His father, Charles, was an engine driver who had migrated to

---

HUGH CONNELL was role model and teacher to WILL RICHARDS at Wickham school in Newcastle. When both joined the army, Connell was determined to protect the under-age boy he had taught for five years.

Australia from Cornwall. His mother, Ada Sproule, was twenty-one years younger than her husband.

Will was born in August 1899, the sixth child. In 1901, Charles and Ada had another daughter, Alberta, who died the same year. The couple split up soon after. Ada took Linda, the youngest daughter, who was about five, to live with her in nearby Hamilton. Will remained in Wickham with his father and four siblings. Charles employed a housekeeper to look after them.

Charles was fifty-two when Will was born – almost an old man by the standards of the time. There is some evidence that Charles had been a drinker: he was charged with a drunken assault in 1895 in Dubbo, when he punched a railway superintendent through a pub window.

Nevertheless, Charles didn't skimp when it came to his children, at least those who lived with him. They were well educated at good local schools; each child learned to play a musical instrument through private lessons. How Charles paid for this on an engine driver's pay is hard to imagine, unless he had a private legacy. In 1907, Ada sued her husband for more child support. Charles responded that he would like her to come home and the court refused her request. Ada moved soon after to Sydney.

At Wickham school, Hugh Connell took a shine to the young William Arthur Leslie Richards, who was small and slight and probably overshadowed in the sporting department. And what boy would not have been impressed with this big sportsman with his kindly air, his strong sense of

> If Will had been looking for male role models – as most boys of his age are – Connell was the perfect fit. During the next four years, that bond only strengthened, as Will grew towards manhood.

right and wrong and his natural authority? If Will had been looking for male role models – as most boys of his age are – Connell was the perfect fit. During the next four years, that bond only strengthened, as Will grew towards manhood.

Connell was an officer in the militia when war broke out, yet he hesitated to join the AIF. His records say he did not enlist until March 1916 – a full eighteen months into the war – but they may be incomplete. A news report puts Lieutenant Connell at Warwick Farm Camp in late 1915; his record also shows that he did a general officer's course at the 'AIF School' in January 1915, six months after the war started. It's possible he joined as a private, then resigned and rejoined when commissioned.

Connell was almost certainly in the army when Will enlisted. The 35th Battalion was raised in Newcastle and Maitland in December 1915. Will was rejected at least once. That may be why he signed on at West Maitland, rather than Newcastle, although he admitted on his papers that he had been rejected for being 'under standard'.

By January 1916, he claimed to be eighteen years and four months old. In reality he was sixteen and four months. He was five feet three inches tall (160 centimetres) and 53.5 kilograms with a chest measurement of thirty-two inches.

Most of the men in C Company, 35th Battalion, to which Will was sent, were coalminers from Newcastle and the Hunter Valley.

Lieutenant Hugh Connell took command of C Company early in 1916. He was among friends, including Will. It's unlikely that Connell knew beforehand that Will was in the ranks, as Connell had been at Warwick Farm when the boy enlisted. Connell could have reported Will for being under-age and had him sent home. Instead, he asked Private Richards to serve as his batman – essentially the military version of a gentleman's servant. If the boy was determined to go to war, at least Connell would try to look after him.

Connell was a popular officer. He knew many of the other officers and men from Newcastle football, the militia and politics. Indeed, his old friend Billy

Dunn from Broken Hill soon arrived in the battalion. He enlisted as a sitting member of parliament in February. Two months later he applied for a commission and was made quartermaster of the 35th Battalion, with responsibility for all stores and transport.

Dunn became a lieutenant on 1 May 1916. Connell became a captain that same day and Will was promoted to lance corporal. This shower of appointments coincided with the mobilising of the battalion. The 35th marched through Newcastle to the station, past huge crowds of stoic fathers; weeping mothers, sisters and sweethearts; and children waving flags. Another large crowd travelled to Sydney to greet them as they arrived. The 9th Brigade embarked the next morning on the *Benalla*. With thirty officers and 1000 men in the 35th, there were at least as many civilians wondering if they would see their loved ones again. In truth, nearly half of them would not.

Will's duties as batman probably began the day they mobilised. He was to serve both Connell and Dunn. In the British army, a batman amounted to a personal servant, who was sometimes paid extra by his officer. In the AIF, where the word servant was unpopular, batmen were expected to be full soldiers who would assist an officer to do his job. Thus, the batman cooked meals, made tea, took care of the officer's uniform and laundry, ran and received messages and often went with him into the front lines, as bodyguard and runner. In other words, a servant with a gun.

The bond between batman and officer was often strong and mutually dependent. A captain was responsible for the welfare of hundreds of men; an orderly was responsible for just one or two men, but this created a sense of obligation on both sides. An orderly might see and hear most of what the officer did, all the highs and lows. He was expected to be discrete, efficient and loyal. He might also know more than the officer about what the men were thinking and saying, so he could be an ear-to-the-ground. Will and Connell had known each other for at least five years by the time they reached England. They were as close as brothers.

The villages around the camp were picturesque and popular with the men, especially their quaint pubs. The camp was not. It was surely one of the most forsaken places on earth, wrote Lieutenant ME Lyne in 1920.

The 35th came late to the party in France. They arrived at Plymouth on the afternoon of 9 July, after ten weeks at sea, via Colombo and Cape Town. An overnight train took them through the English countryside to Amesbury. Here they shouldered their packs and marched to the camp that would provide a good introduction to the discomforts to come.

Major General John Monash, their new commander, was determined that the 3rd Division would be the best trained unit Australia had ever fielded. While their comrades in the 1st and 2nd divisions were dying at Fromelles and Pozieres in July and August 1916, the 9th Brigade was marching up and down the Salisbury Plain, clocking up weary miles on the chalky back roads of Wiltshire, collapsing at night into primitive bunks at Lark Hill Camp.

The villages around the camp were picturesque and popular with the men, especially their quaint pubs. The camp was not. It was surely one of the most forsaken places on earth, wrote Lieutenant ME Lyne in 1920. Pneumonia and pleurisy took a toll on the 35th as the weather turned cold in this 'dissolute hole'. On most days, the men could hear the sounds of a military band playing the Death March at a cemetery nearby, 'playing some poor fellow into his grave'.

In truth, they were lucky to get out of Lark Hill when they did, in late November. The death toll increased there in December and January 1917. By then, the 35th were occupying a part of the line in the 'quiet sector' near Armentières, on the border between France and Belgium. This is where they learned trench life.

Will and his two officers passed a cold winter – one of the coldest in memory – but in more comfort than the average infantryman. Officers had dugouts built from wood and sandbags, or even cement. Will would have had to scrounge for firewood and food and learn how to cook, but he would have slept nearby, warmer and dryer than the men in the line. Except for the nights in the line with Connell, his exposure to danger was reduced as a batman. He probably copped some abuse for being the teacher's pet in a cushy job, but it would have been apparent to the hardened miners of the 35th Battalion that Will was a mere boy.

During the night of 26 or 28 February, Will was in the C Company headquarters dugout, in trenches just behind the lines at Houplines, east of Armentières, when a German 5.9 shell crashed through the dugout wall. According to later reports, Will was making either tea or coffee for three officers when the shell took off both of his legs, leaving the three officers untouched.

The Red Cross Wounded and Missing Enquiry Bureau tried to find out what had happened, after an inquiry from their Sydney office from Will's family. Hugh Connell was among those who responded.

'I am in a position to supply all the information you seek, as the lad was not only my batman, but a personal friend whom I regarded as a younger brother. He was killed on the 26th of Feb of this year in my dugout by a shell, dying in my arms a minute of being struck. He was buried the next day at the Cite Bonjean Military Cemetery Armentières. The grave is marked by a cross with a suitable inscription. I may add that I forwarded full information to his sister in Newcastle, NSW. I should be only too pleased to communicate direct with your enquirers if they desire any further information. I had a big respect for Will, having taught him at school for four or five years before, and his death was a big blow.'

Connell wrote this letter in London in September 1917, while recuperating from a wound. The sister he had written to was Enid D'Arcy Richards, who was nine years older than Will.

> Will was in the C Company headquarters dugout, in trenches just behind the lines at Houplines, east of Armentières, when a German 5.9 shell crashed through the dugout wall.

Hugh O'Connell returned to Australia as a bona fide hero, which helped when he stood in 1920 for the seat of Kahibah in Newcastle.

The shock of Will's death sent his father into a profound depression from which he never recovered. He retired less than a month after Will's death. He died of dementia and heart problems at the Rookwood Asylum in Lidcombe in 1922. One of his great-grandchildren, Charmaine Langford-Budzynski, remembers her grandmother Florence talking of how much she and her sisters missed her brother Will.

Hugh Connell had a good war. He won a Military Cross at Messines, survived being wounded in July 1917, survived Passchendaele in October, and distinguished himself in April 1918 near Amiens where he won a bar to his MC (in effect, a second Military Cross), as well as a Distinguished Service Order.

He returned to Australia as a bona fide hero, which helped when he stood in 1920 for the seat of Kahibah in Newcastle. He represented the area for the next fourteen years in the New South Wales parliament, serving under Jack Lang, until his early death in January 1934, aged forty-nine. The post-war repatriation medical authorities later ruled that Connell died, in part, because of his experiences in the war. He had a heart condition that no-one knew about.

Will Richards' grave, in Cite Bonjean, is in the south-western suburbs of Armentières. He was seventeen years and six months at the time of his death – still too young to join the army. ❧

ALBERT & REGINALD LE ROUX

INTO THE FIRE

ALBERT 'BERTIE' LE ROUX was eighteen when this picture was taken in 1916. He enlisted with his parents' consent. His brother Prosper joined up soon after.

Just outside Lang Lang in southern Gippsland, Victoria, there's an area of high ground once known as Frenchman's Hill. The Frenchman in question was Prosper Henri Victor Le Roux, whose family had farmed in Normandy, France, before he came to Tasmania and eventually to Gippsland. He purchased a barely developed run of sixty-five hectares called Red Bluff, on the shores of Western Port Bay.

Prosper's son, also named Prosper, became one of the more successful farmers in southern Gippsland, raising prize-winning Clydesdale horses, cattle and sheep at Red Bluff. His wife, Caroline (nee Hodgson), had four healthy babies. The first boy was called Prosper Reginald Victor, although he would go through life as Reg. The next child, Henry Reeve, born in 1885, was known as Harry. Then came Dorothy Victoire in 1891 and finally Albert Arthur Le Roux, known as Bertie, who entered the world on 28 June 1897.

By 1914, these three sons had expanded and modernised Red Bluff. The 'Le Roux Bros' name appeared often in the prize lists of the Royal Melbourne shows before the war. They were said to have the best flock of Southdown sheep in Victoria. Bertie was just seventeen and a livewire kid, according to Dorothy. They were close, partly because his brothers were so much older. As war broke out, Reg was thirty and Harry was twenty-nine. Bertie was the baby, although he was showing signs of restlessness. He would soon take a job as a bank clerk.

In the first eighteen months of war, the Le Roux brothers did not beat a path to the recruiting office. Times were hard for farmers. Many of the available farm workers had gone to war. In a year of catastrophic drought, with cattle and sheep dying in the millions, the ships to carry Australia's agricultural exports were suddenly scarce and more expensive. Britain turned to America and Argentina for cheaper produce and left Australian producers without contracts. The Le Roux brothers, like every other Australian farmer, had their backs to the wall as war raged in France, the country their family once called home.

Caroline Le Roux, their mother, was a devout pillar of the local Anglican church. If she disapproved of her sons rushing off to war, she would have been unusual in both her church and community.

The men who left Australia in 1914 often jeered at those who came later. They called them 'deep thinkers', meaning they were too concerned with their own welfare to volunteer. That may be true of some, but those who joined up later in the war knew more about what they were getting into. By late 1916, the full horror of the war was apparent – if not from the censored news reports, then from the casualty lists. In a sense, these late-joiners showed rare courage. The early joiners were more reckless and romantic; the deep thinkers went with their eyes wide open.

Bertie Le Roux presented himself for military service on 1 February 1916, at a recruiting office in Melbourne, but he had been preparing for some time. He sailed through the medical: he was almost five feet six inches tall (167 centimetres), fifty-six kilograms and his chest expanded to thirty-three inches – good enough for the relaxed standards of early 1916. He had a fresh complexion, brown eyes and auburn hair. His eyes, captured in the superb photograph taken before he left, are soft and innocent, like one of the cows at Red Bluff. He looks like a child in dress-up, but Bertie was already eighteen.

Six months earlier, he would have been under-age, but the authorities had changed the regulations in mid-1915 to allow eighteen-year-olds if they had the consent of their parents. The definition of under-age had been shifted to suit the times, the casualty lists, and the needs of the government. Some might have called this expedient and immoral; others might have said it was simply the normalisation of what had been going on at recruiting halls for a year and a half. For an organisation that was supposed to run on regulations, the army had been remarkably slapdash

about enforcing those to do with the age of recruits.

Bertie's forms have two signatures, which suggests that he had his parents' consent. His age may have been the primary reason for the delay: his parents may have hoped the war would be over before he came of age. His enlistment seems to have galvanised his older brother, Reg, because he enlisted a week later. Reg was now thirty-three, a stockier version of Bertie, with those same guileless eyes. It would have been hard for Reg to stay home when his little brother was already in uniform.

That left Harry to run the farm, with his father's help. No shame there: two out of three sons was enough to satisfy any local critics, especially since wool, wheat and meat production were now crucial to the war effort. In early 1916, Billy Hughes had persuaded the British to buy all of Australia's wool crop at a good price. By the end of that year, the British were buying most of Australia's dairy, meat and wheat production as well, to stave off food shortages.

Bertie's role in the army was decided before he enlisted. He had served four years in the compulsory cadet scheme. In the nine months before he joined up, he took a field artillery course at Albert Park barracks in Melbourne. That would have been difficult if he had still been living at Red Bluff, not so much if he was living in Melbourne and working as a bank clerk.

He was assigned to the 8th Field Artillery Brigade as a reinforcement. By May, he was in the 31st battery of that brigade, which sailed from Melbourne on 20 May aboard the *Medic*. They disembarked in Plymouth on 18 July 1916 – the day before the battle of Fromelles – and went into one of the Lark Hill training camps on Salisbury Plain. Like a lot of soldiers who went into these camps, Bertie got sick. He was admitted to the Fargo Military Hospital at Lark Hill in November, suffering from pleurisy. He was readmitted in December for

---

Thirty-three-year-old **PROSPER REGINALD LE ROUX** joined the army just a week after his little brother, Albert, did.

eight days, including Christmas Day, but rejoined his unit as they embarked for France on 31 December.

He arrived back in the land of his forefathers via the port of Le Havre.

A gun battery in the AIF in 1916 consisted of about 120 men, spread across twelve eighteen-pounder guns and four heavy howitzers. The eighteen-pounder was the mainstay of British artillery – light enough to be hauled by six horses, and powerful enough to hurl a range of shell types up to six kilometres. Each gun had a crew of ten men to manage the horses and limbers, carry the ammunition forward, dig a pit for the gun, then lay the gun in position with minute care, the accuracy of the fire being dependent on the skill of the 'gun layer'. Sometimes these gun pits were concreted. Later in 1917, the guns were sometimes moved every day or two, to stay ahead of enemy spotters and in contact with their own infantry. It was exhausting and deafening: men wadded their ears for a firing 'stunt', but still came out of the pits dazed.

Bertie was now part of the most modern kind of war – remote, industrial and deadly. The gunners were largely separate from the infantry and could be sent anywhere. Australian batteries assisted the Canadians in their epic battle for Vimy Ridge, for example. It was a high-risk occupation: if the enemy got a fix on their position, they would be shelled mercilessly. The gunners had two jobs – bashing the enemy's trenches and finding

> Bertie's unit went to billets near Bailleul, close to Armentières, in the dead of winter. With only two blankets per man, each slept in his clothes. Horses died from pneumonia, but the men still thought this place was better than Lark Hill.

and destroying his guns. No previous war had relied so much on artillery – and none had guns that were so destructive. These new weapons killed and maimed more men than any other weapon, including the machine gun, in this war. They struck fear into the heart of every soldier.

Bertie's unit went to billets near Bailleul, close to Armentières, in the dead of winter. With only two blankets per man, each slept in his clothes. Horses died from pneumonia, but the men still thought this place was better than Lark Hill. Food was short: hard biscuits and tinned bully beef plus what they could scrounge from the French villages. French coffee and French wine made all the difference. Some men developed strong friendships with particular farming families, returning again and again to plates of egg and chips and a warm welcome. Others stole anything that quacked, mooed or clucked.

Bertie spent nine months on the Western Front, in northern France and Belgium. His unit took part in the battle of Messines in June, coming under heavy enemy fire designed to knock out the guns. It was a hectic time. One gunner in the 30th battery, the unit next to Bertie's, recorded in his diary that he 'took pants off first time for 5 weeks'.

In September, Bertie's battery moved north towards Ypres, drawn into the British push towards Passchendaele.

By 1917, the effects of the war were bringing down governments, not just generals. The French army was in mutiny after Verdun in 1916, the Bolsheviks were brewing a revolution in Russia and all attempts to break the stalemate on the Western Front in France had failed. The British commanders agreed to a French request to launch an attack from Arras: that resulted in two of the most costly battles of the war for the Australians, known as First and Second Bullecourt. General Haig, commanding the British forces, had wanted to attack in Belgium all along. As the French attacks failed, he prepared to break out of the Ypres Salient (a bulge in the line) in Flanders, pushing east.

The road to Passchendaele was now set. Tactics had changed since the

Somme a year earlier. The aim was not to over-run the enemy in one grand push, but to bite off small sections and hold them, moving by increments. Haig amassed more guns than in any battle in history. The Germans fortified their already strong positions and waited, preferring to defend until winter, when both sides would have to hunker down. The guns turned Flanders into a quagmire, destroying centuries-old drainage channels. This was the ground the British forces would have to cross. The Australian divisions would come together for the first time here, to fight and die beside each other, in appalling numbers. If 1916 had been a bloodbath, unprecedented in the number of casualties, 1917 would be worse.

On 20 September, the 8th Field Artillery Brigade was firing from positions near Hooge, towards Zonnebeke, east of Ypres. Alexander Mackay, who was in Bertie's unit, wrote in his diary that the 'main stunt' began at 5.40 that morning. This was the Battle for Menin Road, part of the Third Battle for Ypres, another name for Passchendaele.

Mackay wrote: 'Our battery consists of six guns. Each fired close on 900 rounds. We are only eighteen-pounders. The big guns have hardly stopped since yesterday. One has to shout to make himself heard above the screaming of shells. It's really awful. You can't help pitying the poor dogs the other side, every yard of ground must be ploughed up …'

On 24 September, German shelling was coming closer to their positions. 'Fritz has had it all on his own here today, shelling and bombing galore. We have had to clear half a dozen times. A while ago he knocked two Tommies the other side of our dugout, also the officers' cook … Just before we left tonight, Fritz got all around us, one shell lobbed right amongst the guns, getting 2 officers, 2 corporals & 2 gunners. I managed to escape by throwing myself flat. We all then acted as stretcher bearers … only one man hit this afternoon is serious'.

Bertie Le Roux was hit on this day. He suffered wounds to both hips that penetrated his abdomen. He was taken down the line to the 3rd Canadian Casualty Clearing Station, where he fought for his life for three days. He succumbed on 27 September. He was buried at the Lijsshenthoek Military Cemetery, adjacent to the casualty clearing station. Lijsshenthoek is the second-largest Commonwealth cemetery in Belgium. More than 10,000 are buried there.

Bertie's older brother Reg, in the 24th Battalion, disappeared a week later in the battle for Broodseinde Ridge, just a little further east from where Bertie was killed. This day, 4 October 1917, was one of the worst for the Australian forces – 6500 men killed, wounded or missing. Reg was one of 1279 men who died taking that ridge. His body was never found.

Back at Red Bluff, the news that both sons had died within a week of each other pitched the Le Roux family into unimaginable grief. Within two years, they sold Red Bluff, the property they had farmed for fifty years. Chris Reid, grandson of Dorothy Le Roux, suspects the place held too many memories. Harry, the third son, bought a new property near Albury, separating himself from his parents. Caroline and Prosper

bought a new property in the western districts of Victoria, at Camperdown.

In 1924, the authorities wrote to Caroline asking where to send her sons' medals. Her response was sharp. 'I think it is time the Defence Department ceased sending out these medals etc. It is just a waste of public money and I for one take no interest in these trashy affairs ...'

Chris Reid remembers hearing from his father that Caroline's grief was profound and long-lasting. She never talked about Bertie or Reg, nor permitted discussion of them. It was apparently no consolation to her to know that Albert Arthur and Prosper Reginald Victor were now buried in the soil of their ancestors in Flanders.

The old man, Prosper, accepted the medals and they are now in the care of Chris Reid, grand-nephew of Reg and Bertie.

Caroline Le Roux died in 1925, aged sixty-four. Her daughter Dorothy had a son in 1920 with James Bruce Reid: they named him Prosper Albert Le Roux Reid. ❧

RUFUS & CYRIL RIGNEY

THE FOUR UNCLES

MILLER MACK (right) was one of more than 1000 Aboriginal men, and one of Doreen Kartinyeri's four uncles to serve Australia in the First World War.

When the late Dr Doreen Kartinyeri was a child at Point McLeay Aboriginal Station, a man named 'Poobley' Wilson used to entertain the children with a song he wrote about his experiences in the First World War: 'He left his left leg in France…'

And he did. Wilson was wounded in the hand in 1917. He was back with his unit in January 1918, at Messines in Belgium, when a shell smashed his left leg. It was amputated in France, then reamputated in England because of gangrene. Wilson survived and returned to Point McLeay on crutches, his sense of humour intact, if not his leg.

He was one of twenty-one Aboriginal men who enlisted from Point McLeay – a former mission in South Australia on the shores of Lake Alexandrina at the mouth of the Murray River, near the Coorong, traditional home of the Ngarrindjeri people. Doreen Kartinyeri was born there in 1935 and documented these men's stories in *Ngarrindjeri Anzacs*, published in 1996. Four of her uncles were among the men who went to war.

The Point McLeay mission was established in 1859 by the Aborigines' Friends Association, but taken over by the South Australian government at the start of 1916, after a Royal Commission. Point McLeay had a population of 380 people – and that was too many for the Chief Protector of Aborigines, William Garnet South. His first annual report, after six months in control of the station, reported a loss of £700. This was satisfactory, he wrote, considering that there were about 70 'full bloods' and 310 'half-castes' 'more or less dependent on the station'. The department had set up a dairy farm with 100 milking cows. He hoped to double that and add a piggery, to provide jobs for all the men. 'The wages system has been initiated on this station as far as possible, but until the dairying and piggery are developed more fully, we have insufficient employment for the support of 380 natives, consequently rations have to be supplied to many who are capable of earning their own living.'

South wrote that the sooner the obsolete system of ration handouts was abolished the better, as it encouraged 'laziness and thriftlessness'.

Doreen Kartinyeri recorded a story told to her by Bill Karpany, one of those who enlisted. 'There were several Aboriginal men sitting down at the River Torrens one day. Some men in uniform came up to them and asked them if they would like to join the army, that if they did, they would get paid and so would their families. This offer seemed a good chance for them to travel overseas and get paid.'

For men who had lived on mission rations and low-paid jobs as stockmen, shearers and horse-breakers, the idea of regular wages – at the same level as every other recruit – must certainly have been attractive.

Aboriginal men had rarely, if ever, been offered equal pay with white men. The war offered a kind of freedom, in that sense, even with all the rules and regulations of army life. They could win some respect, see the world and support their families at the same time. For some, there was a sense that war service would lead to greater human rights for Aboriginal people; for others, there was a strong patriotism. Australia was at war and they were Australians – the first Australians, in fact.

Disenfranchised or not, more than 1000 Aboriginal men, from every state and territory, served in the First World War. At least fifty-six served on Gallipoli, others in Palestine. The largest number served on the Western Front in France and Belgium,

---

Aboriginal men had rarely, if ever, been offered equal pay with white men. The war offered a kind of freedom, in that sense, even with all the rules and regulations of army life. They could win some respect, see the world and support their families at the same time.

---

playing a part in every major Australian battle. At least sixty-two are named on the Roll of Honour (the list of Australian war dead), but the real number is higher, since some concealed their Aboriginality. The roll lists five South Australians. Four of them came from Point McLeay. At least one of them was under-age.

The twenty-one men who left Point McLeay didn't all go together. Two left in 1914, five in 1915. Twelve men left in 1916, after the South Australian government took over. Was this coincidence? Those who were under twenty-one had to have the written permission of the Chief Protector, South – the same man who thought there were too many mouths to feed at Point McLeay.

That may be why South consented to the enlistment of Rufus Gordon Rigney and his brother Cyril Spurgeon Rigney. Cyril went first, signing his papers in Adelaide on 24 April 1916 – the eve of the first anniversary of the Gallipoli landing. Cyril was nineteen years and two months old, the eldest surviving son of Ben and Rachel Rigney. Cyril and Rufus were the fourth and fifth of eleven children.

Cyril had married Constance Maude Varcoe in January. She was pregnant with their first child when he left for the army – an agonising choice to make. He did so, in part, to support them: from his pay of five shillings a day, he assigned four to his new wife. Most soldiers assigned two or three shillings only.

Cyril's uncle, Gordon Wilfred Rigney, enlisted the same day. He was nine years older, a stockman and colt-breaker. Years later, he told Doreen Kartinyeri that he enlisted to take care of Cyril. Cyril's best friend, Eustace Garnet Wilson, known as 'Garney', also signed up. Francis Varcoe and Miller Mack, two of Doreen's four uncles, enlisted together on 23 August. Francis was twenty; Miller was twenty-two.

Rufus was determined to follow his big brother. The problem was that Rufus was just sixteen and a half. His parents said he was too young; his sister Rose begged him not to go. The letter from South is preserved in Rufus's military file:

'As legal guardian of all Half Caste Aboriginal children… I hereby give my consent for Rufus Gordon Rigney to enlist with the Australian Military Forces, he being under the age of twenty-one years.'

Quite a lot under twenty-one, in fact. It's possible that South did not know Rufus's real age, but unlikely. The Chief Protector controlled almost every aspect of the lives of South Australian Aboriginal people, from what they ate and where they lived to which children were removed from their parents. South was a former policeman with patrol experience in north and central Australia. He believed in protecting 'full bloods' from white influence and accelerating the assimilation of all others ('half-castes', 'quadroons' etc.) into white society, by training. And the army offered plenty of training.

Strictly speaking, Aboriginal people were not permitted to go to war. Recruits had to be of European origin. Aboriginal people were non-citizens under the Constitution and not allowed to vote. It depended almost entirely on where the recruit presented himself – and to some extent, on the hue of his skin (the lighter the better). In May

1917, the regulations were relaxed to allow men with one white parent to enlist, but this had little impact, since the rules were so often ignored already.

Rufus got his letter of permission on 7 August 1916. Cyril and Garney had already shipped out in July. Rufus was allotted to the 32nd Battalion, same as his brother, but they would never serve together, as Cyril was transferred to the 43rd. They barely even saw each other once they got to France.

Before he left, Rufus came home to farewell his family at Point McLeay. He had his photo taken with his sister. Rose wore a new dress she had made herself. Doreen found that photo in the mid-1970s and showed it to Rose, who was then in hospital. She cried and cried, wrote Doreen.

Rufus landed at Plymouth in November 1916 and went to Salisbury Plain in Wiltshire for training. This was kept short, possibly because so many recruits were dying in the camps from pneumonia and pleurisy. He left for France on 16 January 1917, catching up with his battalion a few days later, in the Somme Valley near

Montauban. They had just come out of the line, to rest at Adelaide Camp.

The 32nd was a battered battalion. On one night in July 1916 at Fromelles, it had suffered 718 casualties – effectively ninety per cent of its fighting strength. By the time Rufus arrived, it was back up to about 650 men – one-third below par.

Rufus went into the front lines for the first time on 14 February, at Needle and Switch trenches, near Flers. The next day, they were shelled with shrapnel and gas – four officers and nine 'other ranks' killed and fifteen men gassed. On 17 February, rain flooded their trenches. It was a miserable, bloody introduction to modern warfare. Rufus came out of the line on 20 February.

Two weeks later, he copped a 'Blighty' wound, in the same trenches. (This was a wound that didn't kill you, but got you back to England, 'Blighty', for treatment). He had shrapnel wounds in his back and arms. He was admitted to Lakenham Military Hospital in Norfolk, with superficial wounds. After ten weeks, during which he had leave in London, they sent him back to France. He transferred to the 48th Battalion at the end of June. The reason for this is obscure: his brother was in the 43rd, in another brigade. The 48th had many men from South Australia, but so did the 32nd.

If anything, the 48th was in worse shape than the 32nd. It had almost 600 casualties at Pozieres in mid-1916. After rebuilding, it lost another 435 men at Bullecourt in April 1917. It went into its next major action, the Battle of Passchendaele, with just over 600 men.

Of all the battles in which Australians played a significant part, Passchendaele was perhaps the worst – the terrible culmination of a series of battles from July to November 1917. The aim was to push the enemy back to the east of Ypres in Belgium, breaking through a bulge in the line. The British would then swing round and seize the Belgian ports, from which German U-boats were operating. The Battle of Passchendaele started on 31 July at Pilckem. The Australian divisions took part in the battles for Menin Road, Polygon

Wood, Broodseinde and Poelcapelle, all in preparation for taking Passchendaele in October.

By 10 October, the 48th had moved up to Ypres, marching through the Menin Gate and on to Westhoek Ridge. Each man carried 220 rounds of ammunition, five Mills bombs and two sandbags, tied around his shins. Their task was to attack the Passchendaele Ridge from 12 October, beside the Australian 3rd Division, the New Zealand Division and five British divisions. The British commander, General Haig, knew the chance of success was slight, but he needed to take the high ground before winter. His most senior adviser, Brigadier General John Charteris, inspected the ground on 9 October and decided that the advance was doomed.

Shortly after midnight on 12 October, Rufus Rigney went forward in A Company, heading for the jumping-off point near Decoy Wood. They marched out under heavy shelling, then rain. One soldier wrote later that the rain fell 'steadily, soakingly and it seemed to us, vindictively', converting the track into 'a nightmare of mud and slop'. They

arrived at their starting point, exhausted and sodden, after about five hours. They had eight minutes to rest.

At about 5.30 am, they marched out across a lunar landscape of shell holes, filled with water and the putrid remains of earlier advances. The artillery barrage that was supposed to creep ahead of them was thin and unpredictable; a number of friendly shells fell short and killed their own men. German machine and artillery opened up and decimated the rest.

This is where Private Rufus Rigney stopped a bullet. An eyewitness told his story later to the Red Cross Wounded and Missing Enquiry Bureau. Private GW Fox was interviewed at Calais in July 1918: 'There was a man of that name in my bombing section of A Coy, a coloured chap. Like an Australian Aboriginal. He was with me when I was dressing Cpl (TJ) Roachock of A Coy who was wounded in the hop over at Passchendaele on Oct 12th. Then while following me from that shell hole, he got shot through the lungs. He was left in another shell hole, nearer our objective, where no doubt he died, for

At about 5.30 am, they marched out across a lunar landscape of shell holes, filled with water and the putrid remains of earlier advances … a number of friendly shells fell short and killed their own men. German machine and artillery opened up and decimated the rest.

he was very bad. A man named Doran of B Company who got killed later on put a bandage around him. We won our objective after that and dug in, but the Germans counter-attacked and we had to retire after holding on for about ten hours, to where we started from. Nobody got buried that day and the wounded who could not walk were not brought in.'

In fact, Rufus was alive. The Germans picked him up after their counter-attack and sent him to a military hospital. He died there four days later, as a prisoner of war. Rufus was about six weeks short of his eighteenth birthday. The Germans buried him at Iseghem military cemetery. His body was later moved to Harlebeke New British Cemetery, where his grave has been tended for most of the last century by the Commonwealth War Graves Commission.

This day at Passchendaele would never be forgotten by the Australians who were there. John Monash's 3rd Division incurred 3000 casualties, as did the New Zealand Division. The Australian 4th Division (45th to 48th battalions)

suffered 1000 casualties. The 48th lost thirteen officers and 344 other ranks. Overall, II Anzac Corps suffered 7000 casualties for no real gain of territory. Canadian troops relieved the Australians on 18 October and took Passchendaele early in November. By then, the Australian divisions had lost 38,000 men, 12,000 of them dead and missing, in eight weeks. This was worse than Pozieres in 1916. Almost 600,000 men fell at Passchendaele, counting casualties on both sides. One of them was Rufus Rigney.

All four of Doreen Kartinyeri's uncles died as a result of the war. Cyril Rigney died at Messines, on 3 July 1917, in the first stage of Haig's plan to break out of the deadlock. His body was never found. Rufus had only just heard of his brother's death when he was killed at Passchendaele. Francis Varcoe died two months earlier than Cyril at Bulle-court. He has no known grave. Miller Mack survived the fighting but died in a nursing home in Adelaide in September 1919, from broncho-pneumonia and tuberculosis. He was ill before they sent him to France. Arthur Thomas Walker, one of the oldest of the *Ngarrindjeri Anzacs*, died at Mouquet Farm, near Pozieres, in August 1916. Again, he has no known grave.

Point McLeay is now known as Raukkan. In *Ngarrindjeri Anzacs*, Doreen Kartinyeri recalled her family's bitterness about the war.

'When I look back over the history of my people, I see the Protector interfering in all aspects of Aboriginal people's lives, most of the time for no good reason. And yet here they had a good reason to stop the men enlisting. My mother (Thelma Kartinyeri, nee Rigney) and her family always blamed the Protector for the deaths of Cyril and Rufus, her brother-in-law Alban Varcoe and her great uncle Miller Mack. She would sit down with me and my brother Oscar and tell us stories about the time her brothers left Raukkan and she would not let us go to the pictures if there was a war movie on: she would say that the less we knew about the war, the better. Oscar and I could see the hurt in her eyes as she remembered her brothers.'

In 2001, Julie Reece, a South Australian teacher, took students from Mount Barker High School on a trip to the Western Front. On a second trip in 2004, Donna Handke, a student, brought soil from the Coorong to leave at Rufus Rigney's grave. With special permission, she took soil from the grave back to Raukkan. This was distributed over Rufus Rigney's birthplace in a ceremony in 2005. Julie Reece, now retired, continues to take adults and students from the Coorong region to the Western Front, as part of a project called Connecting Spirits. In 2006, Victor Koolmatrie, great-great-nephew of Cyril and Rufus Rigney, performed a traditional Ngarrindjeri dance beside the grave.

FRANCE
1918

GEORGE DRAYTON & DOMINIC NEWCOMB

DYING DAYS

One of seven children in a working-class family, **GEORGE FREDERICK DRAYTON** of Footscray, Victoria, was barely sixteen when this photograph was taken before his deployment.

By late 1917, many Australians had serious misgivings about the war. The people had rejected the idea of conscription on two separate occasions, despite a devious campaign by Billy Hughes, the prime minister, to persuade them to vote yes.

The first referendum, in October 1916, lost by 72,476 votes. The second, in December 1917, lost by 166,588 votes. The soldiers in the field voted narrowly for conscription – about 104,000 in favour, 94,000 against. Both referenda followed battles that produced appalling casualties, and corresponding casualty lists in the Australian papers. Australia would need 5500 recruits per month, just to keep up with the losses. Many citizens no longer had the stomach for war.

George Drayton had a different problem. He did not have the testicles. His brother Leslie had enlisted in August 1916, arriving in England at the end of December. George presented himself at Footscray in Melbourne on 25 January 1917, dropping his strides as ordered. The medical officer Captain Lane noted enlarged veins on the left side of George's scrotum. He had a 'varicocele', which needed an operation. He agreed to have it done, but it delayed his entry to the war by five months. George had just turned sixteen when he took the medical.

He arrived at Broadmeadows Camp in June. By that time, Leslie had already been wounded in France. The wound to his left ankle was slight, but the doctors sent him to England to recover. Leslie returned to France in late July as George was on a ship, steaming towards England.

The Draytons of Footscray were a large working-class family, with seven children. The father, Frederick, worked as a 'striker', a profession usually associated with a foundry or blacksmith. Leslie had recently married. He left his new wife Amelia at home in Spotswood. He was twenty-two years old, a grocer by trade.

George said he was a farm labourer, but he was still a schoolboy, at Footscray Technical School, according to his mother, Annie. When George was finally accepted, he presented a handwritten note signed by both parents. The note said they approved of his enlistment and consented 'to his embarking before the age of nineteen years'. The only condition they placed was that he had to allocate at least half of his pay of six shillings per day to his mother 'for keeping until he returns'. His pay would help support his three sisters and two other brothers.

George was still in England when Leslie was wounded again, on 2 October 1917, near Ypres. Leslie was hit in the head and died the same day at No 2 Canadian Casualty Clearing Station, west of Poperinghe. The news took at least ten days to reach Melbourne, and perhaps another two weeks to reach George at an Australian training camp in Wiltshire. From this point, George went off the rails. His record from 28 October 1917 is a litany of offences, most of them involving disobedience and going absent without leave. These began to escalate in January, when he was given twenty-eight days field punishment (being locked up for part of each day) for swearing at a junior officer and failing to obey an order. He didn't serve the full punishment, because the army required his presence in France. He reached the 60th Battalion on 14 January and lasted a month before reporting sick with scabies.

In April, he was assigned to work at the Australian Veterinary Hospital at Coquelles, on the outskirts of Calais. It's possible someone was trying to protect George as the Veterinary Hospital was a long way from danger, unless he got kicked by one of the 1200 horses. It seems likely that George did not want to be protected, because his 'crimes' continued. These were all minor offences – being late to, or missing a parade – but they weren't all accidental. In August, he was warned about being late to parade, but did it anyway, so they sent him back to the battalion.

The offences stopped once George reached his unit on 12 August 1918, possibly because by then he had all the action he could have wanted.

The war was now reaching its final phase. Both sides were exhausted, but the Russian capitulation in the east had freed up German forces. These were sent west, to join the Spring Offensive in France. The Germans hoped to win the war here, before the newly arrived American troops could become a decisive factor. This German offensive very nearly succeeded. Operation Michael pushed the British back on a wide front in late March 1918, until the attack ran out of steam in June. The British and French then counter-attacked, bringing in tanks and coordinated aerial support. The Battle of Amiens began on 8 August, kicking off what later became known as the Hundred Days Offensive. The Australian divisions took part in most of these battles, pushing the Germans back along the river Somme from August to October. These were exhausting but exhilarating victories, a return to the war of movement rather than an entrenched stalemate.

George rejoined his unit four days after the Battle of Amiens began. The next three weeks took them through a series of victories to Peronne and Mont St Quentin, where the Germans were heavily fortified, along the Hindenburg Line. Taking Mont St Quentin was the last major action for the Australians in the First World War, and the last for George Drayton.

On 2 September 1918, George was in a ration party, carrying food to the front line troops at Mont St Quentin. On the way back, a German high-explosive shell fell directly in front of him.

'He got the full burst and death was instantaneous,' Private WT Longhurst told the Red Cross Wounded and Missing Enquiry Bureau in 1919. Private MJ Henshaw gave a similar account. 'I saw his body a few minutes afterwards. He was quite dead. I was wounded by the same shell, and was told he was buried two days later near where he fell.'

George Drayton was killed two months before the war ended. He was one of the last under-age Anzacs to die – but not the very last.

Dominic George Doubtfire Newcomb's name was as impressive as his colourful background. Dominic came from the kind of family usually only found in novels. He had been born in Adelaide, but his parents, John and Charlotte, lived on Easy Street, Collingwood by 1916.

In fact, their life was anything but, because John Ignatius Newcomb was a career conman and swindler, an English migrant with a gift for the gab and a fertile imagination. He claimed at various times to be an architect, school teacher, barrister and solicitor, law clerk, professor of music, surveyor and real estate agent. He had studied at Merton College, Oxford, he said. He served at least three terms in prison in South Australia for false pretences and fathered enough children to field a modest football team. His second, or possibly third, wife was Charlotte Doubtfire, who gave him four children, of whom three survived childhood – Dominic, Alfred and Dorothy.

Dominic, sixteen years and one month old, turned up for his army medical examination on 4 July 1917. He carried an Application to Enlist signed by both parents – but there was a handwritten note just above the signatures, saying that they consented 'provided that he is not sent into the firing line before he is nineteen years of age'. This appears to have been written by his father, John. Dominic was accepted for the 25th reinforcements of the 6th Battalion and sent to Broadmeadows Camp. He left Australia one month later – on 4

> He carried an Application to Enlist signed by both parents – but there was a handwritten note just above the signatures, saying that they consented 'provided that he is not sent into the firing line before he is nineteen years of age'.

August – on the *Themistocles*.

Ten days later, his brother Alfred Patrick Herbert Newcomb filled in his own papers to enlist, claiming to be an eighteen-year-old cabinet-maker. He arrived at Broadmeadows a week later, but remained there, in limbo, for seven months. He finally embarked in Sydney in February 1918 with the 8th reinforcements of the 39th Battalion. He disembarked at Southampton on 20 May. Six weeks later at Codford Camp, he was transferred to the 46th Battalion, where he was charged with disobeying an order. He copped five days Field Punishment No 2. Alfred went to France on 22 August 1918.

Before he left, Alfred did an amazing thing. On 14 July, while at No 12 Training Battalion at Codford, he wrote a letter to his brother's commanding officer telling him that Dominic was under-age.

'I deem it my duty to inform you as a brother to the under-mentioned Private D Newcomb No 7598 that he is unfit for active service he is far too young being only 17 ½ years of age not only

that but he suffers from heart failure is it possible for him to be sent back out of the firing line.'

He then claimed there were three brothers fighting, the other being a prisoner of war in Germany. This was not quite true: Cyril James Newcomb, an older half-brother from one of his father's other marriages, had enlisted in late 1915. He was wounded in February 1917 but recovered.

Alfred's letter concluded: 'If you see it in the same light as I do sir you would know that a chap of his age cannot realize what he enlisted for. He was born on the 3 day of June 1901.'

What Alfred failed to tell the officer in this letter was that he, Alfred, was even younger – born in May 1902, a year after Dominic. Alfred was fifteen years and three months when he enlisted and barely a year older when he wrote the letter. In the best sense, Alfred was pulling a con, pretending he was the older and more sensible brother, to get Dominic out of harm's way. One part of the letter was true: Dominic did have a dodgy heart.

Alfred waited until Dominic had gone to France before writing the letter. In effect, Alfred saved his brother from the Hundred Days Offensive, in which Dominic's unit was soon heavily engaged. Whether Dominic was grateful is another matter.

Dominic had been in France for a month when he was hauled before the medical officer of his battalion, near the end of July. Captain Clarence Hains determined that he suffered from 'Asthenia and Cardiac Insufficiency' and was not fit for active service. He was sent back to the Australian base at Le Havre for another examination that confirmed his 'aortic incompetence and weak heart'. From there it was back to England and a ship home in October. He was on the water when the armistice was signed, on 11 November 1918.

It's hard to believe Dominic's parents would have let him go if they had known of his heart condition. It is also interesting that the army doctors missed this condition for so long. Perhaps Dominic knew about it before he left, or didn't find out until he was in England. It's likely that Alfred found out in England, especially since Dominic was in camp at Sutton Veny, a few kilometres from Codford, when he arrived. Alfred waited until Dominic had gone to France before writing the letter. In effect, Alfred saved his brother from the Hundred

Days Offensive, in which Dominic's unit was soon heavily engaged. Whether Dominic was grateful is another matter.

Dominic had two years back in Australia after the war, but the heart condition persisted. Dominic George Doubtfire Newcomb died at St Vincent's Hospital in Melbourne on the first day of January 1921, aged nineteen years and six months.

The Australian Roll of Honour lists only those who died in the war, or because of it, within a defined period. In this war, that was between 4 August 1914 and 31 March 1921, when the AIF was wound up. Dominic Newcomb is on that list, but not his brother Alfred. Alfred came home and lived a long life, dying in 1970 at the age of sixty-seven. Both brothers served as under-age soldiers but Dominic was the last under-age Australian soldier that we know of to die in the First World War. 🍁

CODA

LAST POST

PRIVATE ARTHUR ALCHIN, from Gunning, New South Wales, was killed at Passchendaele on 12 October 1917. He was lying on a stretcher among a group of wounded men when a stray shell killed them all. A comrade described him as a 'game little chap'. He was one month from his eighteenth birthday.

Policies toward under-age recruits changed as the war progressed. Boys who had once been seen as plucky were now a problem. By late 1916, the policy was that 'men' who were under-age could not be sent to France until they were nineteen.

In 1917, these regulations evolved from clarity to a state of confusion. In August, an officer at Headquarters, AIF camps, UK, issued guidelines saying that under-age recruits arriving as reinforcements should receive the usual training. Once trained, they should be sent for further training as signallers, cold shoers, saddlers, bootmakers, armourer's assistants, bandsmen and clerks. In other words, cobblers.

In November these orders were cancelled. The new orders were to divide them into three groups by age – the youngest (under seventeen years and nine months) were to be sent home. The others were to be employed in tasks that freed up older men to be sent to France, or kept in training till age nineteen, when they could be sent to France. In June 1918, those orders were scrapped:

under-age personnel once trained in England were now to be sent to a new Corps Working Party in France – behind the lines, but directly aiding the war effort. None would in future be returned to Australia, except on medical grounds. The army hated to lose a man, even if he was a boy.

There's a whiff of punishment about these orders, as if the under-age boys were a damn nuisance. No point sending them home at great cost, when they could be made to work for their sins, until old enough to fight. Lying about your age was indeed an offence in the army – and some of those who were sent back were made to feel like pariahs on the voyage home. In effect, they were inconveniencing the same army that ignored the evidence of their own eyes at the recruitment stage. This was gross hypocrisy.

The recruiters were now encouraging old men and the infirm to join up. The officer commanding the Australian depots in England wrote an angry cable home complaining that half of the 5600 reinforcements who arrived in

England in the second half of August were dentally unfit, 155 were suffering from senility and 394 were under-age. This was a colossal waste of money, he thundered: they could not be sent to France till they were nineteen and meanwhile, they were drawing full pay. The document is undated, but the numbers suggest it was sent around September 1917.

That telegram gives a rare hint of the real extent of under-age recruiting. If a similar percentage applied to every cohort of 5000 men in the AIF, there had to be several thousand under-age boys already serving.

On 7 May 1917, the CO of No 10 Training Battalion at Durrington Camp in Wiltshire counted 107 under-age soldiers in his camp on that day. Multiply that by the number of camps and there may have been somewhere between one and two thousand under-age boys in training on Salisbury Plain in that period. For the army's purposes, it was better not to count them at all, at least not those in France.

The real number of under-age soldiers who served in the first AIF may never be known. Too many lies to unpick, too many imperfect records, too many unregistered births.

The number who died is certainly greater than the 170 listed on the Roll of Honour. Australia sent 332,000 men overseas to fight. Almost twenty per cent of them died on active duty. If under-age boys died at the same rate, there would have been at least 800 under-age boys in the AIF – but it was probably many more. The telegram quoted above gives a better indication: 400 under-age boys in just one batch of 5600 reinforcements. If we assume an

> It's true that many people let them down – from parents to recruiters and politicians and priests, but it's hard to apportion blame. Words like duty and Empire carried more weight than they do now.

average that was just a quarter of that rate, that would mean around 7000 under-age boys went through the AIF from 1914 to 1919.

It's true that many people let them down – from parents to recruiters and politicians and priests, but it's hard to apportion blame. Words like duty and Empire carried more weight than they do now.

Children do not have a duty to fight wars, but teenage boys don't think of themselves that way. It seems incomprehensible to us now that others agreed they could go, but it did not seem so to them, then. We cannot judge them by our standards. We cannot walk in their shoes.

All of the major combatant countries sent boys to fight in the First World War. The politicians and the recruiters did not think it was unusual or even wrong, with the occasional exception of men like George Vowles, who did his best to stop Ernie Pinches. And even he failed.

It is no insult to the memory of the lost boys to say they should never have been there, and no justification to recognise that they fought well and bravely and with all their hearts. Attitudes towards the young may have changed, but only in some parts of the world. Child soldiers remain a terrible fact in others. It would be foolish to think that this could never happen again, given the right circumstances. If we do remember them, it should be with more than sorrow. ◉

It is no insult to the memory of the lost boys to say they should never have been there, and no justification to recognise that they fought well and bravely and with all their hearts.

THE
YOUNGEST
AUSTRALIANS
TO DIE
OVERSEAS IN
THE FIRST
WORLD WAR

1.

JAMES MARTIN, from Tocumwal, New South Wales, born 3 January 1901. He was fourteen years, nine months and twenty-two days old when he succumbed to typhoid on a hospital ship off Gallipoli, in October 1915.

2.

LESLIE PRIOR, who died at Bullecourt in 1917, aged fifteen years, three months and three days. He is the second-youngest to die, but the youngest to be killed in action.

3.

DOUGLAS WOOD (if his date of birth is correct) is the second-youngest Australian to die in action.

4.

ROBERT WARNER, from Kiama, New South Wales, wounded at Pozieres, died two days later on 16 August 1916, aged fifteen years, eight months and six days.

5.

JOHN GORDON, the fourth-youngest Australian to die in action, met his fate on the same day as Wood on the same battlefield. He was aged fifteen years and ten months.

POZIERES &
PASSCHENDAELE

A hot sun hung in a brazen sky,
And the fields we trampled were brown and bare,
And our throats, you remember, were parched and dry
When you got your issue at Pozières

But earth and sky were a sodden mess.
And the mud was churned 'neath a leaden hail;
And we lay in a muddle of filthiness
When I collected at Passchendaele.

Summer and Winter, the seasons pass.
Spring and Autumn, they come and go.
Skies of lead turn to skies of brass,
And where are the Diggers we used to know?

Faster and faster with each swift year
The Diggers go on their last lone trial,
Since you got your issue at Pozières,
And I collected at Passchendaele.

And it may be near, or it may be far,
And it may be a season of sun, or rain,
When we say farewell to the things that are,
With a hope that it has not been all in vain.

And it may be that everything will be clear
When we meet the Diggers beyond the veil.
And we'll find the reason for Pozières
And we'll know the purpose of Passchendaele.

Oscar Walters
3rd Field Company, Australian Engineers

ACKNOWLEDGEMENTS
& THANKS

I am greatly indebted to Jennifer Milward, who has been midwife to this project since the beginning. Her work on the under-age database at the Australian War Memorial was the starting point. She helped me navigate both the corridors of power in the Memorial and the arcane secrets in its files. Aaron Pegram, senior historian, gave valuable guidance on military matters. The staff at the Australian War Memorial Research Centre were patient and resourceful, as were the staff at the State Library in Sydney. Tim Lycett gave freely of his research on Fromelles and other stories. Christopher Pugsley and Ian McGibbon helped to unravel New Zealand's military history.

Special thanks to those who gave generous hospitality in Canberra and Sydney during the research: Peter and Nerida Clarke, Kathy and Ian Pickles, Stephen Schuetz and Michael Bowden, Bernard and Toni Shirley. Michael Grealy found many lost boys during his own research. Our mutual friend Greg Growden introduced me to my agent Jeanne Ryckmans, who made the book happen. Deonie Fiford shaped and honed the text. I could not have had a more supportive publisher than Martin Hughes and the staff at Affirm Press.

My partner Mary Dickie, as ever, gave more help than I can ever fully acknowledge or repay – she was my ideal reader, my psychologist and co-detective, my compass and my map.

Many others helped along the way with particular stories. Their names are acknowledged here in alphabetical order: Kay Ball, Peter Blaxell, Professor Frank Bowden, Thomas Boucknooghe, Rae Casey, Lois Comeadow, Jodie Conn, Tim Cudini, Warren Daly, Jennifer Dore, Martin Edwards, Lina Favrin, Anne Fisher, Anne Giles, Michael Giles, Michael Hallinan, Dr Ben Harkness, Louise Hill-Coleman, Dale Hummer, Steven Jeppesen, Dr Phil Jones, Mal Jurgs, Frank Lampard, Dave Langford, Charmaine Langford-Budzynski, Ann Laver, Peter Lawlor, Shannon Lovelady, Adrienne McConvell, Alexandra McKinnon, Bradley Manera, Allister Mills, Terry O'Neill, Dave Platt, Derek Prosser, Frank Quinlan, Joan Quinlan, Martin Quinlan, Peter Rankin, Julie Reece, Jacqueline Reid, Christopher Reid, Helen Renshaw, Melanie Robb, Adrian Scott, Bob Scott, Moya Sharp, Michael Shelford, Kerry Short, Nick Short, Joanne Smedley, Sundee Strother, Norman Thomas, Veronica Treen, Jenny Ulph, Barbara Vines, Wilma Walls, Klynton Wanganeen, Bob Wills, Janet Wilson, Gina Worboys, Cherril Wynne.

Quotes from the *Official History of Australia in the War of 1914–1918* appear with permission of the Australian War Memorial. Quotes from the diaries of Charles Bean appear with permission of his estate. Quotes from the diary of Walter Eyles appear with permission of the Anzac Memorial in Hyde Park, Sydney. Quotes from private records at the AWM – the letters of Digges La Touche, the letters and diaries of Harry and Dudley Jackson – appear with permission of the Australian War Memorial.

PHOTO CREDITS

Most of the photographs are from the collection of the Australian War Memorial, and appear with permission. They are indicated below by 'AWM', followed by the identifying number of each image. The rest are from other institutions or private collections, as acknowledged. Special thanks to those who allowed me to use some family pictures for the first time.

Page 7: Miller Maffeking Fergusson AWM H06458

Page 9: Ronald Rothsay Wright AWM P01368.001

Page 13: Maud Butler AWM P04683.010

Page 16-17: Chest measuring recruits AWM A03616

Page 23: John Smith and Frank Day, stowaways – Trove, National Library of Australia, ISSN 22059520, published in *The Sun*, Sydney, 16 December 1915, p. 11

Page 31: Albert Scott courtesy of Adrian Scott

Page 36: Hughie O'Donnell courtesy of the Goldfields War Museum, Kalgoorlie

Page 43: John Lyons courtesy of Murchison Historical Society, rephotographed by Kerry Short

Page 49: William Riley courtesy of Jodie Conn

Page 56: John Benson AWM H06079

Page 62-63: The dead at Krithia AWM C01079

Page 70: Leslie Shaw courtesy of Fairfax Syndication

Page 76-77: New Zealand and Australian soldiers landing at Anzac Cove, PAColl-5936-18, Alexander Turnbull Library, Wellington, New Zealand

Page 89: John Harris AWM H06501

Page 101: Albert Cramer and Fred Black, Trove, National Library of Australia, ISSN 2201470, published in *The Australasian*, Melbourne, 21 August 1915, p. 26

Page 113: Norah Edwards and Geoffrey Flemming, courtesy of AWM

Page 117: 'Richard Walter Mayhew' – File No. FL1489835, courtesy of State Library of New South Wales

Page 123: Dudley Jackson – AWM private records file 3DRL/3846, courtesy of AWM

Page 133: William Jackson VC, AWM P01383.006

Page 143: Pte Jackson before VC, AWM P02939.008

Page 147: Douglas Wood courtesy of Peter Lawlor

Page 156-157: Fromelles battlefield, morning of 20 July, AWM A01560

Page 163: James Fitzgibbon Daly AWM H05840

Page 164: William Warren Daly AWM H05841

Page 171: Charles Frank Church AWM DA13633

Page 174: Charles Frank Church and friends AWM DA13550

Page 183: Bernard 'Baby' Haines courtesy of Lois Comeadow

Page 187: Bernard Haines and his brother Royal, courtesy of Lois Comeadow

Page 191: Rowland Lording as 'A Tiveychoc', Trove, National Library of Australia, ISSN 18373763, published in *Western Mail*, Perth, 9 January 1936, p. 6

Page 199: Edward Giles and James Harrington AWM PO3483.023

Page 210-211: Stretcher bearers at Pozieres AWM E04946

Page 216: Cecil Thomas, Trove, National Library of Australia, ISSN 22059520, *The Sun*, Sydney, 6 May 1917, p. 11

Page 222-223: Francis Thomas's family image courtesy Norman Thomas

Page 229: Telegram and cablegram, courtesy of the National Library of Australia, B2455, Collins F, SERN 4171

Page 245: Walter Eyles diary. © Anzac Memorial. Photographer Jean-Francois Lanzarone, reproduced with the approval of the Anzac Memorial

Page 249: The Dawes family, courtesy of Jennifer Dore

Page 254-255: Unloading Australian wounded at 38 CCS, AWM E00003

Page 259: Arthur Hill, AWM P10612.001

Page 262: Thomas Hill, courtesy Louise Hill-Coleman

Page 266-267: Troops embark on the Armadale, 1916, AWM PB0112

Page 271: Albert James Anderson, courtesy of Peter Blaxell

Page 278-279: graves at Sutton Veny, England AWM D00376

Page 283: Ernie Pinches. Courtesy State Library of Queensland. Identifier 702692-19171222-s0028-0005. Published in *The Queenslander,* 22 December 1917

Page 295: Will Daly AWM P05805.001

Page 297: Will Daly and goats, courtesy Joan Quinlan.

Page 305: Will Richards, courtesy of Dave Langford and Charmaine Langford-Budzynski

Page 307: Hugh Connell, courtesy of Adrienne McConvell

Page 317: Albert Le Roux AWM H05544

Page 320: Prosper Le Roux AWM H05543

Page 327: Miller Mack AWM P10608.010

Page 339: George Drayton AWM DA17871

Page 343: Dominic Newcomb AWM DA18487

Page 349: Arthur Alchin AWM

PO8965.001

INDEX:

Note: Most of the under-age boys described in each chapter are listed on the contents pages (2,3), so their names are not repeated here. A few who appear only in a photograph are indexed below. All other soldiers are indexed. Battles are listed under battles, then location.